TWAYNE'S WORLD AUTHORS SERIES

A Survey of the World's Literature

Sylvia E. Bowman, Indiana University

GENERAL EDITOR

FRANCE

Maxwell A. Smith, Guerry Professor of French, Emeritus
The University of Chattanooga
Former Visiting Professor in Modern Languages
The Florida State University

EDITOR

Alphonse Daudet

TWAS 380

Alphonse Daudet

ALPHONSE DAUDET

By ALPHONSE V. ROCHE
University of Arizona

TWAYNE PUBLISHERS
A DIVISION OF G. K. HALL & CO., BOSTON

Library of Congress Cataloging in Publication Data

Roche, Alphonse Victor, 1895-
   Alphonse Daudet.

   (Twayne's world authors series ; TWAS 380 : France)
   Bibliography: p. 179 - 86.
   Includes index.
   1. Daudet, Alphonse, 1840-1897.
PQ2216.Z5R6   843'.8 [B]   75-25549
ISBN 0-8057-6223-X

To
LARRY AND EUNICE

Contents

About the Author

Alphonse V. Roche, professor emeritus of Northwestern University and since his "retirement" a professor of Romance Languages at the University of Arizona, received his B.A. at the State College of Washington and his M.A. and Ph.D. at the University of Illinois. During the last few years he has been a visiting professor in several universities, including those of Wisconsin, Minnesota, Illinois, and Missouri.

Professor Roche is the author of *Les Idées traditionalistes en France...*, *Provençal Regionalism...*, and *Au Pays du Soleil*, which is a collection of short stories edited in collaboration with Mrs. Roche. He has read papers at meetings of professional societies, lectured here and abroad, and contributed to various periodicals and scholarly reviews, encyclopedias and dictionaries of literature.

Preface

During the last quarter of the nineteenth century, Alphonse Daudet became known as one of the most outstanding novelists of his generation. He was admired both as a man and a writer by such contemporaries as Flaubert, Zola, and Mallarmé in France, and Robert-Louis Stevenson, George Meredith, and Edmund Gosse in England.

Brander Matthews, the well-known American critic and scholar, noted that Daudet's popularity "beyond the borders of his own language" surpassed that of Balzac, and was "second only" to that of Victor Hugo. Stevenson regarded him as "incomparably the best of the present French novelists," and Henry James, who placed him "at the head of his profession," wrote that "the appearance of a new novel by this admirable genius" was to his mind, "the most delightful literary event" that could occur.

Yet, like that of other equally famous French writers — Anatole France, Barrès, and even Gide could be named — Daudet's popularity was to fade considerably after his death. He seems to be badly neglected, making a long sojourn in Purgatory, as Mauriac has put it with reference to Barrès. Obviously, this defection of the public and the critics, now more interested in the problems of our time, does not impair or in any way affect the literary value of their works. Nor has interest in them completely subsided.

In the period between the two world wars, many articles in various languages were written about Alphonse Daudet, the man, and his works. A new edition of his *Oeuvres complètes* appeared in France in 1929 - 1930, and his best short stories and some of his novels were published as textbooks for use in American schools. Today, English translations of his works can be found in most of our libraries and bookstores.

Beside the expected doctoral dissertations, there are three

important books that should be recommended to the English reader: *Alphonse Daudet: A Biographical and Critical Study* (1894), by R. H. Sherard; *Alphonse Daudet* (1949), by G. V. Dobie; and *The Career of Alphonse Daudet: A Critical Study* (1965), by Murray Sachs. Sherard and Dobie have treated the subject more particularly from the human, and at times English, point of view — the former keeping his readers interested with anecdotes and new biographical facts, and the latter fascinating them by her enthusiasm and distinctive feminine touch. Professor Sachs, a scholar primarily interested in artistic and literary matters, has thrown a new light on some aspects of the subject in which both biographers and critics are interested.

The purpose of this book is more modest, merely to present as clearly and succinctly as possible a readable and reliable introduction to Daudet. In accordance with the policy adopted in this series, I have tried to include all the material "that may be necessary to the understanding and appreciation of the writer." I have followed step by step the parallel evolution of the man and the writer, because of the unusually close interrelation between them and because of the writer's dependence on outside influences, as for example that which caused him to drop temporarily his work on *Le Nabab* to write *Jack*, or that which led him to put aside the uncompleted *Soutien de famille* to write *Le Trésor d'Arlatan*.

I have not dwelt on Daudet's first and minor writings, nor have I deemed it necessary, in the scope of this work, to analyze him at great length as a playwright. The violent attacks against his person could not be ignored, but going deeply into the subject would have meant disregarding the ideal pursued in this series. A most serious accusation raised against Alphonse Daudet has been that of plagiarism. However, the question having been settled, definitely I think, by Murray Sachs in two excellent articles ("The Role of Collaborators in the Career of Alphonse Daudet," *PMLA*, March-June, 1958; and "Alphonse Daudet and Paul Arène: Some Unpublished Letters," *Romanic Review*, February, 1964), no more space needs to be devoted to it in this short survey.

On the other hand, I have given much attention to the author's southern background, which explains certain aspects of his works, and to the social and historical values of his now less well known "realist novels" depicting life in the French capital. In this respect I have copiously quoted the opinions expressed on his works by his most famous contemporaries.

Preface

For reasons that will be obvious to the reader, a rather large amount of space has been devoted to Daudet's friendship with Edmond de Goncourt, and some perhaps unexpected but helpful information — such as that on the Suez Canal — added for the understanding of the main characters' general behavior and particular activities. A few examples of Daudet's best pages will be found here. Unfortunately, lack of space has made it imperative to leave some remarkable texts out of consideration.

As some of my predecessors have done, I have tried to separate legend from history with regard to that period of Daudet's life which he dramatized so successfully in the first part of *Le Petit Chose*. In turn I have drawn freely from this novel as a source of information and, whenever advisable, commented on new facts recently brought to light in scholarly studies.

Quotations are in my own translation, except where otherwise stated.

Acknowledgments

I wish first of all to offer my thanks to Professor Maxwell A. Smith for the confidence he placed in me and for his never-failing patience and kindness. I also want to express my gratitude to my colleague and friend Professor Robert R. Anderson, who so generously offered to go over my English and ended by doing an editor's job. I appreciate more than I can say the privilege of having had the benefit of his remarks and corrections, which were those of a distinguished scholar with a keen sense of language. Above all, my hearty thanks go to my wife, Lila N. Roche, for her encouragement and helpful comments.

Chronology

1840   Alphonse Daudet born in Nîmes, May 13. Put to nurse in a small town in the vicinity, where he will attend school and speak Provençal.

1845   Lives mostly with family, where speaking Provençal is severely discouraged. Is a pupil at the Frères de la Doctrine chrétienne, and later at the Institution Ganivet.

1848   The Daudet family deeply affected by the Revolution and the setting up of the Second Republic.

1849   The Daudets move to Lyon. Alphonse attends a *manécanterie* (choir school attached to a church), the Collège municipal of Lyon. Teacher calls him "le Petit Chose."

1851   Coup d'Etat of Louis Bonaparte, who will found the Second Empire (1852 - 1870) under the name of Napoléon III.

1857   Alphonse Daudet is appointed maître d'études at the Collège d'Alais, where he stays from May 1 to October 28. Arrives in Paris on November 1.

1858   Is received in various salons where he recites his poems. Publishes *Les Amoureuses*. "Bohemian" life. Marie Rieu liaison.

1859   Meets Frédéric Mistral, in Paris.

1860   Is appointed secretary to the duc de Morny.

1861   Daudet's health affected by damp and cold weather. Doctor recommends warmer climate. Trip to Algeria. Meets Zola in Paris.

1862   Again doctor advises sunshine. Travels to Corsica. Later he will go to Sardinia and Provence. *La Dernière Idole* (one-act play) produced at the Odéon theater.

1864   *Les Absents*, produced at the Opéra comique.

1865   *L'Oeillet blanc* (his third play, in collaboration with Ernest Lépine), at the Théâtre-Français. Death of the duc de

Morny, on March 8. Alphonse Daudet leaves his sinecure. Henceforth he will devote himself entirely to literature.

1866 First "Lettres de mon Moulin" appear in *L'Evénement*. In contact with Zola. Meets Julia Allard. Trip to Alsace, Bavaria, and Switzerland with Alfred Delvau.

1867 He marries Julia Allard. Birth of Léon Daudet (November 16).

1868 Publishes *Le Petit Chose*.

1870 Franco-Prussian War and La Commune. Daudet Joins the
1871 National Guard.

1872 Failure of *L'Arlésienne* at the Vaudeviille theater. Member of the Flaubert group. *Tartarin de Tarascon*.

1873 *Les Contes du lundi*.

1874 *Femmes d'artistes, Fromont jeune et Risler Aîné*.

1875 Death of Vincent Daudet.

1876 *Jack*.

1877 *Le Nabab*.

1879 *Les Rois en exil*. First serious manifestation of the illness that will lead to his death.

1880 Death of Flaubert.

1881 *Numa Roumestan*. Alphonse Daudet at peak of his career (1881 - 1885).

1882 Death of Alphonse's mother.

1883 *L'Evangéliste*. Duel with Alfred Delpit. Birth of Lucien Daudet.

1884 *Sapho*. From now on, his sickness, literary works, and benevolent activities will be his main concerns.

1885 *Tartarin sur les Alpes*. Triumph of *L'Arlésienne* produced at the Odéon theater. His health is worsening.

1886 *La Belle Nivernaise*. Birth of Edmée Daudet.

1888 *Trente ans de Paris, L'Immortel*.

1889 *La lutte pour la vie*.

1890 *L'Obstacle, Port-Tarascon*. A new friend: Batisto Bonnet.

1891 Two years of intense suffering. *Rose et Ninette. La*
1892 *Menteuse*.

1894 Beginning of the Dreyfus Affair.

1895 *La Petite paroisse*. Visit to England.

1896 Visit to Italy. *La Fédor. Le Trésor d'Arlatan*. Death of Edm. de Goncourt.

1897 Finishes *Soutien de famille*, which will be published posthumously. Alphonse Daudet dies on December 16.

CHAPTER 1

Alphonse Daudet's Life: 1840 - 1860

I was born on May 13, 18 . . . , in a town of Languedoc where, as in every southern town, can be found much sunshine, a good deal of dust, a Carmelite convent, and two or three old Roman monuments.[1]

T HIS opening and often quoted sentence from Daudet's semi-autobiographical novel, *Le Petit Chose*, calls for some corrections, clarifications, and additional information. The year referred to was 1840, a year during which were also born in France such famous men as Emile Zola, Claude Monet, and Auguste Rodin. The birth place was the town of Nîmes, where the cotton fabric known as denim (de Nîmes) was originally made. There, the sun shines today as intensely as it did then, but dust cannot be considered any longer as one of the characteristics of the Provence and Languedoc region. Most of it disappeared some fifty years ago, when civil engineers began to cover pebble-paved streets and chalky limestone roads with asphalt. As for the Carmelite convents and Roman remains, it goes without saying that they were never found in "every" town of southern France. However, Nîmes had them, and the latter are still among the most admired monuments of Daudet's birthplace. Here then, as in most literary texts, we must add and subtract, distinguish between life and literature, make allowance for poetry.

I *Alphonse Daudet's Family*

Most biographers have felt impelled to express their view on the origin of Alphonse Daudet's family name, which in the sixteenth century was usually spelled "Daudé." There still exist differences of opinion about its meaning. Some scholars would make it derive from Davidet, a diminutive of David, others from an Arabic word of similar consonance, others from Deodatus — literally, "given to

God." The latter etymology would justify the removal, in the nineteenth century, of the graphic accent on the *e* and the addition of the *t*. Research regarding this relatively minor question can be expected to continue for some time.

On both sides of his family, Alphonse Daudet's parents and grandparents belonged to the world of business and industry. His great-grandfather, Jacques Daudet, had given up farming in the Cévennes to move to the Nîmes region, where he kept on working the land. His son, also called Jacques, went to work as a silk weaver, or *taffetassier*, as the trade was then called at Nîmes. He became foreman of a weaving shop, and soon found himself the owner of a silk store. One of his nine children, a boy born in 1806 and named Vincent, was to be Alphonse Daudet's father.

As he reached the age of sixteen, Vincent Daudet was sent out to sell silk fabrics for his father. He would travel as far as Brittany, driving "night and day, winter and summer," carrying two pistols to defend himself against the highwaymen who still infested the country in those days. With such training, by the age of twenty the young man had experienced all kinds of adventures, learned the value of hard work, and acquired a strong sense of responsibility. It was then that he took into his head to marry Mlle Adeline Reynaud whose family, also in the silk business, had dealings with his own.

It may be pertinent at this point to recall that, along with other industries, that of silk had suddenly developed at a tremendous pace in France. Mulberry trees, originally from China, had been imported from Italy and planted in the Rhone valley as early as the sixteenth century. Silkworms were raised in the region and their cocoons processed in the city of Lyons, which was soon to enjoy a world reputation for its silk goods. That story is common knowledge, but perhaps not so well known is the fact that the city of Nîmes became a serious competitor of Lyons in the nineteenth century, precisely at the time when Vincent Daudet was courting Adeline Reynaud.

Like the Daudets, the Reynauds hailed from the Cévennes, more exactly from the lower Vivarais region, some fifty miles north-east of the Daudets' cradle. Their ancestry has been traced as far back as the sixteenth century. Adeline's grandfather, Jean Reynaud (1723 -1824) had three daughters and six sons. Among the latter were Charles-Henry-Antoine (1789 - 1853), whose son Antoine-Henri (1820 - 1895) was to be the prototype of Tartarin de Tarascon, one of the most famous characters of Alphonse Daudet; and Guillaume (1758 - 1819), a picturesque character nicknamed "the Russian uncle" because he emigrated to Russia, where he became very wealthy. But "l'oncle russe," who had returned to live in France, left none of his fortune to the Reynaud folks. It all went to "his Russian governess," whom he had married. A third uncle who had also an active and rather eventful life was François Reynaud (1761 - 1835).

François took holy orders, was given a small parish, refused to take the oath of allegiance to the Civil Constitution of the Clergy during the Revolution, and emigrated to London, where he learned and taught English. When he returned to France he joined the teaching profession. In 1813, he was appointed principal of the Collège d'Alais (today spelled Alès), to the rebuilding of which he was to devote the rest of his life. He died of cholera, which he had caught while visiting the sick in the hospital during the epidemic. It has been suggested that Alphonse Daudet's appointment at the Collège d'Alais twenty-two years later, owed a great deal to the still vivid reputation of "l'oncle l'abbé."

The Reynauds, who were much wealthier than the Daudets, did not regard Vincent's courtship with favor. But Adeline, then twenty-four and in love, vowed that she would marry the handsome and audacious Vincent, himself "all fire and flame," in spite of her family's opposition — especially that of her brothers. She won her fight, and the wedding took place on September 8, 1829.

Vincent, as enterprising a young man as his father had been, could not be satisfied to remain a mere silk merchant. He accordingly acquired a weaving factory and within a few years became a prosperous manufacturer of silk scarfs, shirts, and neckties which he sold all over France and abroad. He also acquired a family of his own. Some biographers believe that nine children were born to the couple; others that their number reached fifteen. Be that as it may, we know for certain that four of them survived: Henri, born in 1832, Ernest in 1835, Alphonse in 1840, and Anna in 1848. They were all put to nurse, as was then still customary in the well-to-do bourgeois families, and raised in some small towns of the Nîmes region, such as Fons, Bezouce, or Redessan. Alphonse was probably taken to Bezouce, the town which, he tells us, left in his mind the most pleasant and vivid memories. It has not been ascertained in what year he was returned to his parents, but there is no doubt that he made long sojourns in Bezouce, Fons, and other such places during his early childhood.

II *Childhood*

Alphonse Daudet suggests in *Le Petit Chose* that he was the evil star of his family, that from the day of his birth disaster fell upon

them "from twenty directions," that his father, both "happy and
desperate," wondered whether he should cry "like the other fellow,"
for the disappearance of a Marseilles customer, or laugh for his son's
happy arrival. The "other fellow" referred naturally to Gargantua,
Rabelais' famous character. Ernest Daudet was one of the first to
explain, in *My Brother and I,* that the first six years of Alphonse's life
were in reality spent in a happy family atmosphere, totally free from
anxiety, an atmosphere of "domestic well-being" and confidence in
the future.

In Bezouce, Alphonse lived the life of the country folk. He used to
play with the farm boys and he enjoyed speaking their language:
Provençal. Years later he liked to reminisce about this wonderful life
in the open air, when he would climb trees, pick cherries or figs in
the orchards, and pluck grapes in the vineyards. He recalled how on
certain occasions his *nourriciers* ("foster parents") would take him
along in the fields, and how, having been committed to the care of
the nanny goat, he would listen to the crickets and cicadas while
comfortably established in the shade of an olive or mulberry tree. It
was also at Bezouce that he attended school for the first time and
learned how to read. He shed many tears when his parents took him
away to put him in a Nîmes boarding school.

Fortunately, his new home environment did not preclude fun
entirely. Alphonse had a wonderful time playing with his brothers
and cousins. One of their favorite games consisted in donning
ecclesiastical vestments and acting out religious ceremonies and
processions in the empty rooms of his father's factory. Other times
he imagined the factory as a deserted island. There he enacted the
adventures of Robinson Crusoe with the help of the janitor's son who
impersonated Friday by roaring like a lion — as so delightfully told
in *Le Petit Chose*. Ernest Daudet, the "mère Jacques" in the novel,
has recounted, in a less imaginative style, how he and his brother for
a long time enjoyed the family Sunday excursions. He has also
recalled their joy upon receiving the toys or books brought by their
father from the Beaucaire Fair or from other business trips.

It remains however that the above-mentioned "disasters" were
not mere products of Alphonse's imagination. They did occur, but,
as explained by Ernest, only later, after 1846 and in close and rapid
succession: first, several customers of Vincent's firm went bankrupt
and ran off without paying their creditors; then Vincent had to
contend with economic depressions, several strikes, a costly lawsuit,
and two consecutive fires. Next, the Revolution of 1848 occurred,

which turned everything upside down. Embittered, Vincent would make it responsible for all his misfortunes. The last straw came with the death of Grandfather Reynaud, when it was revealed that his sons had let slip all his assets in wild speculations. The Daudets were thus divested of their share of the inheritance on which they counted to solve their financial problems. The situation became so desperate that Vincent had no other choice than to move his family to a smaller apartment while he himself went to seek his fortune in Lyons. He hoped to find a good position in the big city and soon be able to call for his family to join him. However, a full year elapsed before he could send for them. Mme Daudet, the four children, and the "old servant" (she was only thirty) left their sunny hometown for foggy Lyons in the spring of 1849.

III   *Lyons*

The story of their trip, from Nîmes to Valence by stagecoach, and from Valence to Lyons by steamboat on the Rhone river, constitutes one of the most moving and picturesque chapters of *Le Petit Chose*. It took them three days to cover the one hundred thirty miles between the two cities. Their first impression, perhaps the deepest on this southern family, was the one made by the dreary appearance of the "northern" city of Lyons and its people. "I recall," Alphonse wrote in his "souvenirs d'enfance," "a low soot-colored sky and the mist continuously rising from the two rivers. It did not rain. It drizzled."[2] The apartment Vincent had found was still more depressing: a dark apartment on the fourth floor of an old house where, according to the author of *Le Petit Chose*, "the walls wept, the pavement sweated, and the banisters of the staircase stuck to your fingers." Worst of all, the kitchen swarmed with black beetles (cockroaches): "They were everywhere, on the side-board, along the walls, inside the drawers and the buffet, all over."[3] And he found that the appearance of the people, their behavior, their "way of speaking" were in keeping with the dampness of the air. Indeed, no improvement of the situation had resulted from the move to Lyons. Vincent tried to rebuild his business but, bad luck added to lack of capital, and perhaps also to lack of business acumen, prevented him from recouping his losses. He even found it impossible to keep afloat and soon had to take a cheaper apartment and impose more restrictions on his household.

Yet, even during these hard times, Vincent Daudet never lost sight of his sons' education. Against the advice of one of his creditors, a "practical" relative who thought the boys should learn a trade, he managed, in Lyons as in Nîmes, to keep them in school. Henri, who was attracted by the priesthood, attended a seminary. Ernest and Alphonse were sent to a *manécanterie*, a "choir school," where they would be taught Greek and Latin in exchange for choirboy services in the church attached to the school. Ernest, who was quite unhappy in that institution, has humorously written that he could never learn how to serve Mass and that one day he "put all the faithful to flight" by ringing the bell at the Sanctus instead of the Gospel.

Alphonse had his share of mishaps or misadventures, such as being dragged down to the floor in front of the Altar by the weight of the "big book," the Gospel. Nevertheless, he found the school a lot of fun. He liked to swing the censers and ring his little bell when he accompanied the Viaticum being carried to a sick person. He even enjoyed attending funerals and always felt very proud when donning his ecclesiastical outfit.

As a child, he had been generally manageable, but he would occasionally fly into a passion, burst into violent fits of anger. Once when his father had confined him to his room for some petty fault, he threw himself head first against the doors and walls with such a violence that, had they not hurried to free him, Ernest recalled, he would have killed himself. At other times, his fertile imagination carried him away beyond allowed boundary lines. One day, at the manécanterie, he dug a hole in a closet where the priests kept their cassocks and filled it with gunpowder taken from rockets to be used for fireworks. A terrific explosion was heard during a funeral service taking place at that moment.

When he realized that his sons were not learning much Greek or Latin at the manécanterie, Vincent decided to dispense with it as soon as a scholarship could be secured for at least one of the boys. This was done shortly afterward and the two brothers were able to start their formal education at the Lycée de Lyon in 1850. Alphonse was then ten years old.

IV *Alphonse Daudet as a Teenager*

Various occurrences enlivened the life of student Alphonse Daudet during the next seven years. Only a few can be recalled here. His most impressive experience seems to have been that of his first day at the lycée when he found himself the only boy wearing a "blouse" — which in this case means an overall or outer garment worn to protect clothing. At Nîmes, being thus dressed would have been normal. In a Lyons lycée however, it immediately classified him as a *gone* ("a street urchin"). He noticed further that the other boys carried beautiful portfolios, nice smelling inkwells, well-bound notebooks, and new books "with many notes at the bottom of the pages!" His were old, secondhand books with pages missing, soiled, smelling musty and fusty. To cap it all, one of his teachers made fun of his small stature and general appearance.

This particular teacher never called him by his name, although he had been told "over twenty times" what it was and how it should be pronounced: "Daniel Ey-sse-tte". The teacher kept on saying: "Hey, you over there, little thing *(le petit chose)*. What is your name?" As a result, the whole class would refer to him as "Little What's Your (or his) Name." (This rendering by the English translator of the book falls short of expressing all the contempt implied in the three French words *le petit chose*). It may very well be that the disappointment, or rather humiliation, of that first day at the lycée accounted for some of Alphonse's later behavior. It seems indeed that for some time it did prompt him to work hard: "I realized that when you are the holder of a scholarship," he wrote later, and ". . . your nickname is 'Little what's your name,' it is necessary to work twice as much as the others in order to be their equal. . . ."[4] At any rate, it is a matter of record that the lycéen Alphonse Daudet made good grades and soon won the admiration of his professors.

Also a matter of record is the fact that his rebellious spirit, his thirst for independence, and his extreme sensitiveness and imagination could not make of him a model student. And so the story has been told many times how this young freshman began missing classes to go boating on the Rhone and Saone rivers. Not physically strong, at times unable to steer his rowing boat, he would unconsciously imperil his life by getting too close to a paddle-wheeled steamer.

Biographers have also emphasized the quality of his imagination and eloquence which, whenever he arrived home late, enabled him to quickly invent some fantastic and fascinating story to divert his parents' attention from his tardiness. Once when he was caught off his guard as he saw his mother waiting for him at the top of the stairs, he announced dramatically that the pope had just died. The poor woman believed him and was so abashed that she forgot to ask him the expected embarrassing question: "Where have you been?"[5] It should be added that by the time he had reached the age of fifteen, young Alphonse had joined a group of boys who met in a rented room where they tried to emulate the bohemian life of the capital by drinking and smoking. Notwithstanding his behavior, Alphonse amazed everyone around him by his progress in school and by his precocious literary talent. Ernest reports that his brother had begun early to make it a habit of treating in verse every essay subject assigned to the class. A poem entitled "Praise of Homer," which he wrote at the age of thirteen during a two-hour class period, made a sensation. Part of it has been saved from oblivion and quoted many times. He wrote others which, for very good reasons, he did not show to the instructor. These were the kind that later gave his first English biographer an opportunity to vent his feelings on a matter apparently dear to his heart, namely, the superiority of the English system of education over the French.

In 1855 Alphonse Daudet became acquainted with journalists who procured him a minor job in the offices of the *Gazette de Lyon*. He seized this opportunity to show the editor of the newspaper a novel, *Léo et Chrétienne Fleury*, which he had just written. According to Ernest, the editor promised to publish it. Alphonse, then only fifteen, became famous overnight not only in the eyes of his family, but also among the personnel of the *Gazette*. Unfortunately, publication of the paper was suddenly suspended because of an article considered hostile to the government. Alphonse's manuscript was lost in the turmoil: "Though twenty-five years have elapsed since then," wrote Ernest in 1881, "the impression left over my memory by *Léo et Chrétienne Fleury* has remained vivid enough to give me the right to say, that if that novel had been published it would have been quite worthy of a place in a collection of my brother's work."[6]

At the age of sixteen, having taken all the necessary courses and won quite a few prizes at the lycée, Alphonse was ready to take the examination for the baccalauréat degree.[7] Unfortunately, this happened to be at a time when his father's business had completely disintegrated. Unable to find enough money to pay the high fee required for taking the examination, Vincent was about to decide that the precocious Alphonse could defer the ordeal for a year. Then came the news that a vacancy for a *maître d'études* ("assistant") had just occurred at the Collège d'Alais (today spelt Alès).

The family well realized how hard the life of an usher in a French collège or lycée generally was, but they concluded that, all things considered, this was the best solution to the immediate problem.

They hoped further that Alphonse would be able to save enough money to pay the fees and take his examination the next year. Accordingly, an application was made, and the post offered and accepted. Little What's Your Name himself welcomed this opportunity of leaving his dreary environment and starting on a new life probably full of interesting adventures.

He left at the end of April, 1857. The family accompanied him to the boat, apparently the same one that had brought them to Lyons six years before. His father gave him all the sound advice he could think of, while his mother, his brother, and Annou, the maid, cried. "Be a man," mumbled Vincent. "Be a good boy, and don't get sick," advised his mother. Ernest (Jacques, in the novel), was so deeply moved that he could not utter a single word. As for Alphonse himself, "the joy of leaving Lyons, the motion of the boat, the intoxication of the voyage, his pride in feeling himself a man, a grown-up man journeying alone and earning his own living,"[8] excited him beyond measure.

His departure meant the beginning of the breaking up of the Vincent Daudet family (Henri, the elder son, had died in 1855, aged twenty-three). Vincent now tried his luck as a commercial traveler, work which took him all over France, but again he failed to procure sufficient means to support both himself and his household. The only recourse left was to sell the furniture so that the most pressing debts could be paid. All this was carried out perfectly by Ernest, now the head of the house. Annou, the "old servant," had already returned to her hometown. It was decided that Mme Daudet and her daughter Anna would go to live with relatives in Nîmes. They left in July. A few weeks later, having liquidated all the family debts, Ernest in turn left the gloomy atmosphere in which they all had been so unhappy. Paris was his destination and his hope. He had fifty francs in his pocket and several letters of introduction. Fired with the will to succeed, he carried also a beautiful tailor-made suit bought on credit. Both Ernest and Alphonse understood that their first aim should be to rebuild the "foyer," their home. They eventually did so but it took much longer than anticipated.

V *At the Collège d'Alais*

After leaving the boat at Beaucaire, Alphonse had gone to visit his relatives in Nîmes. He reached Alès (called Sarlande in *Le Petit Chose*) a few days later, on May 1, 1857. Because of his slenderness and small stature, the janitor of the college took him for a student.

The principal himself was flabbergasted by his appearance: "Why!," he burst out, "he is a child. . . . What am I to do with a child?" He was about to send him away when the benumbed Little What's Your Name held out a letter from the principal of the Nîmes Academy recommending the grandnephew of Father Reynaud. "The memory of 'l'oncle l'abbé,' " wrote Ernest later, "protected my brother, and they kept him."[9]

During his first weeks at the College le petit chose managed to perform his duties satisfactorily. The youngsters whom he supervised loved him and he loved them. Unfortunately, trouble came a little later, when he was put in charge of the older boys. These were rough fellows who made fun of his physical weakness and at times played mean tricks on him. He found it impossible to establish or maintain discipline. In addition, he realized that the professors looked down upon him, "from the top of their toque." As for his colleagues, the other ushers or assistant masters, they took advantage of his good nature by leaving the whole school in his charge during the Thursday and Sunday afternoon walks in the country while they would "go off to the taverns with the elder boys."[10]

It has been maintained that Alphonse's plight was not so bad as it is described in Le Petit Chose, that he himself was responsible for much of what happened to him, and that he did not work as hard as his readers may be led to think. Whatever the case may be we can easily understand why he longed for the opportunity to join his brother in Paris. In the month of October he received a letter from Ernest in which one word — "Come!" — stood out among all others. According to the story, he immediately resigned his position. But there may be some truth in the suggestion made by several scholars that he was simply fired. In any case, he gave up forever the idea of taking the baccalauréat examination and left for the French capital. His stay in Alès had lasted about six months.

The delightful pages recounting his trip and arrival in Paris are well known. Shabbily dressed and wearing the now famous "Indian rubber socks," or galoshes, with hardly any clothes in his suitcase and not enough money in his pocket even to buy a meal, freezing and starving, he nevertheless felt quite happy, trusting to the future and his lucky stars. He reckoned on his poems and short stories written in Lyons and Alès to start him on his literary career. This thought alone would have been enough to fill his heart with hope and enthusiasm. Ernest was waiting for him at the Gare de Lyon station in Paris, where he finally arrived just before daybreak on November 1, 1857.

VI *First Year in Paris*

Alphonse Daudet was then seventeen, not sixteen as stated in his *Trente ans de Paris*. For the next forty years, that is, till the end of his life, he would live in Paris or its vicinity. Brother Ernest, henceforth called *la mère Jacques* ("mother Jacques") by Little What's Your Name, took him to the small room where both were to live for some time on a rather limited budget, that of Ernest's small salary. Their room was a poorly furnished, miserable garret on the fifth floor of a large building partly occupied by students, in the heart of the Latin Quarter, and called Grand Hôtel du Sénat. It has been wondered which pleased Alphonse most between this high-sounding name which tickled his vanity and the traditional *grenier parisien* ("poet's garret").

Yet, his first days in Paris were not too cheerful. Since Ernest had to leave early in the morning and could not return till late in the evening, Alphonse would remain all day indoors, alone. Being handicapped by the shortsightedness that affected him since childhood, and not knowing a soul in Paris, he dared not, at first, venture by himself into the busy streets of the Latin Quarter. Fortunately, life had already taught him how to keep a stiff upper lip. His will to succeed and his natural enthusiasm having remained unimpaired, he banished the melancholy creeping over him and immediately decided to set about the completion of the book of poems he wanted to publish.

As soon as la mère Jacques had seen to it that he was properly dressed and shod, Alphonse began to walk to the nearby Odéon theater. There he discovered that besides being able to browse among the books of the numerous bookstalls in the arched gallery, he could also learn about the latest literary news and rub elbows with some of the then famous men of letters. One of these was Leconte de Lisle (1818 - 1894) who used to glance through the most recent books "while looking round to see whether he was being recognized." Other times he watched Louis Bouillet (1821 - 69) arrive arm in arm with Flaubert (1821 - 80) and go through the artists' entrance door. Two figures which struck him most were Barbey d'Aurevilly (1808 - 89) and Jules Vallès (1833 - 85), whose names will also be found later in histories of French literature. D'Aurevilly was then in his fifties and already famous, perhaps as much for his eccentricities as for his works. Vallès, only twenty-four, had just published *l'Argent*. Alphonse did not dare to speak to him. He has named a few other habitués of the arched gallery — Cressot, Jules de la Madelène, Amédée Rolland, Jean Duboys, Charles Bataille, Tisserant — who are today almost completely forgotten. Later he ventured a little farther and met other young writers and artists in literary circles as well as in the cafés.[11]

Meanwhile the two brothers lived very frugally, indulging in a good meal only once a week, on Sunday when they would eat at the *table d'hôte* located in the building. There could be seen and above all, heard, a large number of students, natives of Gascony. Among them the noisiest and most eloquent was a twenty-one-year-old law student whose name was Léon Gambetta.[12] The Daudet brothers became acquainted with him on Christmas day when he came to apologize for the noise he and his friends had made during the night.

VII *First Book:* Les Amoureuses

When he thought he had produced enough verses to fill a little volume Alphonse began to visit publishers. He tried first the best ones, such as Michel Lévy and Hachette: " 'May I see M. Lévy? It's about a manuscript.' 'Very well, Sir. Your name?' And invariably, after inquiring the clerk would say: 'Sorry. Mr. Lévy is not in. Or Mr. Hachette is not in.' Nobody was ever in."[13] Perhaps it was all for the best, since his manuscript was finally accepted by a young publisher, Jules Tardieu, who published it at his own expense — which "no well-established firm would have ever done." It is not clear whether Alphonse had first met Tardieu, himself a poet and his neighbor, in front of his shop, as he claimed in *Trente ans de Paris*, or at the library of the Arsenal, as recalled by Ernest. The important fact is that Alphonse had the thrill of seeing his first book, *Les Amoureuses*, come out of the press when he was only eighteen. Now, feeling well started in his career as a writer, he dared to address Jules Vallès.

"Within twenty-four hours," says Ernest, "he was ranked among those beginners of whom people say 'he is somebody!' "[14] A critic went as far as to suggest that he had inherited Musset's pen for poetry, referring naturally to the light and fanciful side of the Romantic master rather than to his gloomy or impassioned side. However, the publication of the volume did not accomplish much more than adding a little to the reputation he had already made in

1858 by reciting his poems to his friends and in front of various groups. These auditors, who had enjoyed his poetry as much as his original way of delivering it, were delighted to find in the book, among other favorites, a light piece entitled "Les Prunes" — those famous plums "qui ont fait le tour du monde," ("known round the world"),[15] wrote Ernest with some exaggeration.

The immediate success and popularity of this poem must be attributed mostly to its simplicity and freshness of expression. As if confiding a secret to his readers or listeners the poet first annouces that he is willing to tell them how plain plums happened to be responsible for the fact that he and his cousin fell in love with each other. After introducing his uncle, who owns a large orchard and a pretty daughter, "belle à ravir mais point coquette" ("ravishing but no flirt"), he shows the young couple romping about through the orchard, where they find a plum tree. She takes one of the fruit, bites on it, hands it to him: " 'Here!' . . . she said. His heart was beating so fast! That was all, but it was enough. This one fruit implied a lot! Had I known what I know. . . ." And our poet concludes in the ninth stanza: "Oui, mesdames, voilà comment . . . Nous nous aimâmes pour des prunes."[16] Here, "pour des prunes" has a double meaning: "because of plums" and "for nothing at all," "for no good result." The poem was probably inspired by one of the author's own experiences.

Among other favorite pieces in *Les Amoureuses* were "Les cerisiers" ("The Cherry Trees"): "Do you remember what you used to say, Darling, in the days of the cherry trees? . . ." and "Aux petits enfants" "To the little children," which opens the book and, perhaps still more than the above, is hard to appreciate fully in translation:

> Enfants d'un jour, ô nouveaux-nés,
> Petites bouches, petits nez,
> Petites lèvres demi-closes,
> Membres tremblants,
> Si frais si blancs,
> Si roses[17];

As can be seen readily, this is only light, fanciful poetry, but it reveals, along with an early mastery of the art of versification, some of Daudet's characteristic traits, especially his sensibility and good-natured irony. He had written "Aux petits enfants" at the age of

sixteen. While *Les Amoureuses* cannot be compared in any way
whatever to Baudelaire's *Les Fleurs du Mal* published a year before,
we can understand why some contemporaries pointed out the
contrast between the two works — and we may wonder with G.
Lanson what "realistic" poetry could have become under Alphonse
Daudet's pen.

Speaking from firsthand experience, Ernest admits that this
"brilliant entrance into literature did not bring them a fortune."
Indeed, the success of the book in 1859 seems to have been confined
mainly to the salons and literary circles. When, some seventy years
later, the editors of the 1930 Ne Varietur edition of Daudet's
Oeuvres complètes looked for significant criticism to quote, they had
to resort to articles published between 1864 and 1898.

Both Alphonse and Ernest had to live on Ernest's salary for a
couple of more years. Alphonse contributed a few articles to such
magazines as *Le Monde illustré* and *Le Musée de famille*, then to *Le
Figaro*, whose editor was the then well-known Villemessant. To
become a contributor to *Le Figaro* had been for a long time his chief
ambition. Undoubtedly Villemessant accepted him partly because
he had been favorably impressed by *Les Amoureuses*.

But the most important gain produced by the book, far more
helpful to the two brothers than copyrights might have been, was the
fact that the Empress Eugénie became interested in the author of
"Les Prunes." The story of how or when she asked the count (later
duke) de Morny (the emperor's half brother) to help the young poet
in want, has been told in different ways, but that remains of
secondary importance. What really mattered was the fact that
Alphonse Daudet was offered a position by the most powerful man
of the Second Empire. This post, that of secretary to the president of
the Legislative Body, was a real and well-paid sinecure that he was
to occupy during the next five years. In addition he was able to
secure also a good position for his brother in the civil service.

It is therefore evident that the year 1860 marked an important
turning point in the life of the two brothers. It meant not only the
end of poverty and insecurity, but also the beginning of a new life
for Alphonse, an easy life full of opportunities which he would find
hard to resist. Henceforth, his real and fundamental problem would
no longer be that of overcoming adversity but rather that of
withstanding prosperity and good fortune, a task particularly
difficult for him on account of both his temperament and his
previous experiences.

VIII *Bohemia*

We have seen that the adolescent Petit Chose had already indulged in some kind of bohemian life in Lyons. In Alès he had spent many hours at the Café Barbette and other taverns or *guinguettes* trying to drown his sorrows in drink. He was not through sowing his wild oats. Soon after his arrival in Paris he began to frequent the cafés of the Latin Quarter and Montmartre and strike up acquaintances with various kinds of bohemians, the beatnicks or hippies of the 1850s. Today, we cannot help thinking of him when we see a young man with long hair, mustachios, and beard. But Alphonse Daudet was not conforming to a new fashion. He had decided once and for all what his physical appearance should be. Even the duke of Morny did not succeed in forcing him to have his hair cut.

The bohemia of the 1850s was as varied as hippyland is probably today. In any case it was no longer the artistic and literary *bohème dorée* of the preceding generation, which included among its members such well-known figures as Théophile Gautier, Gérard de Nerval, and Arsène Houssay. To this gilded bohemia of the Romantic era, bohemian life was less a struggle than an exciting experience. It meant above all independence and freedom to criticize old ideas and traditions, and *choquer le bourgeois*, that is, deride the class to which they belonged. However, although living often from hand to mouth, they never suffered much from want: Houssay received money regularly from his *notaire*, and Gautier, the poorest of the group, lamb chops and bouillon from his mother. Camille Rogier, who illustrated the "*Contes d'Hoffmann*, would use his copyrights to buy beautiful, but extravagant clothes and boots. Even Gérard de Nerval, who seemed satisfied to feed on dreams, could at times indulge in superfluity".[18]

The bohemia represented by those who lived in garrets and suffered from cold and starvation had undoubtedly existed in the 1830s, but its existence remained barely suspected by the general public. It was that part of bohemia which Murger called *La Bohème ignorée*, unnoticed because its members lacked that sense of reality which would have prompted them first to find a way of earning their daily bread, and then find one to make their works known. Instead, whether "true geniuses or false ones", Murger insisted, "they persist in holding that society is solely responsible for their failure." Obviously, Alphonse Daudet never belonged to the Bohème ignorée.

Murger identified also, more than a century ago, those who do not hesitate to leave home and school simply because, he said "they believe that being clad in winter with 'nankin' [Nankeen trousers were fashionable in 1850], sleeping outdoors and skipping a meal now and then constitute the height of felicity." Some of them, he went on, return home after two or three years "to don the black coat of gentility," marry their home sweetheart, take up their father's business or a position in government, and spend the rest of their lives reminiscing about their romantic and stormy bohemian youth, "a story that they tell and retell by the fireside with the gusto and bombast of a tiger hunter."

True bohemia, on the other hand, la Bohème officielle, found worthy of consideration by the author of Scènes de la vie de Bohème, is that consisting of artists and writers who, in one way or another, have managed to make themselves known by their works. Murger refers to them as "bold adventurers whose vices are lined with virtues." To him, a respectable bohemian is one who has plenty of patience, who can show forbearance toward begrudging fools, and "who is courageous, who keeps up his pride, and yet is resigned to the law of vae victis [woe to the vanquished]. Such traits certainly characterize the bohemian Alphonse Daudet of the early 1860s.

"To most bohemians," Murger explained further, "Bohemia is a means rather than an aim, and many leave it as soon as they have made their mark and feel secure in the artistic or literary line they have chosen." This again would apply perfectly to Alphonse Daudet.[19]

By the middle of the nineteeth century, bohemia was no longer the expression of a gay, careless, and more or less irresponsible youth. It was fast becoming an organized group, a sort of social entity with its own laws, customs and morals, quite conscious of unresolved social problems, bitter and socially aggressive. Led by Jules Vallès, who wanted to arm "these shabby, seedy looking intellectuals with guns and drive them to the barricades,"[20] it shifted rapidly from art and literature to politics and, under the Second Empire, became the center of opposition. Alphonse Daudet was one of those who were to leave it. When he did, however, he had experienced it directly, lived through it, observed its various manifestations, and noted a wealth of facts and impressions in little notebooks from which he was later to draw much of his inspiration.

Among his first Parisian acquaintances were two young writers, Charles Bataille and Jean Duboys, whom he had met at the Bal

Bullier in the Latin Quarter. They invited him to pay them a visit in Montmartre and one day took him to the Brasserie des Martyrs, the most popular haunt of bohemia. There reigned the author of the famous *Scènes de la vie de Bohème* which during the past few years had delighted Alphonse Daudet and many others of his generation. Around Murger could be seen Pierre Dupont (1821 - 1870), the famous *chansonnier* ("song writer") and singer of rustic life; Champfleury (1821 - 1889), novelist and theorist of Realism; Alfred Delvau (1825 - 1867), who later accompanied Alphonse to Alsace; and Charles Baudelaire (1821 - 1867), then very much in the public eye because of his recent trial for the publication of *Les Fleurs du Mal*. We may imagine young Alphonse's thrill and excitement upon finding himself in such company.[21]

IX *Marie Rieu*

It was at his friends' apartment that he met Marie Rieu, the girl destined to play such an important part in his life and whom he could never forget entirely. She was an attractive artists' model, a good neighbor, and a charming companion, apparently with a great deal of experience to her credit, but not essentially a "bad girl." She fell madly in love with the handsome young fellow whose originality and superiority over the others had immediately impressed her and, apparently without too much difficulty, succeeded in capturing and monopolizing him.

He for his part found in her both an inspiration and a refuge from loneliness and despair. With her, he saw the future in brighter colors. During his first winter in Paris they faced together all kinds of hardships in a gay mood. Marie, who for some time had aspired to some kind of stability and security, was determined to keep her man. She did her best to make their union last, and they managed to remain happy and cheerful for some time. Unfortunately, unable to control her fears of losing him, she made scenes which she carried on dreadfully. He in turn became bitterly jealous after learning certain details regarding her past life. From then on their happiness was marred by incessant quarrels and separations followed by short-lived reconciliations.

Then the time came when Alphonse, who until then had kept his home with Ernest, decided that moving to an apartment with Marie might help to solve their problems. But the situation kept on worsening until it became unbearable and hopeless. The fact was that they did not belong to the same world. When Marie finally understood there was no hope for her ambition to be realized, they parted. The end of their liaison, which had lasted about two years, meant the end of Alphonse's bohemian life. However, it did not mean at all that he was to become suddenly a well-behaved bourgeois, a man with regular habits. Indeed he did not sever connection entirely either with his good friends of Montmartre and the Latin Quarter or with Marie to whom he could not help returning several times. To her he had dedicated the first edition of *Les Amoureuses* (1858), but in the second edition (1863) he replaced the dedication, "A Marie R . . ." by that of "A J. T. de Saint Germain" and in the third (1873) by the following: "A Madame Alphonse Daudet — Tu as pour te rendre amusée — Ma jeunesse en papier icy — Clément Marot à sa Dame."[22]

The position of attaché de Cabinet of the duc de Morny left Alphonse free to utilize his time the way he saw fit, which he certainly did. It could be said that he had now graduated into a new kind of bohème dorée," a bohemia that meant first of all complete independence: freedom from want as well as freedom from sentimental attachment. He still possessed those fundamental virtues considered by Murger as the lining or natural counterparts of the bohemian vices: the pride of the individual, a deep faith in art, sincerity, courage, patience, and determination to reach artistic perfection. Alphonse Daudet never forgot that he owed it to himself not only to prove equal to the task — which did not present any problem — but especially to achieve a better reputation as a writer.

CHAPTER 2

First Works

I *Apprenticeship Years*

DURING these so-called apprenticeship years, *(les années d'apprentissage)* Alphonse Daudet's works were neither very numerous nor very outstanding. Yet, even among the fifty or sixty pieces of writing that, beside *Les Amoureuses,* he published in periodicals between 1856 and 1865 (in *Paris-Journal, Le Figaro, Le Musée des Familles, La Revue Fantaisiste, La Revue nouvelle,* etc.) can be found a few of a certain merit, such as "Audiberte," a novelette that appeared by installments in *Paris-Journal* during the summer of 1859.

"Audiberte" was his first prose fiction signed Alphonse Daudet, his own name instead of a pseudonym. It is an interesting example of the rustic and regional literature prevalent in those days. It is the story of two teenagers who are unable to decide between love and honor. Professor Bornecque sees in it Alphonse Daudet's first treatment of the theme of fatal love. The story is not to be found in Daudet's *Oeuvres complètes* but Bornecque has summarized and analyzed it in his *Années d'apprentissage d'Alphonse Daudet.*

In 1861, Daudet published in book form *La Double conversion, Conte en vers,* which had already appeared in *Le Figaro,* and in 1862 another little brochure, *Le Roman du Petit Chaperon rouge.* It was apparent, however, that his literary activities were slowed down by ill health due to excesses in his stormy and dissolute bohemian life. In the summer of 1861, Alphonse, weak and overworked, suffered from an acute tracheitis. In the fall, he was advised to leave Paris and spend the winter in a warmer climate, the only way, his doctor insisted, to prevent permanently ruining his health. He left for Algeria in November, 1861. In February, 1862, while he was enjoying the African sunshine in the Cheliff Valley, he received a dispatch from his brother Ernest informing him that *La Dernière*

Idole, a play he had written in collaboration with Ernest Lépine, had just been produced with great success at the Odéon theater. According to what he said later to his brother, "the news left him entirely cold"; but other reports, including Alphonse's own written account, show convincingly that far from remaining calm and indifferent he, on the contrary, became very excited over this first success: "I read and reread it, this blessed dispatch, twenty times, one hundred times! My first play!" To be sure, this was only a one-act play written in collaboration, but the most and the best part of the writing belonged to Alphonse. We can imagine what a thrill it must have been for a young man of his age (only twenty-one) to feel as a successful playwright. And so, forgetting the doctor's orders he immediately decided to rush back to Paris: "To see my play on the stage, nothing else counted. . . . I arrived in Paris around six o'clock. It was dark and I did not think of eating. 'Driver, to the Odéon.' Oh! jeunesse!"[1]

Was he on his way to becoming a great dramatist? He may have thought so himself at the time. In any case, there is no doubt that the theater attracted him. He hastened to write a one-act farcical comedy which failed at the Opéra comique the following year; but in 1865, another one-act comedy, *l'Oeillet blanc*, again written in collaboration with Lépine, enjoyed a certain success at the Théâtre-Français — a kind of *succès de sensation*. He had two more produced during that decade, *Le Frère aîné*, again with Lépine in 1867, and, in 1869, *Le Sacrifice*, a three-act comedy which he wrote alone. They enjoyed only a mild success. He wrote others later, either alone or in collaboration, until the end of his life. But, as we shall see, his real triumph as a dramatist was not to come until 1885, with the revival of *l'Arlésienne*.

Meanwhile, toward the end of the summer 1862 his doctor insisted again that he should spend the winter in a warm climate, and again there was no difficulty for him to secure a leave of absence from the duc de Morny. This time Alphonse went to Corsica. There, as he had done in Algeria, he observed life around him and filled notebooks with his impressions of the land and of the people. When he returned to Paris his health had improved a little but not enough to satisfy the doctors. They again recommended a cure of sunshine during the next winter, that of 1863 - 64.

II   *Provence and the Felibrige*

For this third sojourn in a warm climate he chose Provence, this time a place already quite familiar to him, where he expected to find old and new friends such as Timoléon Ambroy and the Felibres. The Ambroy (of Fontvieille, near Arles) and the Daudet families had been united for some time, and Alphonse and Timoléon had grown fond of each other through the years. The Felibres were the Provençal poets who ten years before had vowed to work together for the "rehabilitation and restauration" of the Provençal language and literature. By the time he had reached the age of twenty-three, Alphonse Daudet had already met the most prominent of them: Roumanille, Aubanel, and particularly Mistral, who, as the author of *Mireille*, had been for some time in the limelight.

The Felibres had soon been recognized as the real initiators and true leaders of the nineteenth-century Provençal Renaissance which, under the name of Felibrige developed later into a well-organized association extending all over southern France. As it reacted against excessive centralization, the Felibrige had immediately acquired a political social character. Its basic claim however was the recognition of Provençal as a language deserving to be taught in French elementary schools. Alphonse Daudet never thought such reform could be realized, but he understood his friends and sympathized with their cause. He has recalled how, when still living in Lyons (he was then fifteen or sixteen) his family would wait anxiously for the arrival of the *Armana prouvençau*, the official organ of the Felibrige. The origin of Provençal influence on him may well go back to those days.[2]

Later he found in the *Armana* inspiration for several of his short stories, as for example the well-known "Curé de Cucugnan" or "Les Etoiles." It may be assumed that during his first two years in Paris he was indeed too busy trying to solve his many problems and adapt to life in the capital to give much attention to Provence and the Felibres. However, when in April, 1859, he heard that Mistral had come to Paris to thank Lamartine for heralding his budding fame in the world of literature, he had no rest till a meeting with the author of *Mireille* could be arranged.

This was done thanks to the Provençal-born poet Adolphe Dumas who had discovered Mistral's genius a few months before. Dumas brought Mistral to Alphonse's garret where the three southerners enjoyed a scanty, "wretched dinner" but a dinner enlivened by conversation. Mistral spoke and answered questions "with a soft and singing voice," Alphonse wrote later. However, when asked why he wrote in Provençal, Mistral's voice rose high: "Why? Why I write in Provençal? Because Provençal is my language, the language of the land where I was born . . . where the very birds sing their song in Provençal." And he spoke at length of that land and then recited some passages from *Mirèio* (*Mireille* in French). Alphonse himself declaimed "Lou Prego-Dièu d'estoublo," a poem Mistral had published the year before in the *Armana prouvençau*. "The whole evening passed after this fashion . . . it seemed to me that the narrow room was filled with a delicious odor, fresh and living, exhaled from my own country, left so long before. . . . From that first meeting on we were friends, and before leaving him I promised to come very soon to see him in his fields of Maillane, whither he was in haste to return."[3]

Mistral returned home, and Alphonse Daudet to his works and worries. But he kept his word and managed to go to Maillane in the summer of 1860, a journey that he considered as "one of the most delightful reminiscences" of his life. He described it profusely and with great gusto in the article in the *Century Magazine* quoted above. He went back in 1862, and again in 1863 on his way to, and back from, Corsica.

Now, in the winter of 1863 - 64, his visit lasted a good deal longer. Those were the days when his friendship with Mistral deepened, turned into one that was to last a lifetime. It was also during that visit that he became better acquainted with Roumanille, Aubanel, Anselme Mathieu, and other Felibres, and gathered most of the material he later used in his famous *Lettres de mon Moulin*. It is with reference to those sojourns in Provence that Mrs. Dobie writes that young Alphonse Daudet, "full with the joy of living . . . would embrace with ardour the maidens of Provence while Aubanel chanted his 'Vénus d'Arles.' "[4]

III   *His Marriage to Julia Allard*

Eighteen sixty-five was for Alphonse Daudet a climacteric year during which various events compelled him to look at life and the world in general more seriously than he had done until then. This was a time of prosperity for France, but also one during which its foreign policy tended to create an international crisis. The death of the duke de Morny (March 10, 1865) affected him more directly. Added to his personal sorrow and perhaps worries about his immediate future, was the sudden realization that the problems raised by philosophers about the universe and Man's fate were more than metaphysical abstractions, that they applied directly to real and practical life.

He felt the time had come for hard thinking and great decisions. As soon as he was convinced that his position at the Legislative Body would no longer be a sinecure, he decided to leave it and devote all his time to literature, or, more exactly, to the theater, which he still thought was the best road to fame. The government continued to pay his salary for several months but, even though *L'Oeillet blanc* had thirty-seven performances between April and July, his plays did not enjoy all the success he had expected, and he began to sink deeper and deeper into debt. A few months later he started on a trip to Alsace and Switzerland with his bohemian friend Alfred Delvau. It has been assumed that *Le Figaro* financed part of the adventure. This time Daudet did not take any notes, but he has reminisced about it. Delvau wrote an interesting account of their experiences in *Du Pont des Arts au Pont de Kehl*.[5]

Perhaps the most consequential event of that year for Alphonse took place in December when, through his opera glasses, he saw for the first time Julia Allard, the girl he was destined to marry. The occasion was a performance of the Goncourt brothers' new play, *Henriette Maréchal*, which, for political reasons, a band of young men had vowed to scuttle. In order to counteract their action, the authors had filled the hall with people willing to applaud loudly enough to drown the hissing and shouting. Since the play had already acquired a bad reputation "because of its realism," Mr. Allard and his wife, who had been invited, wondered for a while whether they should take their daughter to see it. They did after being assured that, in any case, Julia would not be able to hear anything because of the uproar.

On the other hand, there was no hesitation whatever on the part of the Daudet brothers who had been invited to sit in the box of Villemessant, the famous editor of the *Figaro* to which Alphonse had just resumed contributing articles. We may presume that both he and Ernest considered this invitation as a great honor and perhaps as a sort of tribute to Alphonse's own achievements in the theater. Moreover, Alphonse was a great admirer of the Goncourt brothers' famous novel, *Germinie Lacerteux*. We are told that for this occasion he had donned a beautiful new plush gray jacket ("en peluche gris de souris à reflets blancs") which attracted notice. At one time, as he cast his eyes over the boxes, his attention was suddenly fixed on the box occupied by the Allards. He stopped, stared a long time, and finally turning to Ernest: "See over there, that beautiful girl? Wonder who she is. Any idea?" he inquired. "How intelligent, self-controlled, determined she seems to be! . . . Well, if I should marry, which of course will never happen, she would be my type. . . ." And,

according to the story as told some thirty years later by Lucien
Daudet, their second son, at that very moment Mademoiselle Allard
was asking her father: "Who is that fellow in that ridiculous
garb? . . . Just the same, he has an unforgettable look in his eyes, and
what a poetic forehead! He is surely somebody. . . ." The Allards'
host (the painter Anatole de Beaulieu) answered the question:
"Indeed dear child, he is a rather gifted young writer. . . .
Unfortunately, he has turned to Bohemian living and, I am afraid,
he will never get anywhere."[6]

Respectable bourgeois as they were, the Allards did not represent
the type constantly bantered by the romantic bohemians. Both
father and mother had flirted with poetry in their youth and were
capable of appreciating and enjoying the arts. Julia was well versed
in literature and had even published a little piece under a pen name
at the age of eighteen. She was now twenty-one, had a mind of her
own, and was determined to choose her husband herself.

We do not know whether the impression she made upon Alphonse
lasted very long during the following days or weeks, or whether it
had any bearing upon his intention to leave again for the South. His
final decision may have been caused, as he claimed, by his desire to
concentrate on a new play or, as it seems more likely, first of all by
the more or less conscious urge he felt to free himself from all his
Parisian ties and worries, especially from the bondage into which his
dissolute life had plunged him.

IV Le Petit Chose

In any case, two or three weeks later, in January, 1866, he
departed again for Provence, this time not so much to see his friends
in Fontvieille, Maillane, or Avignon as to isolate himself in a small
country house, a kind of homestead that his cousin Louis Daudet
had put at his disposal. There he could work! But inspiration for the
play in question did not come. It suddenly occurred to him that what
he really wanted to do was to write an important work, more
important than any of those he had so far published, and at the same
time a kind of work that would allow him, so to speak, to get rid of
the past, the old as well as the recent past. This would naturally be
accomplished by writing an autobiographical novel. Thus came to
Alphonse Daudet the idea of writing Le Petit Chose, his first
important book, to which he would owe his first popular success.

There he stayed for several weeks absolutely alone. The only
human being he saw was the farmer's wife who brought him his

meals, a little bewildered woman who served him silently and "left in a hurry without turning her head."[7] Without any plan or notes, he said, just by following his inspiration, his memories assailing him, he began to write feverishly on wrapping paper or any kind of paper he could lay his hands on. He kept working like this for several weeks. He had just finished the first draft of the first part of the book and begun making a second copy of his manuscript when an "unexpected visitor from Paris" came to visit him. They had lunch together, talked about literature, life on the boulevards, the plays being performed there, the newspapers. The Paris fever seized him again, and, apparently without much hesitation, he decided to leave for the capital that very evening. His manuscript was to remain for several months at the bottom of a drawer.

This was the time when he began writing his famous *Lettres de mon Moulin* in collaboration with Paul Arène. It was also the time when they lampooned the Parnassian poets, in *Le Petit Parniassiculet*. The publication of this thin brochure almost drew Alphonse into a duel with Catulle Mendès, who was then well in the limelight as a poet and novelist. However, a far more exciting and significant event was to happen during that summer of 1866.

Because of an epidemic of cholera now raging in Paris, Alphonse had decided to move to Ville-d'Avray, where his parents and his brother were living. One day, the Daudets entertained neighbors who had brought with them one of their relatives, a well-educated young lady whose name happened to be Julia Allard. It has naturally been assumed that brother Ernest, the former "mère Jacques," now more than ever deeply concerned with his brother's happiness, had something to do with the arrangement of the party. It may be further assumed that neither Alphonse nor Julia had forgotten the feelings they had experienced a few months before after seeing each other through their opera glasses. In any case, the direct result of this first meeting was love at second sight, soon followed by betrothal, and a few months later by marriage. The wedding took place on January 27, 1867.

There is no doubt that, to Alphonse Daudet more than to the average man, marriage meant an important turning point in life, a change which was to affect, in fact transform, the writer as well as the man. From then on, his story would be mainly that of his works. Julia Allard knew his weaknesses, but she believed in his genius and felt confident that she could develop in him all the good qualities he possessed. After a short honeymoon spent mostly visiting his friends in Provence, the manuscript of the *Petit Chose* was rescued from the drawer and, with Julia's encouragement and help, finally carried to an end. It appeared in 1868, and was praised by reviewers. But, again, it failed to make him wealthy.

V   Lettres de mon Moulin

The publication of the *Lettres de mon Moulin*, begun on August 18, 1868, in *L'Evénement* and interrupted in the fall at the time of the merging of that newspaper with *Le Figaro*, was resumed by the latter in 1869. Critics called attention to the work of this young writer who had already mastered the art of expressing himself in a clear, classical prose, and yet poetical language. These "letters," or rather short stories, have lost none of their charm or interest. While modern readers may be disappointed not to find in them a good plot, or an expression of deep emotion, they cannot help admiring the author's understanding of human nature and his sureness and lightness of touch in bringing it out in his characters, whether these are human beings, animals, or plants.

Indeed, we could hardly imagine a reader of "La Chèvre de M. Seguin," for example, not appreciating the tenacity of this now famous nanny goat who could not stand being tied to a post all day long; who wanted her freedom at any cost, and felt nothing but contempt for her master's good care and devotion. Nor can we imagine a reader of "La Mule du Pape" forgetting Daudet's short but vivid and colorful description of Avignon in the days of the popes, and in that setting the pope's mule; that very human mule who loved her daily bowl of wine "with sugar and spices," who would amble along by the music of the farandole when crossing the river on the famous bridge; that papal mule "as gentle as an angel" who nevertheless delivered that terrible kick which she had kept for seven years. And finally, who could forget the story of "l'Elixir du Révérend Père Gaucher," the devoted monk who damns himself for the sake of the community, which blesses him for it? Or again the tale of the Provençal shepherd who, pointing to the stars above his head, so poetically tells their love stories to his master's daughter and then dreams that she is one of them, the brightest and loveliest one in the firmament that has come down to rest her head on his shoulders?

Those stories appeared in book form in 1870 under the title of *Les Lettres de Mon Moulin: Impressions et Souvenirs*, but, for some unknown reason, they did not enjoy so much success as they had four years before, when they first appeared in the newspapers. The volume contained other pieces of an entirely different character such as "L'Arlésienne" ("The Woman of Arles"), a very brief but powerful short story from which the author drew later, in collaboration with Georges Bizet, the well-known lyrical drama by the same title, and "La Diligence de Beaucaire" or "Les Deux auberges," in which the presence of the tragic element is perhaps not so evident but can nevertheless be intensely felt. Others are mere sketches or anecdotes. Yet, every one of them possesses a charm of its own, an original and penetrating charm, that of pure poetry. Alphonse Daudet wrote later that this book was his favorite "not from the literary viewpoint," he specified, but because it reminded him of "the best hours of [his] youth. . . ."[8]

While most of the "Letters" were written in Paris, and not in the mill in question, it remains that they were mostly inspired by Provence and Provençal life. Such also was the case of *Tartarin de Tarascon*, even though most of the action of this very popular novel takes place in North Africa. Tartarin was to appear in its final form only after the war.

Now, in 1869, Alphonse Daudet still believed in his future as a playwright. He had not been discouraged by the failures or mediocre successes of his recent plays such as *Le Frère aîné* and *Le Sacrifice*, and he had decided to apply all his energy and enthusiasm to a new one, *L'Arlésienne*, whose story he had already told in one of the *Lettres de mon Moulin*. Since his marriage, he had steadily made an effort to give up his bohemian habits. Surely, he had not abandoned his old friends and he still spent a good deal of time with them in the taverns, or at home where Julia was willing to receive them. Nonetheless, owing to his wife's patience and understanding, he was well on the road to a regular, well-ordered life, that of a good husband and father. Their first child, Léon, was born in 1867.

VI *The Franco-Prussian War and the Commune*

This unexpected change in his general state of mind did not take place overnight. As we have seen, his spiritual development had manifested itself unequivocally in 1865, and in 1866 when he went south to write *Le Petit Chose*. Now it was to be suddenly accelerated by the Franco-Prussian War of 1870 and the Commune of 1871. He himself has explained how these two calamities achieved the transformation of this bohemian into a well-behaved bourgeois, a serious man who now felt responsible not only toward his country and humanity as a whole but also toward himself and his family.

When the war broke out, Alphonse Daudet and his family, including the Allards, happened to be settled in the country at Champrosay, some fifteen miles southeast of Paris. On July 14 (not yet the national holiday), 1870, a day when excited crowds in Paris were demonstrating over the pending official declaration of war, Alphonse had the misfortune of breaking his leg as he was enjoying a friendly bout with the sculptor Zacharie Astruc. This accident kept him immobilized at Champrosay for some six weeks. As soon as he had recovered, however, the family decided to return to Paris, about to be besieged by the German armies. Like thousands of others, they loaded their most precious belongings on a truck and left for the capital where, in spite of his poor health and myopia, Alphonse managed to get himself accepted in the National Guard. He remained with it until the capitulation of Paris, on January 28, 1871.

Alphonse Daudet did not have much opportunity to fight the enemy as a national guard, but he could observe life in the strained atmosphere of the besieged capital and fill his notebooks with new facts, impressions, and ideas. These formed the substance or basic material of his first two war books, his *Lettres à un Absent* and his *Contes du lundi*.

VII   Lettres à un Absent, Contes du lundi

The *Lettres à un Absent* began to appear in 1871, in the Versailles edition of the newspaper *Le Soir*. Some of them were purely informative accounts of the author's observations. Others, in the form of stories, revealed more of a literary concern, but most of them had a documentary value. Students of French of a generation ago have read "le Siège de Berlin," the moving story of an old colonel of the French army who falls dead when he discovers that the triumphant troops parading on the Champs Elysées are not French, as he had been led to believe, but Prussian; "Nos Pendules, de Bougival à Munich" (republished in *Les Contes du lundi* under the title of "La Pendule de Bougival"), which is the amusing story (Daudet calls it "une fantaisie") of a Parisian timepiece that cannot keep time (striking eight o'clock while showing three), and upsets and demoralizes a German family, to whom it symbolizes French levity. "Les Mères," — a little on the sentimental side to people who have not had this kind of experience — is the story of a soldier's mother whose visit to her son in the barracks is cut short by a bugle call.

The *Contes du Lundi (Monday Tales)*, also published at first in newspapers, appeared in book form in 1873. Again well-known are: "La partie de billard," which tells of the scandalous, ignoble behavior of a field marshal who is more concerned about his game than about the fate of his men; "La Dernière Classe," which depicts the class of an old Alsatian schoolmaster the last time he is allowed to use French in a school of the recently conquered province; and "Les Trois messes basses," a Christmas story which was added to the 1876 edition and had nothing to do with the war nor the Commune. It is a humorous and somewhat irreverent satire of a priest who hurries his mass service to get sooner to his Christmas dinner.

VIII   Robert Helmont

Robert Helmont, journal d'un solitaire, 1870 - 1871 was Daudet's third work inspired by the war. As suggested by its subtitle, it is presented in the form of a diary, that of an artist painter who decides to remain in the zone of the investing army instead of leaving town to take refuge in Paris. Robert Helmont hides in the forest of Sénard, jots down his thoughts, impressions, and experiences, which, in addition to his contemplation and enjoyment of nature — and his grief when he hears the roar of the big guns in the distance — include such daily chores as his search for food and a way to cook it without attracting attention; and his discovery and acquisition of ingredients to make bread, cider, or candles. He is deeply impressed by the destruction of life, or signs of its disappearance, in a recently deserted town where windows deprived of their awnings "look at you with dead eyes."[9] He beholds the pillage of empty homes and other acts of vandalism; hides from the enemy patrols, discovers corpses of murdered Prussian soldiers, and meets the old peasant who has killed them; catches a carrier pigeon, and attempts, unsuccessfully, to return to Paris through the Prussian lines. It is a very impressive, dramatic book, full of suspense.

When, after the war and toward the end of the Commune era, Alphonse Daudet decided to take his family back to Champrosay, he had filled enough pages in his notebook to provide him with material for several stories related to "Paysages d'Insurrection" or "Au Marais," which is the title of the first story in the part of the *Lettres à un absent* devoted to the Commune. Others of the same inspiration are "Le Jardin de la rue des rosiers," the tragic story of the execution of two hostages, and "Les Tricoteuses." Classified with *Les Contes du Lundi* are the delightful story "Les Petits Patés," the horrible one

"La Bataille du Père Lachaise" and others like "Le Turco de la Commune," in which man's cruelty and stupidity are amply illustrated. The notes transcribed in "Autour des *Lettres à un absent*" will be found as interesting and equally if not more fascinating than, anything that has been written on the subject.[10]

These three volumes then constitute the bulk of Alphonse Daudet's contribution to war literature. Daudet limited himself to recording his personal observations and reactions to events without theorizing much on philosophical implications or political questions.

At the beginning he had been eager to get into action, to serve his country, and apparently was optimistic regarding the conclusion of the war, but he became discouraged after hearing about the various defeats of the French armies, and especially when, during the siege of Paris, he realized the inability or incapacity of the army, the National Guard, and the governments to turn the course of events. He observed the hordes of war profiteers and was thoroughly disgusted when the incompetence of the leaders or their indifference regarding the fate of the country had become evident. Nevertheless, as it appears clearly in many of his stories, his wrath having vanished, Daudet treated the subject with marvelous understanding, a sweet irony and sensibility, even though in a serious and occasionally — but only occasionally — bitter mood.

Today, the realistic elements that he stressed remain worthy of consideration. His experiences in the war had indeed furnished him with a tremendous opportunity to probe into the human soul, to uncover what really motivates men's actions and general behavior.

IX   L'Arlésienne

Two important events in Daudet's career took place in 1872: the already mentioned publication of *Tartarin de Tarascon* and the first performance of *L'Arlésienne*. The former was to contribute a great deal to his reputation abroad; the latter, which has been in France one of the most popular plays since 1885 and for a long time a stock piece of the Odéon theater, failed miserably in 1872. Even the now famous overture of Bizet fell short of expectation: "It was a most glorious fall [chute] in the midst of the nicest music in the world,"[11] Daudet quipped a dozen years later.

L'Arlésienne is the story of a young farmer, Frederi, who has fallen deeply in love with a city girl from Arles (the Arlesian woman) and commits suicide when he learns that she has been someone's mistress for two years. The girl herself never appears in the play.[12]

On the other hand, life on the farm and the conflicts arising first between the boy and his parents, then within his own soul, which is the keynote of the play, are dramatized masterfully. The gloomy, tense, and tragic atmosphere of the play is somewhat relieved by the presence of L'Innocent, Frederi's younger brother. The "innocent" is the simpleminded, mentally retarded child whose mere existence is supposed to protect the family, to be its safeguard. L'Innocent awakens, sharpens his wits and gains full possession of his faculties on the day when his brother hurls himself from the hayloft of the farm. The mother, Rose Mamai, and the self-effacing Vivette, whose love is spurned by Frederi, are perhaps the two most admirable characters.

Like the producer, both the author and composer of *L'Arlésienne* were literally appalled by this unexpected disaster of 1872. To explain it, some put forward the regional character of the play and its simplicity, or lack of action. More important may have been the fact that the Parisian public of the time, that had just emerged from "l'année terrible," was not the kind that could get interested in a rustic play, even though presented with accompanying music. Indeed it is hard to see how it could have been apreciated for its poetry and classical beauty by an audience consisting mainly of half-educated, cynical, and noisy upstarts. As for the critics themselves, they were no more appreciative than the crowd whose reactions they had espoused.

In his "Histoire de mes livres," Daudet recalls how, during one of the dress rehearsals of *L'Arlésienne*, the idea occured to him that getting the Parisians really interested would require a work closer to them, one dealing with contemporary life in Paris, and he had immediately imagined a new drama inspired by this thought of a Parisian background. Following the failure of *L'Arlésienne*, however, he lost faith in himself as a dramatist and decided to transform the intended drama into a novel. Then, a couple of weeks later, when he heard that *L'Arlésienne* had been removed from the playbill of the Vaudeville theater, Alphonse was thoroughly discouraged and declared that he would give up literature altogether and apply for a position in the civil service. He wrote a long letter to Ernest entreating "la mère Jacques" to find him a job. He may well have meant it, as another of his plays, *Lise Tavernier*, had also failed miserably a few months earlier. However, his despair was not to last very long. Julia did not have much trouble convincing him that he should remain the man she had married, that is, Alphonse Daudet

the writer, not Alphonse Daudet the bureaucrat — and the letter was
never mailed. Instead, Ernest was asked to use his good offices to
have him appointed to the *Journal Officiel* as dramatic critic, which
was done successfully.

Alphonse Daudet, who was to keep this position for some sixteen
years (see the *Pages inédites de critique dramatique* in *Oeuvres
complètes*, vol. 18), assumed his duties immediately. He also began
writing a few short stories and resumed work on his novel. Upon
Julia's suggestion, they had returned to Champrosay, where they
could more easily practice strict economy. Yet their income was
hardly sufficient for the family to make ends meet. It was then that
M. Allard, aware of their deplorable situation, came to the rescue. By
dint of tact he succeeded in overcoming Alphonse's pride and made
him accept his father-in-law's financial help.

Old debts were paid off and life suddenly made easier. Both
Alphonse and Julia returned to their literary work, each more filled
with enthusiasm and faith in the future. One day Mme Allard, who
had come to visit them, complained that she could hardly see them
except at meal time: "This is no longer a home," she wrote to her
husband, "it is a literary factory."[13] Fortunately, as if fate had willed
it so, one of his most popular books, *Tartarin de Tarascon*, was also to
come out that same year.

X   Tartarin de Tarascon

First published as "an embryo of the novel" in *Le Figaro* of June
18, 1863, under the title of "Chapatin, le tueur de lions," then in
1869, in part and by instalments in *Le Petit Moniteur universel*, as
"Barbarin de Tarascon," and in 1870 again in *Le Figaro*, this time
completed and under a third title, "Le Don Quichotte provençal ou
les aventures prodigieuses de l'Illustre Barbarin de Tarascon," the
story finally appeared in book form in 1872 as *Tartarin de Tarascon*.
The change of titles was due partly to the failure of the first two
narratives to please the readers, and partly to the protests of the
Barbarin family in Tarascon, who threatened to go to law if author
did not remove their name immediately — as told humorously in his
"Histoire de mes livres."

Like the name of Tarascon itself, which Daudet picked up only
because "it boomed beautifully in the southern accent" and, when
railway stations were called, "triumphed over others as would have
the war cry of an Apache warrior,"[14] the name of Tartarin was to
become famous under his pen. The book deserves to be summarized.

Tartarin de Tarascon opens with a description of the hero's house, which, "from the basement to the attic, had an heroic look." The walls of his study were covered with firearms and swords from all times and countries, such as Hottentot clubs and tomahawks, Mexican lassos and Caribbean arrows, Catalan and Corsican daggers and fancy rifles and carbines. His garden was filled with all kinds of undersized exotic plants and trees, including coconut palms, and a giant baobab tree *(arbor gigantea)* small enough to fit into a mignonette vase, a sort of Japanese bonsai tree.

Like his baobab in its pot, the owner of the house, the dauntless, intrepid Tartarin himself — whose prototype was a cousin with whom the author had gone to Algeria in 1861 — felt confined, boxed up in the little town of Tarascon. And this is why Tartarin spent most of his time reading travel books, filling his head as he filled his house and garden, feeding his imagination with *Voyages Round the World* of Captain Cook, the novels of Fenimore Cooper and of Gustave Aimard, and numberless hunting stories of wild animals. This is also why he had become so famous as a "cap-shooter," the sport to which the Tarasconians, all sportsmen, had to resort when all game, ground and winged, fur and feather, had disappeared from the region. In this strange sport each hunter would fling up his cap as high as he could and fire at it in the air. The man scoring the most hits would be proclaimed "king of the hunting," and Tartarin was always the winner of the title. Because he knew the huntsman's code in every detail, including that of tiger and elephant hunting, they recognized him as the arbiter to whom all disputes should be brought for settlement.

Tartarin had other achievements to his credit. The Tarasconians considered him as the best opera singer in town — even though he would limit himself to "roaring" a few bars of Meyerbeer's *Robert le diable* at gatherings in the Bézuquet's drug store or other "salons." They also admired him for his strength and his "double muscles." The author remarks that "only in Tarascon one can hear that kind of things." And yet, in spite of his "double muscles," of his various talents and his popularity, Tartarin found life in Tarascon decidedly stifling. Many times, forgetting that he was at home in his study, he would get excited at the sound of his own voice, and carry his reading into action. He would get up, grasp weapons from the wall and roar: "Let them come!"

In case one should wonder why, then, in view of these circumstances and in this state of mind, the forty-five-year-old

Tartarin had never spent the night away from his hometown, the author has dramatized amusingly for his reader the fact that within Tartarin there were two men unceasingly fighting each other: idealistic Don Quixote and down-to-earth, matter-of-fact Sancho Panza; the former animated by the urge of accomplishing great feats and the latter primarily concerned with his own comfort, Tartarin-Quixote inflamed by his reading and shouting "I shall set out!" and Tartarin-Sancho, his rheumatism in mind, saying: "I shall stay home!"

Tartarin-Quixote (very exalted): Cover yourself with glory!
Tartarin-Sancho (very calm): Cover yourself with flannel.
T.-Q. (more and more exalted): How I would like a good double-barreled gun, daggers, lassos, moccasins!
T.-S. (calmer and calmer): How I enjoy good knitted waistcoats, and warm knee-caps, and a cap with earflaps!
T.-Q. (beside himself): An axe! Give me an axe!
T.-S. (ringing for the maid): Jeanette, my chocolate!
    Thereupon, Jeanette comes in with a cup of excellent chocolate, hot, with a sweet savory smell, waving, undulating, rippling like watered silk [*moiré de soie*], and some delicious aniseed toast all of which makes Tartarin-Sancho laugh while stifling Tartarin-Quixote's cries. And that is how it happened that Tartarin de Tarascon had never left Tarascon."[15]

But Tartarin would eventually leave. In fact, he almost did once to join a business firm in Shanghai where they offered him a position as manager of an important office, exactly the kind of work he wanted to do. In addition, some excitement could be expected there. Since the Tartars occasionally visited the place, that meant closing the doors, grasping the guns in a hurry, and "bang, bang through the window at the Tartars!" Naturally Tartarin-Quixote wanted to seize this opportunity, but Tartarin-Sancho objected violently. He got the upperhand and plain Tartarin did not start on the great adventure. Quite an event in Tarascon!

A little later a menagerie came to town with a number of wild animals among which was a magnificent lion from the Atlas. Tartarin went bravely to look at the beast through the bars of his cage. When people heard him muttering that this was "a beast well worth hunting," they started the rumor that he would soon be leaving for Africa. Tartarin was the most surprised man in town upon hearing about his impending departure. However, the first time someone asked him about it, his vanity prompted him to let it be understood that he might well go. The second time he ventured to say that he probably would, and the third time he would certainly.

While Tartarin-Quixote and Tartarin-Sancho were still fighting, the hero explained that it would take him some time to get ready. He had to read all the accounts of the great African hunters and then prepare himself accordingly. He trained himself to withstand thirst and hunger by existing only on *aigo boulido* ("boiled water"), which is a garlic soup consisting of hot water with a clove of garlic, a sprig of thyme, a bit of bay leaf, olive oil, and a few slices of bread. He acquired the habit of long walks by hiking every morning seven or eight times around the town; he got accustomed to chilly nights, fogs, and dews by staying in his garden till ten or eleven at night, and to the roaring of the lion without shuddering by walking to and fro behind the menagerie, at least as long as the latter remained in town.

However, when, at the end of three months it became known that he had not packed a single trunk, the Tarasconians lost faith in their hero. They soon began to deride him in various ways, especially in a song concerning a man whose terrific gun could easily "exterminate all the lions of Africa." Unfortunately, that strange gun would never go off, although they kept on loading it. The allusion was clear, and Tartarin-Sancho had to give up the fight.

Tartarin left Tarascon wearing an Algerian costume and with it all the necessary equipment to go after the lions in the "Teur" country, which to the Tarasconians meant a very large country consisting of such places as Algeria, Africa, Greece, Persia, Turkey, and Mesopotamia. Tartarin's adventures were to begin on the ship, soon after leaving the port of Marseilles (of which Daudet has sketched a wonderful picture comparable to, but richer and more realistic than, that of Avignon in "La Mule du Pape").

As for Tartarin himself, a caricature symbolizing the French southerner but nevertheless a portrait composed of many observed fundamental human traits, he will henceforth interest the reader and arouse his sympathy as much as his mirth. Whether we read about the various positions of Tartarin's fez during the crossing from Marseilles to Algiers or about the Montenegro "prince" who robs him, the lioness Baia in whose arms he forgets the lions, his unintentional killing of a burro and of a blind tame lion, or again his vain attempts to get rid of his faithful camel, we congratulate plain Tartarin for having been able to reconcile within himself the souls of Don Quixote and Sancho Panza. And we feel relieved when, at the end of his disastrous expedition, Tartarin de Tarascon is welcomed home as a true hero by his countrymen. Suddenly rejuvenated, having recovered his composure, he can explain his camel's cumbersome faithfulness by declaring that he is a noble animal who saw him kill all his lions.

At first, the story was not well received, its humor not appreciated, neither by the readers of the *Petit Moniteur du Soir* nor by those of the *Figaro*. In Provence, especially at Tarascon, it aroused the anger of many people. The Tarasconians refused to recognize themselves in the portrait Daudet had made of them. They regarded themselves as having been ridiculed and personally insulted, and it took some time for the book to achieve the success and the popularity it now has in southern France as elsewhere. Meanwhile, Daudet had the pleasure of seeing it fully appreciated by men like Flaubert and Anatole France.

What has been said regarding the lasting impression left in the reader's mind by the *Lettres de mon Moulin* applies similarly to *Tartarin de Tarascon,* although, for various reasons neither the language nor the style are quite the same in the two works. The important fact to keep in mind at this point is that Alphonse Daudet's third book made him famous as a humoristic writer.

The progress made by Alphonse Daudet in the art of storytelling during these Provençal-inspired "apprentice years" is quite obvious when we compare for example, *Tartarin de Tarascon* to "Audiberte," the novelette he had published ten years before in *Paris-Journal.* Like his other southern stories, "Audiberte" was inspired by the author's personal experiences, not in Provence but in the Languedoc region, where he had spent his childhood. Now he would work on his first novel with a Parisian background.

CHAPTER 3

The Realist Novels

I   Fromont jeune et Risler aîné

THE new drama turned into a novel was finished by the end of 1873. It appeared under the title of *Fromont jeune et Risler aîné*, at first by installments in a periodical called *Le Bien public*, from March 25 to June 18, 1874. As recognized by the author himself, the structure of the novel suffered somewhat from the fact that it was at first conceived as a drama: "I should have changed the plot, changed the order of the gradation of feelings,"[1] he wrote. Nevertheless, its success was genuine and spontaneous. Readers wrote to ask him questions and express their own views on the characters and their actions. This was indeed a new experience for Alphonse Daudet. For the first time in his career he felt that people entertained an earnest interest in his work. "There is nothing better in life," he commented, "than this rise of popularity, this communication between the reader and the author."[2]

As could be expected, *Fromont jeune et Risler aîné* was written in accordance with the decision he had made after the failure of his last two plays. Its action takes place in Paris. It deals with the industrial and business world, a world which Alphonse had known in his childhood but which he could now observe in a different setting, specifically in the neighborhood called le quartier du Marais, where he lived with his family. There, from his apartment window, he could watch men working in old aristocratic mansions that had been transformed into factories, and women in small workshops making those fancy goods called *articles de Paris*. There he found all the details on Parisian life that he needed to create his characters. In fact most of these are drawn directly from life and are perfectly integrated with, and conditioned by, the environment in whch they move and evolve.

The plot develops around the conflict between Risler, an honest, hardworking man devoted to the success and good reputation of his firm, and Sidonie, his unfaithful wife, a heartless social climber whose misdeeds and betrayal bring ruin to the firm and death to her husband. Among the minor and now famous characters should be recalled Delobelle, the vain, would-be actor who personifies the *raté* ("the washout"), unwilling or unable to recognize the fact that he is a failure, not only in his profession, but also as a man; his devoted wife and daughter who similarly delude themselves with vain hopes; and Mr. Chèbe, Sidonie's father, a very minor but nonetheless interesting character who symbolizes the pretentious braggard who wants to impress his listeners, who is always on the point of closing a big deal and finally has to rely on others — on his son-in-law in this case — to get out of trouble.

The novel appeared in book form in 1874, with the significant subtitle of *Moeurs parisiennes*. Unlike what happened to the *Lettres de mon Moulin* four years before, the success of the story was immediate and at least equal to what it had been when published in serial form. Although reviewers had some reservations, it can be said that their general attitude was quite favorable, even genuinely enthusiastic. Zola hailed his friend as one of the few authors whom he deemed capable of writing a novel permeated with "the breath of modern life."[3]

Indeed Daudet's ideas concerning the nature and aim of the novel corresponded closely to those of his time, as can be seen in the following quotation taken from a text he wrote two years later:

> The aim of the modern novel, such as Balzac conceived it is not simply to amuse. With him, observation comes before imagination. Instead of dispersing interest on several characters, of scattering it over a thousand adventures, he confines it, condenses it, at times in one single fact, on a sole character. But, above interest, he still puts truth. . . . The public is beginning to understand that a fiction, a work of imagination, is not necessarily an "amusing" one, in the banal commonplace meaning of this word, and that the study of morals by Balzac or Flaubert must be taken as seriously as any book of science, philosophy, or history.[4]

Two weeks after the appearance of *Fromont jeune* Alphonse, accompanied by his six-year-old Léon and a little apprehensive, went to inquire about the sales: "It is quite a success, a huge success," answered publisher Georges Charpentier. "Go and see the cashier!" Léon reminisced some sixty-five years later that his father "was beaming with joy" and had asked to be paid with gold:

I still can see the rolls of gold coins which we put in a little bag. We immediately rushed home. Mother was reading in the living room. "Here, look at this!" said the author of *Fromont*. He pulled the twenty franc pieces from his pocket and scattered them through the room. Then he asked me to join him in the "gold dance," which we did laughing. . . . Mme Daudet kept her composure and smiled: "I never had any doubt about it," she said gently.[5]

During the first two years after its publication, *Fromont jeune* ran into numerous reprint editions. The work was crowned by the French Academy in 1876 and translations were made into several languages. The American poet Edwin Arlington Robinson felt that Alphonse Daudet was "the greatest artist in fiction now living."[6] It had become clear that Alphonse Daudet's status would no longer be that of a young author resorting for inspiration to his provincial background and youthful experiences. Henceforth, it would rather be that of an accomplished novelist and master of his art, looking at life from a more general and objective point of view. To be sure, his personal experiences were not to be ignored in the future, nor was the Midi to be excluded from the rest of his works. Reminiscences of the far-off country would be found later, not only in *Numa Roumestan* and the sequel to *Tartarin de Tarascon*, but also in other novels such as the *Nabab, Sapho, and Les Rois en exil.* The difference, however, was that from then on his main source of inspiration would be that of a new and recently observed environment. By the same token his works were to reflect more and more a realistic approach to literature.

As a writer, Alphonse Daudet now appreciated, perhaps more than anything else, the freedom given him by the success of his book. His mind now free from petty financial and other worries, he could devote himself entirely to his writings and, with the help he received at home, apply himself to the full development of his particular talent. He did not have any more to beg publishers to consider his manuscripts for publication. They came to him. They even discovered that his previous works deserved more attention than they had received hitherto, and they began to publish new editions of *Le Petit Chose*, the *Lettres de mon Moulin*, and *Tartarin de Tarascon*. Obviously, another turning point in his career had been reached.

Whether they lived in Paris or at Champrosay, the Daudets' home was fast becoming a kind of literary and artistic center. Their circle of friends and admirers had suddenly extended considerably. Among their regular guests of those days must be named the novelists

Gustave Droz and Léon Cladel, the journalists Edouard Drumond and Adrien Hébrard, who was then editor of *Le Temps*, the cartoonist André Gill, the impressionist painters Manet, Renoir (a very close friend), Monet, and Sisley. The Daudets themselves were often invited by such important people as Victor Hugo, who had become very fond of them, and later the Princess Mathilde, in whose salon the celebrities of the Second Empire used to gather.

But it is quite evident that the Daudets did not attach undue importance to these social activities: the book or play to be written was always given priority on their agenda. Priority was also given to meetings with writers like Gustave Flaubert, Edmond de Goncourt, and Emile Zola who had recently become Alphonse's most intimate friends. In 1874 these four men decided to have dinner together once a month, every time in a different restaurant to satisfy their taste for varied food. Their main interest however lay in the opportunity thus created for the discussion of their works and exchange of ideas on art and literature. It should perhaps not be found too surprising that they availed themselves of the occasion to give vent to their feelings about the publishers and the unappreciative public.

Their dinner was characterized by the fact "that everyone could express his thoughts, and even his thoughts carried to extremes through contradictions, on anyone and on anything."[7] Since all of them had had at least one play badly received, they thought it would be appropriate to refer to the monthly event as "the booed author's dinner," *(le dîner des auteurs sifflés)*. Their friend Turgenev having testified that he, too, had had one play booed in Russia, was admitted as the fifth member of the group. Many references to those dinners will be found in the *Goncourts' Journal*.

The years 1874 - 1884 turned out to be the most productive of Alphonse Daudet's career, the decade during which he published his best and most important novels: *Fromont jeune, Jack, Les Femmes d'artistes* (also in 1874), *Le Nabab, Les Rois en Exil, Numa Roumestan, L'Evangeliste,* and *Sapho.*

II Jack

The author of *Fromont jeune,* who was not going to sleep on his laurels, began writing *Le Nabab,* a novel to deal with big business and politics during the Second Empire. However, he soon decided to put it aside temporarily and devote his time to another subject which he could not get off his mind: the fascinating life story of a young man named Raoul Dubief in whom he and Mme Duaudet had become interested. Raoul's fictitious name was to become Jack in the novel, and *Jack* the title of the latter.

The story of Jack, which does not follow exactly the life of his prototype, is that of a child whose father is unknown and whose mother is a "kept woman" not too much concerned about the well-being of her illegitimate son. Ida de Barancy, as she wants to be called, is at first obsessed with the idea of being reckoned among the nobility. She is a confused being, capricious, irresponsible, alternately generous and selfish, but not quite an "unnatural mother," even though she ends by sacrificing her son to d'Argenton, a literary failure, another *raté*, with whom she has become infatuated. Jack dies at the age of twenty-two after enduring, through his short life, an incredible amount of physical and moral sufferings. He has dearly loved his mother almost to the end.

Interest, in this long two-volume work, is naturally centered on the hero, However, all due consideration is given to the society he lives in, a society consisting of many different groups and social types. In fact, the very subtitle of the book, *Moeurs contemporaines* (ContemporaryMorals and Customs), suggests the importance attached by the author to the social element. The dedication, an homage to Flaubert which points out the kind of spirit and passion that endow the work with life, is equally purposeful and significant:

> This book of compassion
> of anger and irony
> is dedicated
> to Gustave Flaubert
> my friend and master

Daudet has explained how he started writing *Jack* with feverish haste and let the *Moniteur universel* begin its publication by installments long before it was finished. He has also written at length on the genesis of the work, his various sources, and his ideas regarding the plot and creation of its characters. He has pointed out, for example, that the whole episode of Indret — an iron manufacturing center where Jack worked — is entirely imaginary, that Raoul never lived there and never was, like Jack in the novel, a stoker on a ship, and that his mother was actually worse than Ida de Barancy. As for d'Argenton and most of the ratés around him, Alphonse Daudet had only to look twenty-five years behind him, when he lived among them. Other characters in the book had been observed more recently either at Champrosay, Indret, or Paris.

Jack appeared in book form at the beginning of 1876 and was generally well received by the press. But its success did not compare with that enjoyed by *Fromont jeune*, and did not, like the latter, prompt the author to perform another "gold dance."

Several reasons have been given to explain this colder reception. Daudet himself seemed to accept Flaubert's opinion that there was "a little too much paper in it." The often quoted "un peu trop de papier, mon fils," inferred clearly enough that condensing and streamlining the author's longest and most rapidly written novel would have improved it and probably increased its sale.

George Sand wrote to Daudet that Jack's pains and miseries had so deeply affected her that for three days after reading the book she could not work. Some fifty years later, critic Albert Thibaudet noted that *Jack* had caused as many tears to be shed as had *David Copperfield*.[8] While such statements are not necessarily derogatory they help us to understand why, more often than seems justified, mere pathos and sensibility should have been reacted against as plain sentimentality.

One critic defined *Jack* as "an indictment against society in favor of neglected or forsaken children."[9] Another has called it "the book of failures."[10] However, it is neither a treatise of sociology nor a *roman à thèse*, that is, a novel with a purpose — that of demonstrating the truth of a theory. It is essentially a description of life as the author observed it around him, without any long dissertations or theories regarding the social problems that arose in his mind. Yet, we can well see how certain pages or chapters may have led one to the above interpretations and definitions.

It has also been emphasized that the plot as well as some of the characters lack verisimilitude, are short of "psychological truth." Perhaps more correct is the idea that, rather than such deficiencies, the main reason for the public's unfavorable reactions was precisely the presence of too much truth, too much of that observed, realistic truth which could not possibly please the average reader. Daudet was to comment later: "Yes indeed, this is a cruel, bitter, dreary book. But what does it amount to, when compared to the real existence that I have just related."

Daudet felt that the time he had spent writing *Jack*, particularly the few months at Champrosy where the family moved every spring, had been the happiest in his career. There he daily enjoyed what he called "une ivresse de pensée et de travail" ("a drunkenness with thought and work").

Back in Paris, he was soon ready to resume his work on *Le Nabab* (*The Nabob*), the novel he had laid aside to write *Jack*. It took him a long time to do the necessary research and recapture the atmosphere of the period he wanted to revive — a period which, because of recent political events and social changes, seemed now very far removed. By the end of September, 1876, it became imperative for him to take a long rest: "I am dog-tired, puffed up with unhealthy fat, exhausted,"[11] he wrote to his Provençal friend Timoléon Ambroy. Some time later the Daudets arrived at Fontvieille for a short visit. From there they went to Marseilles, Cassis (where Alphonse and Julia had spent their honeymoon), Monaco, and then Bordighera on the Italian Riviera.

As soon as he had sufficiently recuperated they returned to Paris. It was then that they left their apartment on Rue Pavée, now too small for the family, and moved to Place des Vosges where Julia had found a "pavillon entre cour et jardin," a detached building in the old Hôtel Richelieu which gave Alphonse the feeling of inhabiting a house in the country. Once installed he was again able to devote all his thought and energy to the piece of work at hand. On October 8, 1877, Edmond de Goncourt wrote in his journal: "Daudet is done up. For the last five months he has been working from 4:00 AM to 8:00, from 9 to 12, from 2:00 PM to 6 and from 8 to Midnight — a steady twenty hours' work."

III   Le Nabab

Le Nabab was serialized in the newspaper *Le Temps* from July 12 to October 21, 1877, and appeared in book form a few weeks later, at the end of November. Five days after its publication, a noted journalist could write without too much exaggeration that people now rushed upon a new novel by Alphonse Daudet as soon as it came off the press. Another gave him first rank among those who "dare" to replace the "old conventional fiction" by truth as seen and taken directly from life.[12] There was to be sure adverse criticism, as we shall see, but Alphonse Daudet's reputation as a great novelist had been well established and could not be challenged.

The title *Le Nabab*, here meaning simply a man rolling in wealth, suggests naturally that the character so designated is the hero of the novel, while the subtitle, *Moeurs parisiennes*, purports vaguely that Parisian morals constitute its subject matter. Some critics have found it misleading and have warned that it should not be taken to the letter. Indeed it can be argued that the customs and manners described in the book will be found anywhere. They are inherent in that portion of society consisting mainly of financiers, politicians, and minor personages who thrive in politics. They are indeed universal in character rather than distinctly Parisian. *Moeurs politiques* might have been a more appropriate subtitle.

The dedication, which appeared only on a few volumes of the first edition, reads thus:

> To the devoted, discreet
> And untiring collaborator
> To my beloved Julia Daudet
> I present with my
> grateful thanks and affection
> this book which owes her so much

Mme Daudet having disapproved of the wording, order was given to the printer to replace it by the phrase "To my dear wife." This was to be the only dedication known to the public until the late 1920s, when the true one was finally restored in the Ne Varietur edition of the *Oeuvres complètes*.

When, some fifty years later Julia's second son Lucien begged her to tell him why she had been so adamant in her refusal of that first "message" (the dedication for *Le Nabab*), she answered that, while modesty had a part in her decision, the main reason had been her desire for privacy. She felt that the dedication was revealing a secret which to her mind should remain entirely hers and her husband's. She had thought, also, that this "secret" would be misunderstood by the public — some people remaining within the truth and others overstepping it, some imagining "the sad role of a secretary," and others a "greedy collaboration." In reality, wrote Lucien, it was a question of something very complex, namely "a feminine presence in a masculine work." After quoting Balzac who said that genius is bisexual ("le véritable génie est bissexué"), Lucien wondered whether the popularity of his father's works did not derive precisely from a kind of bisexuality due to this "feminine presence."

As many other critics and biographers have done, Lucien quotes also his father's following acknowledgment: "My wife has taken such part in all that I have written, that there is not one single page of mine on which she has not scattered some of her beautiful azure and gold powder." Worth quoting are also these lines from Julia herself: "Our collaboration: a Japanese fan. On one side, the subject, the characters, the atmosphere; on the other, sprigs, flower petals; whatever amount of color is left on the painter's brush: that is my work. . . ."[13]

While Julia, not too much concerned with the sales or the critics' opinions, enjoyed a cloudless, unalloyed happiness, Alphonse on the other hand was very much concerned with the success of the book. According to Goncourt, he heard, or thought he did, "what people whispered about him and his novels." He worried about "articles that would be written and about those that would not."[14] He did not approve of his wife going to hear a review of the *Nabab* by "cette brute de Sarcey." Furthermore, he decided to cancel a trip to Vienna where *L' Arlésienne* was to be staged in his honor: "This is a book that will arouse protests and I do not want to appear as if I was running away," he wrote to his friend Ambroy. He was right. *Le Nabab* made some people cry shame.[15]

Daudet has not written a "story" of *Le Nabab* telling why and how the book was written, but through his notes, sketches, prefaces and forewords, comments and conversations with his friends, it has been possible to establish the main facts concerning the genesis of this novel for which he probably drew more from his recollections of the past he had observed than he did for his other books: "Skimming through his past," Daudet wrote about himself, "the author recalled a strange episode of the Paris of fifteen years ago. The romantic element of a swift and dazzling life flying across the Parisian sky, evidently served as a frame for the *Nabab*, for this picture of morals at the end of the Second Empire."[16] The "swift and dazzling life" in question is that of the historical personage nicknamed le Nabab, whom Daudet called Jansoulet in the novel and whose real name was François Bravay. A summary knowledge of the main facts concerning his activities and those of the duc de Morny, the man who protected him, will help us to understand the excitement that took place upon the publication of the novel.

IV *François Bravay*

François Bravay was born in 1817 at Pont-Saint-Esprit, a town on the Rhone river. At the age of twenty-five, after the death of his father, he moved to Paris where he secured a position as a traveling wine salesman. This made it possible for him to support his mother and his brother for some time. Later, his business took him to Alexandria, Egypt. There he founded an importing firm which prospered very rapidly. He was soon recognized as one of the most prominent men in the French colony of Alexandria. This happened at the time when, because of the policy of peace at any price inaugurated by Louis-Philippe I, French prestige had fallen to a very low ebb. When mobs began scoffing at the French flag and started a riot against the French Consulate, Bravay intervened energetically and won the confidence of the viceroy Saïd-Pacha. Then Bravay made good speculations and, within a relatively short time, managed to pile up the immense fortune which won him his nickname. They also called him "Boud-Saïd," which in Arabic means "the father of happiness."

Now feeling all powerful and knowing he could count on Saïd-Pacha's protection, he took it upon himself to try to restore and extol French influence in Egypt by encouraging all sorts of enterprises by his countrymen. The most important of these was Ferdinand de Lesseps's proposal to dig a canal through the isthmus of Suez. Saïd-Pacha having become interested in the project, Bravay, now a multimillionaire, put his fortune at his disposal, and a so-called "Compagnie universelle du Canal maritime de Suez" was created as a result. It remained naturally in the hands of the viceroy and a majority of French shareholders.

In 1859 work began under the direction of French engineers and executives, and the canal was open for traffic ten years later. It has been said that this company has since then served as a model for similar enterprises supported by international capitalism. In France, it aroused much admiration and stirred up envy among businessmen on the lookout for an opportunity to get rich quickly.

Bravay returned to France in 1862 with the intention of entering politics. Convinced that his fortune (now estimated to be around one hundred million francs) entitled him to a seat in the Chamber of deputies, he was ready to do anything in order to realize his aim. He began by securing the support of such a prominent figure as the duke of Morny, then he created a new company, the "Compagnie des eaux du Midi," whose purpose was to make irrigation possible in the dry region of Nîmes, where he presented himself as a parliamentary candidate. He was elected "député du Gard" in 1863, but his enemies succeeded in having him arraigned before the Legislative Body to answer charges of having bought votes or unduly influenced his constituency. His election was cancelled, and he suffered the same humiliation in 1864, after he had been elected a second time. Finally, in 1865 the Legislative Body had to bow to public opinion and Bravay's election was validated. Alphonse Daudet, who was present at one of these sessions, was deeply impressed. Later, in the novel, he rendered homage to the Nabab's sincerity.

In 1869 Bravay returned to Egypt to supervise the management of his business interests. He had incurred the disfavor of Ismaï Pacha, the successor to the late viceroy Saïd. Bravay's enemies were quick to unite against the man fallen into disgrace and they succeeded in divesting him completely of his millions. François Bravay died in 1874 a poor man in every sense of the word. Such was the perhaps not too unusual but certainly exciting, impressive personage that inspired Alphonse Daudet.

V *Le duc de Morny*

However, in fiction as in real life, the figure of François Bravay was overshadowed by that of his protector, the duc de Morny, called in the novel duc de Mora. De Morny, who had organized the "coup d'Etat" in 1851, had remained the most powerful man in France, especially in financial and political circles. He was a master politician. Like Talleyrand, his grandfather, de Morny possessed the talent for reconciling contraries, whether opinions, situations, or people. In 1856 Napoleon III sent him to Russia as *ambassadeur extraordinaire* to represent France at the coronation of Alexander II. He gained the czar's sympathy and the admiration of his court, which he entertained lavishly. On that particular occasion as on many others, he combined perfectly the qualities of a statesman and those of a man of the world. In Paris he was regarded as the perfect dandy and arbiter of taste, the true incarnation of the society he lived in.

On the other hand, the duke was known also as a man of no scruples, often mixed in bubble schemes in which he played a shady part. It has been said that the phrase "Morny *est dans l'affaire* ("is in the deal") was the supreme argument used to convince reluctant prospective subscribers for shares in a new enterprise. Both he and François Bravay were therefore easy targets. The legends created about each of them and the verified facts regarding their business and political deals furnished sufficient ammunition to whoever wanted to attack them. But they were also greatly admired for their accomplishments and the services they had rendered to the state as well as to individuals.

The idea of introducing the duc de Morny in a novel on the

French society of the Second Empire had been in Daudet's mind for some time when, in 1875, he discussed the matter with his friend Edmond de Goncourt. When he mentioned his intention to bring the duke into his work only accessorily, as an incidental character, de Goncourt argued that de Morny deserved a special study and that he should appear with all his faults. Daudet agreed and, to a certain extent, followed the advice. The question was again raised at the dîner des auteurs sifflés (Turgenev seems to have been absent) with Zola insisting — in opposition to Flaubert's opinion — that there was enough material for a book in the facts and anecdotes related by Daudet.[17]

Daudet did not write a book on Morny, which would have entailed an analysis of the statesman's activities, but he did assign him enough importance as a character in the *Nabab* to make the reader wonder which, between the duc de Mora and the Nabab, should be considered as the true hero of the novel.

When he was reproached for introducing his contemporaries in his novels, and accused of having defamed some of his benefactors, particularly de Morny and Bravay, Alphonse Daudet felt he should defend himself:

"As for me, sir," he wrote to the editor in chief of *Le Figaro*, "if I occupy in Parisian society the distinguished position that was assigned to me in your paper, I can assure you that I do not owe it to François Bravay. I saw him only twice in my life, just long enough to judge him, to pity him and to portray him."[18] Apparently, with all his faults and shortcomings, François Bravay was fundamentally a sincere and good man.

Referring to de Morny, Daudet wrote in his preface of 1878 that he had described him "such as he liked to present himself. . . . History will take care of the statesman," he continued, "as for me, I have shown him as the man of the world that he was and wanted to be. I am convinced that during his life he would have enjoyed to be thus represented."[19]

The nabob Jansoulet and the duke of Mora were unquestionably the two most important characters in the book. They were at the same time the easiest to identify. But there were others of lesser importance whose prototypes could also be found. Such was for example Dr. Jenkins, the physician who prescribed pills sprinkled with arsenic to create a temporary recrudescence of activities in the jaded bodies of his patients. The duke of Mora died, like de Morny, a victim of the famous "Jenkins pearls." Jenkins, prototype seems to have been an Irishman by the name of Dr. Oliffe who had become the most popular doctor among the smart set of the 1860s.

Another identifiable character was Montpavon, the man who in the novel apes the duke of Mora and to his death remains his most intimate friend. He was correctly identified as the marquis de Montguyon. But Felicia Ruys, the famous sculptress who ends by marrying the despicable Dr. Jenkins, had not much in common with Sarah Bernhardt, with whom some try to identify her. In the above quoted letter to *Le Figaro*, Alphonse Daudet protested also against the identification of Cardailhac with his friend the theater producer Carvalho, and he insisted that La Levantine (Jansoulet's wife) and her masseur were purely imaginary characters.

There is no doubt however that the intense interest created in the reading public by these portraits contributed a great deal to the success of the book, considered by some as a great historical novel and by others as a mere "roman à clefs," a story with no central plot but consisting, essentially, of a succession of plots, scenes, and episodes, and a display of portraits. *Le Nabab* possesses naturally other merits which have justified not only the enthusiasm of these first reviewers, but also that of later critics.

The names of Balzac and Saint-Simon were evoked in conjunction with the author of *Le Nabab*. Among the most often mentioned or quoted passages are the pages devoted to the death of the duke de Mora (de Morny) and his funeral, Jansoulet defending himself before the Legislature, and the dance of "La Crenmitz" in the chapter entitled "Un jour de spleen."

Le Nabab, a play based on the novel, by Alphonse Daudet in collaboration with Pierre Elzéar was put on the stage in 1880.

VI   Les Rois en exil

We learn through the Goncourt *Journal* of January 6, 1878, that while still trying to ward off attacks on *Le Nabab*, Alphonse Daudet had begun working on a new novel which he recounts and develops to his friends. This novel will deal with dethroned and dispossessed foreign royalties, and its title will be that of *Les Rois en exil*. The subtitle, *Roman parisien*, again will suggest life in Paris, but this time not the life of the cosmopolitan, financial, political, and artificial society of the "fast set" found in *Le Nabab*. It will not be either that of the industrial and business-minded bourgeois world of *Fromont Jeune et Risler Aîné*, nor that of the working classes and the bohemia that constitute part of the environment in which the characters of *Jack* moved. This will be the Parisian life of a very peculiar and small fragment of society consisting mainly of the said exiled former kings and queens with their servants and the lower class upstarts, loose women and usurers with whom they are in daily contact. The dedication, this time to Edmond de Goncourt, presented it as another *roman d'histoire moderne.*

As usual, Alphonse Daudet had had the subject in mind for a long time: "Of all my books this is the one whose title and outline I have carried longest in my head," he wrote later in his "histoire de mes livres."[20] The idea had come to him one evening after the Commune, as he was watching the ruins of the Tuileries palace against the sky. This sight apparently led him to imagine the effect it might have on deposed royalty chased from their country by revolution and having come to Paris to seek safety.

And thus indeed begins *Les Rois en exil* with Queen Frédérique on the balcony of her hotel located in the nicest part of Rue de Rivoli. She is at first enchanted with what she sees in the street: the line of sparkling carriages rolling toward the Bois through a "luminous confusion" of blond hair, light white dresses, and dazzling silks. Then suddenly her eyes fall on the remains of the Tuileries palace at which sight she is greatly moved. She recalls that some ten years before she had been welcomed there with her young husband Christian, king of Illyria and Dalmatia. She had danced with monarchs and potentates, with lords and nobility of all ranks, and had been admired by all of them, now "all dead, exiled or gone insane." But the sad view also reminds her of the horrors she has just witnessed during the past few days when she and her husband and child had to flee from their country laid in ruins by a revolution. As for her husband, he thinks only of the good life Paris can offer him. Such is the beginning of the new novel whose action will be based on the conflict between the queen, who wants to save the crown for her son, Prince Zara, and the king, whose only concern will always be his own pleasure.

Les Rois en exil is the book that up to 1880 had given Daudet "the most trouble to work out" (*le plus de mal à mettre debout*). He soon realized the difficulties involved in treating a subject so far removed from his mode of life and way of thinking. In his eyes, the main difficulty consisted precisely in getting the information he needed from life itself rather than from dusty archives. The fact of having heard, as a child, a great deal about Henry V (the pretender to the throne of France who was exiled in Austria), or that of having, as a

young man, "brushed past" the duke of Brunswick in a night club —
and the king of Hanover at the door of the music conservatory —
was hardly enough to enable him to write about the private or social
life of royalty. Citron le Taciturne (nickname of the prince of
Orange) was his prototype for the character of the prince d'Axel, the
man who initiates King Christian to the pleasure of Parisian life, but
much more data had to be collected. This involved numberless visits
and calls on all his friends and acquaintances "from top to bottom of
the social ladder." Daudet tells us how he snatched society secrets,
skimmed through police records, tradesmen bills, and work
estimates. Along with decrepitudes, seared or hardened consciences,
and chinks in the sense of honor, he discovered pride in persons in
dire straits and truly heroic devotion beside manias for self-sacrifice.
When he felt the need to refresh his mind on the theories of
monarchy, he reread the works of the theorists and Catholic
philosophers of the nineteenth century such as Joseph de Maistre,
Louis de Bonald, Blanc Saint-Bonnet, and no doubt Balzac, who
himself had frequently referred to the above-mentioned *prophètes
du passé*. One day, in an old book bought secondhand on the quays,
he found a note recommending a certain Constand Thérion as a
well-educated and eloquent young man.

Thérion was now dead, but Daudet remembered having met him
soon after his arrival in Paris, when Thérion could be seen in the
cafés of the Latin Quarter pleading passionately the cause of
monarchy. Daudet decided to introduce him in his book under the
fictitious name of Elysée Méraut, as the private tutor of Prince Zara.
Elysée Méraut can be considered as the veritable hero of the novel.

Now *Les Rois en exil* was progressing satisfactorily and, from the
surface, it seemed indeed that nothing more important mattered in
Daudet's life. Yet, the winter of 1878 was to mark another turning
point in his life. Preparing and organizing the material for the book
had been a very demanding task, a "strenuous and tyrannous job"
which he had carried on enthusiastically. Then one day his abused
body, "the overworked machine," broke down. That began, he said,
with short one minute naps, a kind of "bird slumbers," then a
disturbing and insuperable listlessness, sluggishness which made it
impossible for him to concentrate, forced him to stop in the middle
of a page. His handwriting had become shaky.

The doctor having recommended a long rest in the country, the
family left for Champrosay in early June. By the end of the month he
felt completely rejuvenated: "For a week I enjoyed such a fullness of

life that I would have embraced trees."[21] The work on the book was again progressing splendidly when, suddenly one night, without warning, he was waked up by a violent hemoptysis, a clot of blood in his mouth. This time he was really frightened, thought the end had come and that he would have to leave his work unfinished. He could gather just enough energy to ask his wife to finish his book. He was then thirty-eight years of age.

However, after spending a few days motionless in bed, the danger disappeared once more. Meanwhile, since he believed that "everything can be useful," he had analyzed his sufferings and the feeling undergone during those moments of anguish. He later utilized them in his account of Elysée Méraut's death. Little by little with Julia's help, he resumed his work and finished the book. But he felt that something had broken down in him. He knew that from now on he could no longer treat his body like a rag, deprive it of exercise and fresh air or bring it, by "making evenings last until morning," to experience the fever of joy due to the fine literary lucky finds which at that moment used to come to his mind.

Les Rois en exil appeared serially in *Le Temps* between June and November, 1879, and in book form a few months later. It can be said, granting naturally some adverse criticism, that the new book enjoyed genuine success. Twenty thousand copies were sold during the first few weeks. The subject which, oddly enough lent itself as well to comedy as to tragedy, became a popular one. Several novelists and dramatists were later to treat it, but none with comparable success. When *Les Rois en exil*, his fourth important "realistic" novel, appeared, Alphonse Daudet had already begun writing a new one: *Numa Roumestan.*

VII Numa Roumestan

While *Les Rois en exil* was the book whose preparation and writing gave Daudet the most trouble, *Numa Roumestan* was apparently the one that gave him the least. He claimed having dedicated himself to it more thoroughly than to any other ("celui où je me suis le mieux donné"), and that no fatigue resulted, "as is the case," he adds, "with anything natural, coming from the heart."[22] It did not require any specially active, hard, or bold research. All he needed to do was to refer now and then to his old notebooks and think of his own experiences.

Numa Roumestan appears unequivocally as the main character, the hero of the novel, but *Moeurs parisiennes* is again a misleading subtitle. Rather than an objective study of Parisian customs and morals, the subject of study is the problem of North and South in France, as suggested by the cryptic epigraph, "The Latins have conquered Gaul for the second time. . . ." ("Pour la seconde fois les Latins ont conquis la Gaule. . . ."), which the author himself deemed appropriate to place at the head of his book.

The story itself can be summarized in a few lines: Numa Roumestan is presented as a typical meridional, or more exactly a Provençal, with whom are found all the traits attributed to his "race." He is a likable fellow, a great talker but a brilliant one, without much energy or ambition as a young man. He goes to Paris to study law, becomes a lawyer, and later a shrewed and deceptive, though artless, politician. He marries a girl from northern France, Rosalie Le Quesnoy, the daughter of a distinguished counsellor to the Court of Appeal in Paris. Rosalie shows herself an honest, responsible, and proud woman. She is supposed to personify the North as Numa is to personify the South. Harmony between the two will be utterly impossible. Numa will deceive her a number of times. Hortense, Rosalie's sister, also falls in love with a Provençal, this one a complete failure. She does not marry him, however, and she dies after having reconciled Numa and his wife.

Daudet explains that he wanted to sum up his native province, its climate, the morals of its people, their temper and temperament, their accent and pronunciation along with their gestures, frenzies, superstitions, etc, in addition to the "ebullitions of the Provençal sun," which he considers as the cause of their excessive imagination and propensity to exaggerate and to lie.

It seems therefore understandable, if not quite justified, that *Numa Roumestan* should have been characterized as a *roman à thèse*. Fortunately, Daudet's talent is such that the uninformed reader is likely to enjoy the book to the end without realizing the existence of the so-called thesis. Moreover, if unable to detect where irony and satire begin or end he may be prone to take literally and seriously what was meant only as a joke.

As could be expected, *Numa Roumestan*, like *Tartarin de Tarascon* five years before, produced violent reactions in the South where the people, for reasons that will become clear in the light of history, are extremely sensitive regarding the attitude of northern France toward them. In Paris the novel was unquestionably better appreciated as a work of art, but many readers, among them distinguished literary critics, blindly accepted the statements and generalizations that seemed to confirm centuries old prejudices.

The North-South question in France has naturally little in common with that which existed in the United States except for the sufferings endured in a civil war — from which each was to emerge as a unified nation — and abuses inflicted later by the winning party. In France that war took place in the thirteenth century and is known as the Albigensian Crusade. The origin of the conflict however can be related to the historical antagonism between the countries of northern and southern Europe. This antagonism intensified, at times even started anew, by the theories of racism that were propagated by scholars, historians, literary critics, and men of letters of the nineteenth century.

The Felibrige movement (cf. pp. 34 - 36) contributed its share to its development by reviving race-consciousness. Its theorists always referred to Provence as a nation and linked the idea of nation with that of race. To one of them the Felibrige's main accomplishments consisted precisely in the "proclamation, affirmation and proof" of the existence of a "race méridionale" or "race provençale," which he naturally labeled as a "race majeure et supérieure."

As could be expected, the exaltation of this so-called race had its counterpart in the North. Theorists and conservative politicians of northern France complained bitterly that the South held sway over politics — especially after Numa Roumestan's braggadocio concerning the second "conquest" of Gaul by the "Latins." Evidently, if the Latins (i.e., the French southerners) had invaded France for a second time, two thousand years after the true "Latins" or Romans, it could indeed be attributed to the Republic and the parliamentary system that had made it possible for them to do so. Moreover, it is common knowledge that while the North is conservative, except in industrial centers, the South leans more generally to the left. Numa Roumestan himself was a conservative and a strong advocate of "l'Ordre moral" — an expression applied ironically to the government of the duke of Broglie who, under pretext of restoring public order, harassed the republicans from 1873 to 1877. But Numa was in this respect the exception that proves the rule. Today the situation is no longer what it used to be in Daudet's time.

As far as the general public is concerned, this North-South antagonism does not go beyond the feeling and prejudices that are inevitable when any two groups of different languages and traditions live within the same nation. The average méridional is not "still fighting the civil war," a war that took place almost eight hundred years ago. Nevertheless, a few people can still be found who view the

North chiefly as the country from where "the barbarians came," and there are of course a good many "northerners" who still regard the South as a wonderful land inhabited by the wrong people, precisely the type portrayed in *Tartarin de Tarascon* and *Numa Roumestan*. Ironically, the trials and miseries of the two world wars have done more to attenuate the North-South antagonism than any amount of theorizing or preaching might have.

Such is the situation and such are the main facts that should be known in order to fully understand, not only *Numa Roumestan* and the varied reactions to it, but also its author, the man and his works. However, it should not be concluded, either from the book or from the above, that France is a country divided in two irreconcilable parts, as implied in the novel, where Numa and his wife are identified with "North and South facing each other without any hope of ever merging together."[23]

This is precisely one of the points where Daudet's pessimism does not seem justified. Perhaps more than any other of his novels, this one which he prized so highly should be read critically, with full knowledge of the facts concerning the subject.

In fact, upon rereading *Numa Roumestan*, it becomes quite evident that, while the author's purpose of summing up his native land must be accepted as he stated it, the result has been first of all an examination and account of his own case rather than that of the Midi. Numa facing Rosalie represents better Alphonse facing Julia than it represents North and South face to face. For indeed, in spite of all appearances, the Daudets' married life at this point was far from harmonious. Their son Lucien, who believed that whenever it is a question of a great man whose dissolute life has become exemplary "no one has a right to keep it in the dark," has dispelled any doubt that might remain on the subject.[24]

Lucien Daudet explains why the sudden great changes observed in Alphonse's private life during the first years of his marriage had not been, and could not be, as radical and permanent as it had been expected. Deep in him were some well-ingrained, deep-rooted old habits, some acquired in Lyons and developed in Paris, that could not be eradicated by mere willpower or determination. Moreover, he had to contend with his impetuous, ardent temperament which, it can be argued, had not so much to do with the South as it had with the mere fact that he was a plain human being, incidently an individual quite different from his brother Ernest who was raised in the same way and in the same environment.

The young and handsome fellow whose charms had attracted Julia Allard in spite of his disordered, loose living — of which she was perfectly aware — had not lost any of the fundamental traits of his personality. In addition, he was now a man in the public eye and his ever growing fame made him more popular than ever with women. Some of these were quite aggressive and tenacious. "Only a saint could have resisted them" ("il aurait fallu être un saint . . .") suggests Lucien, and Alphonse Daudet was not a saint.

And so Lucien Daudet expressed the belief that between 1873 and 1881 his mother had to fight in order to keep her man. The fact that their marriage, which from the start had seemed doomed to failure, had been saved until then, could be regarded as a miracle. Now, they knew and appreciated each other and they were still in love, and Julia was determined to make the miracle continue whatever the odds. This did not mean however that Mme Alphonse Daudet surrendered on the essentials. She never accepted the status of some of the wives he had described in his *Femmes d'artistes*, who put up with all kinds of humiliation in order to "keep a name." She fought and kept both her husband and her dignity. When *Numa Roumestan* which had appeared serially in *L'Illustration* from May to July, 1881, was published in book form a few weeks later, it bore the dedication: "A ma chère femme."

Alphonse Daudet had now reached and passed the age of forty. Since the alert of 1878, when he underwent a violent crisis of hemoptysis, he had enjoyed fairly good health, except for rheumatic pains which harried him once in a while. They had worsened in 1880, the year during which he was greatly saddened by the death of his friend Gustave Flaubert.

In the fall, the Daudets decided to move from Place des Vosges to Avenue de l'Observatoire, where they would have more room for young Lucien, now two years old. They took an apartment on the fifth floor commanding a magnificent view on the Luxembourg Gardens and rows of beautiful chestnut trees. In Alphonse's study, now that of a most successful and prosperous man, could be seen a portrait of Julia by Renoir that the famous artist had painted at Champrosay in 1876. In that workroom , where *Numa Roumestan* was finished, work went on as usual notwithstanding their much increased social activities. The Avenue de l'Observatoire apartment was to become one of the great literary and intellectual centers in Paris for more than a decade.

They had servants. Julia hired maids to take care of Lucien who, in any case, was never neglected either by his mother or his father.

Alphonse's old friend and secretary, Jules Ebner, now on a full-time basis relieved him of such chores as correspondence and business transactions with editors and translators. Julia enjoyed being a hostess to the ever increasing number of new friends. They themselves, now quite in the public eye, were received in various kinds of famous salons such as those of the Princess Mathilde, Victor Hugo, and Juliette Adam (1836 - 1936), the founder of the *Nouvelle Revue*. In short the past two years had been busy and eventful ones whose importance soon would be reflected in both his physical and spiritual life. Alphonse Daudet had reached the peak of his career.

Basing himself mostly on his father's famous notebooks, Lucien infers that, like the previous ones, this last move into the new historical neighborhood (the vicinity of the Latin Quarter) influenced Alphonse Daudet's attitude on life and inspired him with new literary ideals. He suggested also that his age and perhaps the premonition of the terrible sufferings he was about to endure, plus the idea of death which obsessed him and his friends — as can be verified in the Goncourts' *Journal* — accounted for the important changes that were then taking place.

It is a fact that from then on Alphonse Daudet would not be satisfied any longer with winning his readers' attention and keeping them interested simply by making them laugh or by moving them to tears; that without preaching or assuming the priggish, learned tone which he loathed so thoroughly, he would henceforth strive to make them think over the problems of life directly concerning them. As a result, "his pen became sharper" and his gentle irony turned occasionally into a bitter and sometime unfair satire.

VIII   L'Evangéliste

Alphonse Daudet's next novel, *L'Evangéliste*, a deeply moving book, was like *Jack* based on a tragic true story related to him by its principal victim, with whom he was then closely acquainted. The victim was this time a foreign teacher, Mme Lima (in the novel Mme Ebsen) who came twice a week to Avenue de l'Observatoire to give Léon a German lesson.

As remarked by his sons, Alphonse Daudet had always been attracted by, and interested in, unpretentious, simple people of the humbler classes — an interest which undoubtedly went back to his childhood and probably also to the influence of Mistral and the Felibres, who never missed the opportunity to exalt the virtues of the nonsophisticated.

In any case, Léon's German lesson would be regularly interrupted,

not by a coffee break, but by what they called an entr'acte or inter-
mission, when a glass of Frontignan wine would be offered to the
good lady teacher and Alphonse Daudet would come in to chat a
while with her. Once, having noticed she looked very sad, he asked
what made her so unhappy. Sobbing, Mme Lima answered that she
had just received a postcard from her daughter, a card without the
sender's address and bringing the same message that for years had
been brought by similar ones. For years, the message read: "Mother,
I am well. I hope it is the same with you. Your daughter in Christ."
This time the "Frontignan break" lasted a little longer than usual.

Mme Lima explained that her twenty-year-old daughter had been
gradually alienated from her and finally dragged from home by a
fanatic evangelist, the wife of a well-known banker who attracted
girls of various nationalities to a kind of lay convent workroom she
had founded. after a period of training during which they were made
to renounce all ties with their families, the girls would be dispatched
through Europe to preach the Gospel. Mme Lima's daughter was
thus fanaticized by the lady evangelist to the point of repudiating
her past life and her mother. Mme Lima had done everything possible to obtain her daughter's address from the Evangelist, but it was
all in vain. The "wall of gold" that protected the latter had discouraged all those wanting to help Mme Lima, who was not even
able to find a lawyer willing to fight her case, even though everyone
acknowledged its merits.

At first Alphonse Daudet regarded this story as a gross exaggeration on the part of the abandoned and disowned mother. But after a
serious and thorough investigation, he became convinced that the
facts were actually as she had reported them. He saw in this affair
first of all the sad plight of an unfortunate mother and a cause worth
fighting for. When he realized that the only way for him to do so
would be to denounce the evil in a well-documented and convincing
novel he immediately put aside all other plans he had in mind and
dedicated himself to this task.

He selected the part of Paris where he was now living as a setting
for most of the action, but as a rule followed Mrs. Lima's story very
closely. He naturally added some new situations and characters
destined to better dramatize or bring out the evidence of the facts.
His most admirable creation in this respect proved to be that of the
old minister Aussandon, who, commenting on the text of the Sermon
on the Mount, does not hesitate to condemn the arrogant pride and

bumptiousness of false prophets as severely as he condemns the "miracle merchants" who keep on committing crimes "in the Lord's name."

L'Evangéliste appeared first in *Le Figaro*, in the period between December, 1882, and January, 1883. Before the last installment had come out strong feelings for and against the author and his works were voiced either by various kinds of messages sent to Avenue de l'Observatoire or through the press. By the end of February Alphonse Daudet had answered a few letters and accepted to be interviewed by a newsman in order to defend himself against various accusations regarding *L'Evangéliste*. He denied having attacked any particular religious sect. His only purpose, he maintained, had been to exemplify cases of fanaticism and to show the dangers of excessive proselytism wherever it occurred. Fortunately, he had the satisfaction of reading some favorable and even enthusiastic reviews and articles from prominent Protestant ministers and other spokesmen for both the Protestant and Catholic churches.

When the volume was published, in the spring of 1883, discussions ensued and polemics arose among diverse political and religious periodicals, both in France and abroad, where translations had appeared at almost the same time. *L'Evangéliste* was dedicated to famous Dr. Charcot who was then a pioneer and outstanding authority in the field of nervous diseases.

A l'éloquent et savant professeur
J.-M. Charcot
Médecin de la Salpétrière
je dédie cette observation

In addition to pointing out the objective and scientific aspect of the book, this dedication may have discouraged possible future attacks against the author. Most critics praised highly the literary and artistic qualities of the book, its terse and yet harmonious language, its light, free, natural style and the simplicity of its well-knit plot.

However, Daudet had been so deeply affected by grievous happenings and circumstances during that winter that he remained for some time almost completely insensitive to either the most laudatory or adverse criticism of his works. He was now deeply concerned by the state of his health. His rheumatic pains had increased considerably during the preceding few months and the course of treatment he had undergone at Néris-les-Bains in the summer of 1882 had not brought him any relief whatever.

Then it so happened that his mother, Mme Vincent Daudet, whom he loved so much, passed away at the very moment when he was correcting the proofs of the opening scene of *L'Evangéliste* in which Mme Ebsen grieves over the death of her own mother. Alphonse Daudet could never entirely dissociate the book from the funeral atmosphere cast over it by this deplorable fortuitous coincidence. In addition, he had been afflicted by the death of his friend Léon Gambetta, then by the news that Turgenev was losing his mind, the third one among his friends (the other two being Duboys and Bataille) to suffer such a tragic destiny. Perhaps a more important reason for remaining unmoved by either excessive high praise or plain cursing was that his most recent successes had given him a new faith in himself, a kind of pride that enabled him to enjoy a greater feeling of independence toward criticism.

Nonetheless, in May, 1883, he decided to assert himself by challenging Albert Delpit, who had "insulted" him in a recent article, to a duel with swords. Daudet, for whom fencing had become a favorite sport, wounded his opponent, not too seriously, at the first thrust. He was duly proclaimed the victor and he came home triumphant. But this adventure, evidently a great event in the Daudet family, proved to be for Alphonse more of a trial than a relief from sorrow and physical pain.

CHAPTER 4

From Sapho *to* L'Obstacle

I Sapho

ALPHONSE DAUDET was determined to carry on to the end.
As usual, work on a new book was started long before the
publication of the old one. While the fuss about *L'Evangéliste* continued he had already begun writing *Sapho*, his sixth novel with a
Parisian background. Unlike the *Rois en exil* and the *Evangelist*, the
new novel did not require research in any particular social group or
environment. It may be even assumed that the author did not have
to refer much to his famous "petits cahiers," even though it has been
ascertained that he utilized them. *Sapho* is basically the product of
mature thinking, deducing from observation and personal experiences in bohemian life. We know, again through the Goncourt
Journal, that the idea of this novel had been on his mind for a long
time.

The story is essentially that of a young man, Jean Gaussin, trying
to extricate himself from the clutches of a courtesan named Fanny
Legrand, but better known as Sapho, since a renowned sculptor had
her sit for a statue of the famous Greek poetess. Her nickname
evokes naturally some of the characteristics attributed to the latter,
which she seems to possess.

The novel begins with a conversation between these two
characters who have met by chance at a masked fancy-dress ball in
Paris. Fanny makes Jean talk and "seduces" him, apparently
without too much difficulty. They leave the place together and go to
his apartment. He romantically carries her upstairs, climbs to the
second floor in one breath, has to slow down as he proceeds to the
third, fourth, and fifth flights. He finally reaches the fifth completely out of breath, thoroughly overcome. She sighs: "Already!"
He, unable to pronounce a single word, thinks: "At last!" And thus

ends the first chapter, which the author closes with this seemingly listless remark: "Their whole story, the climbing of those stairs in the gray sadness of the morning."

She remained with him for two days. Upon leaving she gave him her card and uttered: "Whenever you want me, let me know, I will always be ready." Jean Gaussin, who was studying for an examination to enter the diplomatic service, did not want to get involved and failed to heed the suggestion. One or two weeks later she came back as he was setting out to work, and she eventually returned several times. He did all he could to get rid of her, all in vain.

Once she said: "Whether you like it or not, I will indeed make you love me" ("je te forcerai bien de m'aimer"). Then Jean fell very sick and for ten days she took care of him, in fact saved him. When she thought she was pregnant, she announced it "with such a joy that he could but share it." Meanwhile, he could not sleep any more than she did. . . . It proved to be a false alarm, but now he realized "how heavy, cold and well forged his chain was."

Later on they took an apartment and lived together as husband and wife. They were "stuck" together, as implied by the French slang term *collage*, which describes perfectly this kind of situation. It was agreed of course that their union would terminate when time came for Jean to join his post, that the breaking off would take place quietly, smoothly. Fanny had been warned, and "they spoke of it as of death, as of a distant, remote fatality, but ineluctable."

One day he learned certain facts about her former life, discovered that she had had many lovers. He became jealous and they began to quarrel. He felt many times like beating her "for in this flesh-love in which esteem and respect of the beloved one do not exist, brutality always springs up, either in wrath or caresses." He became afraid of himself, scared of what he might do. They decided that he would take a short trip home, to southern France, to facilitate the breaking apart of their liaison, but this half-separation was like the cut of "the pruner's billhook which revives the tired tree." Jean rushed back to Paris, "defeated by his own weakness." He now loved her:

There is in certain words that we ordinarily use a hidden spring which suddenly opens them down to the base, discloses their depth, explains to us their exceptional, innermost meaning; then, the word coils up, returns to its commonplace shape and rolls along insignificant, worn-out through perfunctory and mechanical use. Love is one of these words. Only those for whom its clearness has been once felt, translated in its entirety, will understand the delightful anguish in which Jean lived.[1]

Thus does the author limit himself to suggesting the nature of this kind of love and its effect on his hero.

At the end of the book, powerless Jean has broken with his family and decided to keep Fanny and take her to Peru, where he has been appointed a consul. She is supposed to join him in Marseilles. He waits for her but she does not appear. Finally he receives a letter explaining why she has decided to let him go alone:

"Well, No! I am not going . . . ," she writes. "Five years ago I would have followed you to the end of the earth . . . for you cannot deny that I loved you passionately . . . but now I am broken down. . . . Don't try to find me . . . you would not succeed. There you are, free! Farewell. . . . A kiss, the last one, on your neck . . . darling. . . ." And the emptiness of his ruined life appeared to him " as a bare field with the harvest gathered without any hope of return . . . and for that woman who was now escaping from him."[2]

Such is the main action of the novel. It contains also vivid portraits of Fanny's former lovers, some of whom have been identified in real life, and of a few "ancient beauties" of the bohemia of the 1860s and seventies. There are two or three interesting sketches of *faux-ménages* or *collages* and a few picturesque but minor southern characters. However, its interest lies principally, as we have seen, in the two main characters and their problem, whose universality explains the tremendous success of the book.

Sapho has been regarded as the story of a common type of *collage*, that is, the situation of a man and woman living together out of the bonds of marriage. But experts on the subject point out that in the average *collage* the man is usually the seducer and the one who assumes responsibility for the household until he decides the time has come for him to quit, while in *Sapho*, they explain, it is the woman who is passionately in love. Moreover, she is older than the man (Fanny is thirty-seven and Jean twenty one), and it is finally she who decides to break up. Jean, who has always been concerned with his family and his career, is the one who at the end is willing to sacrifice everything to his love, while Fanny turns out to be the wise and strong character.

The fundamental question however is that of love itself, the power of love understood as a force that, while inseparable from purely physical, sexual desire, goes far beyond it and is not as such national or regional but fundamentally human and universal in character. Gustave Lanson regarded *Sapho* as a "scabrous heartrending subject treated by Alphonse Daudet with incomparable tact, vigor, and unerringness."[3]

Evidently, the work was inspired by the author's liaison with
Marie Rieu. It is equally clear that he added characters and episodes
born of his imagination. We may also take it for granted that, as
suggested by Lucien Daudet, he had wondered what his life would
have been had he not married and forsaken bohemia.

Sapho began to appear serially in a recently founded newspaper,
L'Echo de Paris, in April, 1884, and was published in book form by
Charpentier the following month. The dedication, "For my sons
when they are twenty" (not twenty-one, as printed in *The Novels,
Romances and Writings of Alphonse Daudet*, XIV, xxi) has been
heeded and commented upon by practically every critic and
biographer. It suggests the didactic character of the novel — "didactic," that is, instructive but not moralizing. No more than in his
previous novels had Daudet in this case overly indulged in any form
of preaching or idle philosophizing. Sapho is a plain realistic analysis
of a passionate love whose history, to quote Henry James, "omits
nothing but shows everything in the fullest possible light."[4]

Some French critics regarded *Sapho* as the best, the most perfect
expression of Naturalism, and one of them went as far as saying it
was the only true naturalistic novel of the century. Yet, not a single
vulgar word or expression is to be found in the book. To quote
Adrien Remacle, a reviewer of *la Revue indépendante*, Daudet
"kept the decency and tone of well-bred people [*le ton de bonne
compagnie*] peculiar to him."[5]

Léon Daudet has given a lively account of the excitement caused
in his family and among the Parisian elite by the publication of
Sapho:

. . . Alphonse Daudet had just finished his novel *Sapho* on which he had
worked unceasingly for several months. My great friend Jules Ebner, my
father's secretary, had told me: "It is an astonishing book, the most beautiful
book your father has written."
"Well then he will have trouble."
"Not at all, it does not deal with politics. . . . It's a book on love."
"Is it a story that happened to him?"
"Yes and to many others. . . ."
I said to mother: "It seems that papa's new novel is a very fine one. . . ."
"Yes, that is true, it is dedicated to you and to your brother."
That made me laugh, for Lucien was quite young. A book dedicated to a
young man of eighteen and to a young boy. Queer indeed! I knew much
more on the subject in question than my mother ever suspected. . . . You
may imagine how much *Sapho* intrigued me!

The family decided that my father would read the first chapter to my maternal grandparents and that I could attend the reading. I can still see my grandfather Jules Allard sitting near Alphonse Daudet who read bending under the lamp, his long hair sweeping the page. First he read the dedication "For my sons . . . ," then the famous opening dialogue at the ball between Fanny Legrand and Jean Gaussin — which later I knew by heart, then the climbing of the stairs, first charming, exciting, then heavy, tiring, then exhausting, a symbol of the liaison that had started with kisses and would end with tears.

Grandfather was weeping, grandmother — was deeply moved. Mother kept her eyes down to hide her tears. I shivered . . . realizing perfectly that something great had just appeared in the firmament of French literature. This was also the opinion expressed by Jules Allard whose judgment the reader [i.e., Alphonse Daudet] valued highly, being himself more moved than he cared to appear. . . .

I went to see the publisher, Charpentier, launch the book. I remember that he began by ordering eighty thousand copies printed. Good Charpentier exulted: "Don't you see that, that success . . . something never seen before!" . . . Indeed this quick and solar success was to exceed anything one can imagine. In the Luxembourg gardens, in all public places [endroits] people had the little yellow book in their hands. At the Lycée Louis-Le-Grand professors of the upper classes would congratulate me. I became the son of the author, then Alphonse Daudet 'the son's father of the author.' Satirical songs were written and sung in night clubs: 'It's for my sons when they are twenty. . . .' With notes and letters of congratulations the mail brought us newspaper clippings from every country. . . . Father of course was happy. . . .

The excitement went on. . . . Suddenly I was informed that I had passed my B.A. examination with honors. Believing that I had a right to have my registration fees reimbursed, I went to the Sorbonne to ask for my money. They laughed at me and answered that I had to produce an indigency certificate. Just think!

Among friends of the family, Céard and Geffroy were the most enthusiastic. The former proclaimed that *Sapho* was one of the best written books in our language, which is still my opinion. The latter brought with his own testimony that of Clemenceau. . . . Lemaître, it was said, would read with his golden voice the passage he preferred. Théodore de Banville would announce that he had read the book three times. . . . One of the most enthusiastic among the confrères was Heredía, Leconte de Lisle one of the least. . . . Naturally, Edm. de Goncourt and Zola had been among the first to express their admiration.[6]

With *Sapho* ends the series of the great masterpieces with a Parisian background. The six or seven novels or novelettes published during the next thirteen years have each a value of their own, but none added anything to the author's fame. Daudet's life and his literary career remained inseparable till the end, but his health preoccupied him more and more and his suffering conditioned more and more the nature as well as the value of his work.

The excitement caused by the publication of *Sapho* did not affect much the ordinary trend of life of the Daudet household. To be sure they were now more than ever in the limelight. They went out quite often in the evening and Julia had a regular "at home" once a week, but she continued most of her afternoons in his study copying or reviewing her husband's manuscripts. Her principal aim was to divert his thoughts from his ailment and keep alive his enthusiasm and confidence in the future. This became an extremely difficult task after the famous Dr. Charcot informed Alphonse that he was in the early stages of a spinal complaint.

In his book, Lucien Daudet regards his father's existence, starting with the year 1885, as consisting of three distinct "parts" of equal importance: "First, his sickness, which Alphonse called '*la doulou*' [Provençal for pain, *la douleur* in French]; secondly, his work, which continued as if pain did not exist; and third his love of life — which developed into . . . that of humanity."[7] There is no doubt that owing to his almost ceaseless suffering and his complete loss of any hope for recovery, Daudet's preoccupation with the idea of death became more persistent than ever and in consequence intensified his love of life. His determination to pursue his work whatever the cost can be ascribed in part to the common belief that work remains the best way to forget one's worries and secure some kind of relief from both moral and physical distress.

Alphonse Daudet began to record minutely all the manifestations of his illness as well as his thoughts and impresssions in a little notebook which he intended to utilize for a study or perhaps a novel dealing with la doulou. When he confided to his wife his intention of laying aside temporarily his other works in order to write this one, she warned him that such a book would constitute a sort of ending or conclusion and that he would not be able to write anything else. There is no evidence that she convinced him, but the book was never written. His notes and observations were published by Julia under the title *La Doulou* in 1931, thirty-four years after his death.

II Tartarin sur les Alpes

The novel he had projected to write after *Sapho* was to deal with the French Academy. He suddenly decided to lay it aside temporarily, not because of la doulou, as some believed, but because he had signed a contract to write one on a different subject, as recorded in the Goncourt *Journal* on the date of October 20, 1884:

> . . . he [Daudet] confesses to me that he is not working on the novel he was to write after *Sapho*. Without admitting it to anyone, he is writing, for an international company, a kind of "Tartarin in Switzerland," a work *[une machine]* for which they are paying him two hundred seventy-five thousand francs! Do you hear, manes of Gautier, Flaubert, Murger, etc. who were paid by Lévy four hundred francs for one volume, and at that without royalties! In relation to me [*vis-à-vis de moi*] Daudet feels a little ashamed of what he has confessed and he is expecting some recomforting words. "Well," I told him, "such a sum is big enough to justify a bit of commercialism in the course of a whole literary existence. And then, you are not alone on this earth as I am. . . . Heck! You have children!"

The new novel, the Tartarin sequel, did not appear serially in a periodical like the previous ones. It was published directly by Calman Lévy under the title of *Tartarin sur les Alpes*, in 1885. As usual, the editor of the 1929 - 1930 Ne Varietur edition of the *O.C.* gathered under the heading "Autour de . . . [title of book]" every bit of information, notes, and documents, excerpts of book reviews and criticism, likely to help the reader as well as future scholars to interpret correctly the work in question. After a few remarks on the main characters and various episodes of *Tartarin sur les Alpes*, he wrote that Alphonse Daudet had gone to Switzerland several times to prepare the background for his novel — a statement which has been repeated in subsequent biographies.

In reality Daudet, who had set foot in Basel for only a few hours with his friend Delvau in 1865, did not return to Switzerland until 1884. He then went on a pleasure trip with his family and two friends, the de Nittis. Their intention was to visit the country, then intensely advertised by the Swiss, and rest for some time in a setting different from that of Néris-les-Bains, where the Daudets had just experienced three weeks of "dreadful boredom." They traveled through most of the country and had many interesting experiences. Alphonse naturally took notes as he always did on such occasions, by sheer force of habit, as today's tourists take photographs. But it has not been proved that he went there, in 1881, with the express purpose of gathering material for that particular book.

However, this may well have been the case three years later when the Daudet family returned to Switzerland for another extensive vacation, again after an unsuccessful course of treatment at Néris-les-Bains. They went via Aix-les-Bains and Chamonix and traveled as far as the latter in company of the publisher Alphonse Lemerre and his wife. Then the Daudets proceeded to Geneva and Montreux, where they settled for the rest of the trip. According to Lucien, this last sojourn was partly spoiled by the large number of autograph seekers who came at meal time to ask the author of *Sapho* to sign books and pictures.

In Chamonix, Alphonse enjoyed conversations with mountain guides and, in spite of his "rheumatisms," ended by making an excursion to the Bossom glacier and the "mer de glace," as Perrichon, the famous character of Labiche had done. This experience was apparently sufficient to enable him to imagine all the impressions, sensations, and reflections provoked by true mountain climbing.

Not only some of the notes taken in 1884 but also many of those that filled his notebook in 1881 were utilized in *Tartarin sur les Alpes*. He had recorded his feelings of admiration for both the country and its inhabitants, whose customs he found original and interesting. At the same time, he reacted against the industrialization and commercialization of its natural beauties, "tout cela gâté par le décor des hôtelleries et la chamarure des portiers" ("all spoiled by the gaudy, tawdry ornamented hostelries and their bedizened porters").[8] Neither did he hesitate to exercise his irony or satire on tourists of various nationalities (some of them as irritating by their freezing and disdainful silence and complex of superiority as Tartarin was by his disconcerting artlessness and deafening loquacity) or on such absurdities and oddities as the firing of a cannon for VIPs arriving at Interlaken, a cannon which, he said, could be heard "every five minutes."[9]

The adventures of the colorful and most intrepid Tartarin — at first proclaimed by the Tarasconnais "king" of the cap hunters and later acclaimed by them as a great wild-beast hunter and lion killer — had remained in the minds of the readers of *Tartarin de Tarascon*. Now, a dozen years later, these readers wanted to hear more about their great hero and apparently asked for a sequel to the story. Hence the attractive inducement received by its creator to meet their wishes.

In the opening chapter of *Tartarin sur les Alpes* Daudet informs his reader that during the past years the good people of Tarascon had lost their enthusiasm for "cap hunting" and replaced it by one for mountain climbing, the new fad then sweeping Europe. Their old club, where the elite of the small town used to meet to listen to its most distinguished members telling tall stories or singing, had been transformed into a "Club des Alpines" patterned after the famous London Alpine Club. Tartarin, then still considered a great hero by his fellow countrymen, was naturally selected as its president.

According to the author, it was not a question for the members of the new club to go and conquer high peaks in the Alps or Himalayas. In fact they were quite satisfied with spending part of their weekends picnicking in the thyme and lavender scented Alpilles (a name now more popular than "Alpines"), which are little hillocks not higher than eleven or twelve hundred feet at most, and located at the very gates of Tarascon. As to Tartarin, he lived happily in ease and comfort, still covered with glory for his past achievements. It had never occurred to him that now, in his early fifties, he would have to regain the respect and admiration of his countrymen in order to keep his position as PCA (President du Club des Alpines).

However, when he realized that his enemy, the jealous Costecalde, coveted the presidency and was making all the ascents one by one, Tartarin felt that time had come for him to perform some heroic deeds that would save his prestige and reputation. And so it came about that after much hesitation, followed by a period of intense training in his garden during which he read many books and filled his head with all kinds of Alpine words and expressions, Tartarin decided to dare the perils of a journey to the Swiss Alps, face avalanches, crevasses and glaciers, abysses and precipices, and start on his way to raise the banner of the Tarascon Club des Alpines on the Jungfrau, and perhaps later on the Mont Blanc, the highest peak in Europe!

He then procured all the equipment needed for mountain climbing, to which he added a few items recommended in the books he had read, plus a rope of his own invention, waterproof coverings, and a cooking lamp. His preposterous adventures began when he burst into the dining room of the Riga-Kulm Hotel, loaded with this equipment, an apparatus that made him look like a traveling tinman. In the last chapter we find Tartarin safe and sound in Tarascon, telling his listeners how he "did the Mont Blanc on two sides. . . ."[10]

Daudet has been criticized for introducing in his book the activities of the Russian nihilists then hiding in Switzerland and plotting the assassination of Czar Alexander III. The beginning of a mild sentimental love affair is suggested when Tartarin, seduced by the deep blue eyes of Sonia, the girl in the group, is about to get deeply

involved with her and fall into their hands. He is saved by the unexpected arrival of Tarascon delegates bringing him the banner of the
Club des Alpines.

This somewhat artificial amalgam of two unrelated subjects —
sports and politics — is perhaps a blemish, but if so, only a minor one
that does not seem to deserve all the importance that has been given
to it. A similar remark would apply to the discussion and dramatization of Schopenhauer's philosophy, an episode filling only a few
pages and equally defensible and justifiable. It cannot be denied
that Tartarin's sad plight is intensely dramatized when the Swedish
student threatens to hurl himself into a crevasse, which would drag
to death all the ascensionists tied to him by the rope.

At all events, the success enjoyed by *Tartarin sur les Alpes* could
have gratified the most deserving author as well as the most demanding publisher. It created a stir in the least expected quarters,
such as the Club Alpin Français, which immediately made Alphonse
Daudet an honorary member. Still more remarkable was the case of
the famous British Alpine climber Whimper, the first man to reach
the summit of Mount Cervin, who took Daudet for a confrere
climber and sent him his last book. Edward Whimper (1840 - 1911)
was himself an artist and writer whose books on mountaineering
have been very favorably appreciated for both their literary merits
and pictorial value.

III   *Worsening Health*

Alphonse Daudet was finding it harder and harder to adjust to his
worsening health. In the spring of 1885, Dr. Charcot recommended
a course of treatment at Lamalou, in the Cévennes, and that summer
the whole Daudet family betook itself to this watering place. But
they soon discovered that it did not constitute the right kind of environment for Julia and Lucien. The following year Alphonse went
alone with Léon, now a medical student, and until 1893 returned
there every year. Unfortunately, these "seasons" or spells of treatment never produced any real relief. Neither did a treatment by
baths taken in Paris (spring, 1886) under the supervision of the then
best-known hydrotherapist. By now it had become clear that rather
than mere nervous prostration, rheumatism, or arthritis, the malady
he had to contend with was the terrible and incurable locomotor
ataxis.

Alphonse Daudet now hesitated to cross a street in Paris for fear of
being unable to avoid the traffic. Once, while playing with his young

son Lucien in Champrosay, he was suddenly paralyzed, unable to move his legs. At Victor Hugo's funeral he could not control his shaky hand when asked to sign the register. One day, after seeing himself in a mirror Alphonse jotted down the following in his notebook: "What an emaciated face! What a funny little old man I have suddenly become! Leaped from age forty-five to sixty-five. Twenty years which I have not lived through!"[11] "He knew there was no hope for his condition ever to improve, and that it would keep on getting worse. Only through chloral and morphine could he now get some relief, and some sleep at night. Evidently, such a physical and mental strain could hardly be conducive to an appreciation and enjoyment of honors bestowed upon him or glory attached to his name.

The first Lamalou sojourn had been followed by a far more pleasant one in nearby Provence, where Alphonse and his family had been invited by their friends the Parrocels, to spend a few weeks. According to Lucien Daudet their stay there proved more beneficial to Alphonse than the one at Lamalou, for there, in the land and among people whom he loved, he found again the best memories of his youth. Old friends such as Mistral and Timoléon Ambroy came to see them. The Parrocels had been the Daudets' host several times in the past. They were wealthy, cultured, sophisticated, and very generous people who enjoyed entertaining distinguished guests on their property of Saint Esteve, near the town of Orgon, southeast of Avignon. Among their guests that year was Edmond de Goncourt, who, after a good deal of coaxing, had finally arrived unexpectedly one fine day (*un beau matin*). His surprise visit added a great deal to his friend's hapiness. Alphonse, delighted to introduce him to Provence, which Goncourt hardly knew, took him to such places as Les Baux, Saint Rémy, and Lamanon which he himself wanted to see again. Lucien marveled at the "miraculous excitement" that overtook "this sick man," his father.

At the beginning of 1885 the Daudets had moved from Avenue de l'Observatoire, now considered too far from the center of Paris, to Rue de Bellechasse, just across the river from the Gardens of the Tuileries. Their third child, a daughter, was born to them the following year in 1886. Edmond de Goncourt accepted the honor of being her godfather. Momentarily at least, this birth helped Alphonse to forget his growing sadness and physical torture. For the next ten or eleven years, little Edmée was to be his pride and joy.

At Champrosay a few weeks later it was realized that the apartment they occupied in the Allard's house was too small for the now larger family. Since they could easily afford to have a house of their own, they immediately bought one in the neighborhood, "not luxurious," said Lucien, but large enough and comfortable. It had several bedrooms and large outbuildings. The property extended down to the Seine river, through nearly fifteen acres of land. There were beautiful alleys bordered with trimmed bushes and trees (linden, sycamore, tulip trees, etc.), terraces and lawns, an ornamental lake, and a quadrangle (*cour d'honneur*), flowers, and kitchen gardens.

One of the guest rooms was reserved for Edmond de Goncourt whose expected and unexpected visits were quite frequent. Alphonse did much of his work in one of the several pavillons in the park. In another they put a billiard table for Léon and his friends. It is easy to imagine why this house in the countryside, in the midst of that nature which he had loved all his life, became for Alphonse Daudet another great diversion: "I, a landed proprietor! That's incredible," he would say laughingly. No doubt he would have enjoyed it much more had he been in good health, but it diverted his thoughts and somehow, temporarily at least, gave him a new lease on life.

IV *Revival of* L'Arlésienne

Among the other events and good news that came to alleviate pain and sorrow in the Daudet family in 1885 must be recalled the revival of *L'Arlésienne*. When the famous actor and theater producer Porel (Désiré-Paul Parfouru, *alias*), then director of the Odéon theater, suggested that time was ripe for another trial of the play on the stage, Daudet, who had not quite forgotten the failure of 1872, hesitated for a while to give his consent. He finally agreed to work with Porel, and nothing was neglected to insure the success of the play.

The first performance took place on May 5 before an enthusiastic audience and was followed by many others which met with equal success. It may be assumed that this belated triumph of 1885 gave Daudet one of the greatest satisfactions of his life. On the other hand we can understand why he could not enjoy it in the manner he might have some twelve or thirteen years before, when it would have put him on the road to fame as a dramatist. In this connection he remarked wistfully that "there are some successes that come too late," a feeling he had already expressed in 1875 at the time of

Bizet's death. Referring to the latter's complaint that the public of 1872 did not even listen to his overture of *L'Arlésienne,* Daudet commented: "They listened later . . . they applauded, acclaimed it. . . . When I think of him, I think of that endless bargaining and haggling over success and glory during which the most valiant perish, die sometimes just as they are about to triumph."[12] It remains that Daudet's somewhat dampened enthusiasm for the theater was revived by this genuine triumph of *L'Arlésienne,* now a classic of the French stage.

Taking advantage of his sojourn at the Parrocels, Alphonse Daudet rewrote — or, rather, revised, with the help of his son Léon writing under his dictation — the dramatization of *Sapho* originally made by Adolphe Bellot. The revised play, performed at the Gymnase theater in December, turned out to be another considerable theatrical event, Daudet's second dramatic triumph in the year 1885. It was duly celebrated in the Daudet apartment, Rue de Bellechasse, at a "souper traditionnel" attended by a dozen guests among whom were Edmond de Goncourt, the Zolas, and the Charcots. As the translation for possible performances in New York was being discussed, a brief telegram brought the message that *Sapho* had been found "objectionable." This was a disappointment for everybody concerned, but perhaps more specially for young Léon who had got excited over a promise made by his father to pay for his trip to the United States should the deal materialize.

V   La Belle Nivernaise

In 1886 Daudet published *La Belle Nivernaise, histoire d'un vieux bateau et de son équipage,* which is a story for children. According to his secretary Jules Ebner "it was the result of a bet," the author having wanted to prove that it was possible to write a book in which almost every sentence could start with an indented line, that is, constitute a paragraph, without disrupting the harmony of the whole. Apparently not in a mood to give much attention to it, Daudet dictated the story to Huges Le Roux, a young writer whom he wanted to help. Later, Le Roux pretended that he, and not Alphonse Daudet, was the real author of the book. The dedication of *La Belle Nivernaise* reads thus: "I dedicate this New Year Book to my dear son [*mon cher petit garçon*] Lucien Daudet." (Lucien had had another book dedicated to him in 1884. This was a "picture-book for children," *Les Cigognes* for which Daudet had written the text. It was dedicated to Lucien by the artist, G. Jundt.)

La Belle Nivernaise is neither a great book nor what might be called a polished, perfect work. But it filled its primary purpose. Adults themselves can find it enjoyable to read.

Presumably encouraged by the big successes of *L'Arlésienne* and *Sapho*, Daudet began to make a stage version of *Numa Roumestan*, this time without any collaborator. The play, performed at the Odéon in 1887, was well received. It was to be revived for a short period in 1891. During that year Daudet had collected a certain number of articles he had written in the past. They were published in two volumes: *Trente ans de Paris* in the spring of 1888, and *Souvenirs d'un Homme de Lettres* in the fall of that same year. Some of the texts they contained had appeared in the Parisian press as early as 1859 and 1865, others in Russia in the 1870s, one more recently in the United States. A few were new. They were all interesting, most of them dealing with important people in both the literary and political worlds and a few about himself and his work, such as the delightful "true story" entitled "Premier habit."

VI L'Immortel

Meanwhile, Daudet had not forgotten the work he wanted to write on the French Academy, his most important publication of that year, which appeared under the title of *L'Immortel*, first serially in *L'Illustration* (May, June, and July, 1888) and soon after in book form, published by Alphonse Lemerre.

The work aroused a storm of protests and was immediately condemned as an unfair and vicious attack against the venerable company Richelieu had founded some three hundred years ago to preserve the purity of the French language and improve the quality of French literature. In 1888 as in our days most people in France regarded the Academy as a respectable, almost sacred, institution with which nobody should "take familiarities," as Alphonse Daudet had done. But the latter could easily defend his position. He began by showing that both his criticism and the incidents dramatized in the book were supported by verified fact and he confounded those pretending that his work was one written out of spite by an unsuccessful candidate.

Daudet had been approached years before, at the time of his first great triumphs as a novelist, by academicians who urged him to offer himself as a candidate. Indeed, he had referred to the Academy and academicians in an ironic vein as early at 1874 in his *Femmes d'artistes*, and later in *Les Rois en exil*. He had been particularly angered in 1883 when during a rehearsal of *Les Rois en exil* it was made clear

to him that *le parti des ducs* would not support his candidature unless he withdrew his play from the stage. After the publication of the
Evangelist, and especially when a seat was left vacant by the death
of Jules Sandeau, his friends (among whom were delegates of the
Academy) insisted again that he should present himself immediately.

However, while feeling naturally much flattered by the offer,
Daudet remained apprehensive and avoided committing himself.
After discussing the matter with his family and with Edmond de
Goncourt and Emile Zola, who both encouraged him to canvass for
the seat, he decided first to inquire about the formalities to be
observed by a prospective candidate. To that end, he applied to the
most reliable and direct source of information, to the perpetual
secretary of the Academy himself. Appalled by what he learned from
the latter, Alphonse Daudet made up his mind, "right then and
there," first, never to be a candidate himself, and second, to write a
book on the subject.

Later, as his name kept on coming to the fore in the press every
time a vacancy occurred, he made it a point to make his position
clear by having the *Figaro* print the now often quoted statement: "I
am not, I never was and never will be a candidate for the French
Academy."[13]

While it procured him "some respite," this declaration fell short of
convincing everybody, as he explained to a newsman. His academician friends in particular resumed coaxing him to join, saying or
suggesting "with an ironic smile" that he "would come to it" as
others had, as one "always ends by coming to it." And that, he
added, was the reason why he wrote *L'Immortel.* He wrote it "to
prove once for all" that he would not "come to it." He wanted it to
be known that he abhorred coteries and cliques, "whatever they may
be and whatever may be said about them," and that he was an independent writer, "in nobody's tow": "When I have written a good
book, I feel rewarded specially by the pleasure — or the pride if you
will — of having written it; and that means leaving aside official
praises, academic prizes, and even commendations from my contemporaries."[14]

L'Immortel could be summarized as the story of the scholar
Astier-Rhéu who has become an academician, that is, an "immortal," as the members of the French Academy are called. He owes his
elevation to this high national dignity partly to the intrigues of his
wife and perhaps mostly to her marital unfaithfulness. He has a son,

Paul, but he does not enjoy any more love or respect from him than he does from his wife. Paul Astier belongs to that new breed of young men "who use the Darwinian theory of the struggle for life as a scientific excuse and pretext for all kinds of villainies and infamies."[15] Daudet dubbed them the "struggle-for-lifeurs," an expression which, he informs us, he had coined in English "to please the Parisians, who like nothing so much as to murder foreign words, and already counted *high lifeur* in their vocabulary." Paul is a type, he wrote later, "that did not exist among us before the war."[16]

Astier Rhéu senior falls victim of a forger who sells him false documents, letters, and autographs, which make both him and the Academy appear ridiculous. Having realized the futility of his work thus reduced to naught, discovered his wife's disloyalty ("It's strange," he said once, "I do not smoke and my wife's veils smell of tobacco"),[17] and considered the emptiness of his life, he commits suicide by throwing himself into the Seine river.

However, what impressed the readers above all was the number of contemptible actions, intrigues, and machinations to which the would-be "immortals" resorted in their effort to be elected members of the French Academy. In the novel the traditional candidate is personified by the writer Abel de Freydet, who has been "inoculated with the virus of the Academy." Another character, his friend Vérdrine, is his exact antithesis: the spokesman for the author in his criticism of the Academy, the man who compares glory to "a good cigar put in your mouth by the burning and ash side," and whose *joie personnelle* is to create and to express himself.[18]

Furthermore, Daudet insisted on the influence of the academic atmosphere upon the newcomers. He conveyed the idea that the academicians felt keenly — though very few would admit it — the inanity of their function and the depressive effect of their conventional and traditional attitude toward life, which he considered as detrimental to the writer's creative power.

L'Immortel has been called an original novel, not only because of the newness of the subject, which had never been treated in a work of fiction, but also because of its spirit, style, and tone. It is an aggressive work, almost completely devoid of Daudet's characteristic humor, tenderness, and compassion usually found in his other works. He later expressed his regrets for having been "a little harsh" on the "old lady," that is, the Academy. True enough, he made this statement at a time when both his fortune and reputation were well established, when he could afford to disregard official praises and prizes — and even public approbation — which would seem to emphasize its validity. Nevertheless, it may be taken for granted that deep within he felt "rewarded," happy for having been so outspoken. And yet, we may wonder to what extent poor health had contributed to his change of attitude.

Violent protests and insults from angry critics that reached him at Champrosay were "muffled," according to Lucien Daudet, "by the calmness of the countryside," but his suffering did not subside. The Lamalou treatments remained ineffective and he realized he had come down to the point of no longer having a desire to be cured, that his only desire was to be able to hold his own, to last.[19]

VII   *Treatment by Suspension*

When he was back in Paris in the summer of 1888, Dr. Charcot decided to try on him a new treatment. It almost cost his life. This very painful and dangerous treatment referred to as "the treatment by suspension" consisted in having the patient suspended in the air at stated intervals. Alphonse Daudet was subjected to it twice a week: "I remain as much as four minutes in the air, two minutes during which I am held up only by my jaw. Pain in my teeth. Then, when they take me down and untie me, an awful malaise in my spine and the nape of the neck, as if all marrow was melting. I have to crouch and rise little by little as if, it seems to me, my stretched marrow returned to its place."[20] His suffering had been so intense that year, that for some time he thought seriously of suicide. But he decided that one has no right to take his own life. Beside, his task was not over and he felt he could still gather enough energy to carry on.

During that fall he took a lively interest in the performance of Goncourt's *Germinie Lacerteux* (based on the famous novel published in 1865) which Porel had put on the stage partly on his recommendation. He attended several rehearsals and the opening performance at which he applauded as loudly as he could to cover the noisy protests and hootings of various antagonistic groups in the audience. At the dinner offered by the Daudets to celebrate the success of the play, Julia and Alphonse reminisced about a similar noisy evening at another performance of a Goncourt play, that of *Henriette Maréchal* in 1865, when they saw each other for the first time.

Some time in February, 1889, during the night following his thirteenth "suspension" or "pendaison," as he would call it,

Alphonse Daudet had a violent hemorrhage reminiscent of his experience of 1878 (See p. 66 of this work). He remained between life and death for several days, throughly exhausted. He recovered slowly but was for a long time in a dangerous state of prostration. Moreover, he was saddened by the death of M. Allard, his father-in-law for whom he had a great respect and deep affection.

VIII   La Lutte pour la vie

Nevertheless, his active mind always ready to move, he went on working alternately on two projects, a new play, *La Lutte pour la vie*, and a new novel, *Port-Tarascon*, which he carried through during the year 1889.

Deeply concerned about the ever increasing number of "struggle-for-lifeurs" among the younger generations, Daudet decided he would complete the portrait of Paul Astier which he had sketched in *L'Immortel*. He made him the main character of *La Lutte pour la vie* and, mostly through him, suggested the possible effect of the Darwinian phrase "the struggle for life" when applied to human society. His ideas on the Academy were not to be found in the play itself, but he summarized and discussed them in the preface.

La Lutte pour la Vie introduces a more or less aristocratic environment and cosmopolitan society. Most of the action takes place in an historical château of the Loire valley and in a beautiful residence (the Hôtel Padovani) in Paris. In addition to Paul Astier and his wife Maria-Antonia former duchess of Padovani who used to monopolize the dukes in her salon, are the following recurring characters whom the reader had already met in *L'Immortel:* The Marquise de Rocanère from the neighboring château across the Loire river; Count Adriani, the papal nuncio's nephew who exclaims "Cristo! qu'elle est bella!" every time he sees a woman; the duke of Bretigny of the French Academy, who holds there the seat reserved for the "man of the world," and Countess de Foder, with "her pointed nose bustling with curiosity in a mass of enticing laces." Among the new characters must be mentioned a couple of "struggle-for-lifeurs" (Astier's friends and employees); Antonin Caussade, a scientist who is partly the author's spokeman; Countess Esther de Seleny ("de la noblesse de ghetto") whom Paul Astier wants to marry because of her wealth; Lydie, one of his mistresses who, unable to stand his desertion, takes poison; and her father Vaillant who at the end of the play kills Paul Astier to avenge his seduced and betrayed daughter.

La Lutte pour la vie was played for the first time on October 3,

1889, at the Gymnase dramatic theater. Calman Lévy published it in 1890. It had a rather good run, about one hundred performances, and then was completely forgotten. Half a century later Lucien Daudet was at a loss to understand why it had not been revived. In fact *La Lutte pour la vie* deserved a better fate. There is certainly more to it than in many plays of the time which have been kept in the repertory of some theaters. But public interest in the analysis and dramatization of the modern physiognomy of the "struggle-for-lifeur" was partly due to the prevailing, but temporary state of mind of that period. It reflected the reaction then taking place against nineteenth-century "scientism," or more precisely against blind belief in the power of science to solve all human problems. It was bound to fade out rapidly. The "struggle-for-lifeur" himself, the type dramatized by Daudet, was not to disappear. In fact, it seems to be more common today, in 1975, than it has ever been in the past. Perhaps an attempt should be made to revive the play.

IX L'Obstacle

Encouraged by the success of 1889, Alphonse Daudet began to work again for the stage, but over one year elapsed before he had any work ready for either the theater or the publishers. By the end of 1890, however, he had written *L'Obstacle*, a play on the then much discussed question of heredity. It was performed for the first time on December 27, 1890. The "obstacle" in question is the belief that a mental disease developed as the result of a sun stroke is likely to be inherited by the victim's son. The latter, the hero called Didier d'Alein, is about to marry a beautiful girl, Madeleine de Remondy. They are both deeply in love with each other, but Madeleine breaks her engagement when she is advised to forestall a possibly tragic predicament. It turns out however that the sun stroke having occurred after Didier's birth, its consequences could not have affected him. The wedding finally takes place and all is well that ends well.

The play was well received but it did not hold the stage very long. In spite of some interesting scenes and one or two somewhat original characters it lacks the dramatic quality that made the success of *La Lutte pour la vie*. It reflects the discouraged, pessimistic state of mind of the author.

CHAPTER 5

From Port-Tarascon *to* La Petite Paroisse

I   Port-Tarascon

AND yet, although in the midst of physical and moral tortures, of fears and nightmares, more and more beset by the idea of death, Alphonse Daudet had not lost entirely his sense of humor and had managed to introduce it in the third volume of the Tartarin trilogy under the title of *Port-Tarascon, dernières aventures de l'illustre Tartarin* (Paris: Dentu, 1890). It was translated into English by Henry James in 1890, and W. P. Trent in 1889 - 90 (Little, Brown & Co.).

In an amusing kind of foreword or introduction to this book, in which he continuously blends truth and poetry, fiction and reality, Daudet refers facetiously to the actual threats he has received in the past, during and after the publication of the first Barbarins and Tartarins (Cf. pp. 46 ff): " 'Father, how pale you are!' said my son, and I could hardly find the strength to whisper as I pointed to King René's castle whose four towers seemed to watch me come, 'There's Tarascon!' " However, his fear proved to be unwarranted.

Nothing moved in the streets. All was silent and it looked as if life itself had stopped. Obviously the old town had been abandoned: ". . . no dogs or cats, children or chickens . . . nobody." The flies themselves had disappeared . . . and so had "the exquisite odors of garlic soup which at this time should have come in puffs from every kitchen in town. . . ."[1]

This idea of a completely deserted Tarascon had been suggested to Daudet by an experience he had in 1886 as he and his son Léon, accompanied by Frédéric Mistral, were on their way to the Tarascon railway station on a hot, sultry, dusty summer day. In such weather, the Provençaux, who normally prefer outdoor life, seek relief from the oppressive canicular heat in the relative coolness of their closed houses, and they stay indoors till the end of the afternoon. This much, then, was reality. It remained for the author to imagine a situation which would justify, at least in literature, a complete desertion of the city by its inhabitants.

Daudet felt it advisable first to inform the reader that he intended to comply with Pascal's doctrine according to which, in literature, "the agreeable and the real are necessary" and that *Port-Tarascon* was "taken from the true." And he added: "When you find here and there some "tarasconade" altogether too extravagant, may I be hanged if I invented it!"[2]

The story of *Port-Tarascon* is indeed based on actual facts. These are related to the famous "Affaire de la Colonie libre de Port-Breton," an affair which ironically did not concern the South but the North, specifically Brittany and the Bretons. It was an awful mystification in which a few thousand Bretons had been swindled out of their savings with the promise that they would be taken to a rich island in the South Pacific, a kind of promised land where they were to find happiness, and rapidly become wealthy. Four ships were actually freighted by a certain Marquis de Rays, but only hardships, disease, and distress, and for some death, were to be found by the emigrants (The relation of the events by one of the surviviors, M. Villetèle, was published in the newspaper *L'Intransigeant* from November 28, 1883, to January, 1884. Part of it has been reprinted in the *O.C.* XIII, 157ff). The case, taken to the Court of Appeals, had considerably excited public opinion between 1878 and 1884. Daudet thought rightly that it would have been just as easy to fool the Provençaux as the Bretons and so did not hesitate to transfer the scene to Tarascon and to an imaginary "Port-Tarascon" settled by Tartarin and other Provençal recurring characters.

In *Port-Tarascon* the tragedy of the situation has not been belittled in the least, but, somehow, it has been submerged, superseded by the comic element found in almost every character concerned, including the villain, the duc de Mons himself.

Nonetheless, the duc de Mons had been able to assert himself immediately, on his first visit: "A duke! Can you imagine? No duke had ever come to Tarascon. To be sure, . . . a camel, a baobab, a lionskin, a collection of poisoned arrows and alpenstocks of honor could be seen there . . . but a duke, never!" In addition to his title, the mere fact of being a genuine northerner was decidedly in his favor: "No gestures, few words, and such a composure! . . . He never got excited . . . saw things as they are, calmly. . . . You could rely on him."[3]

The "duke" had immediately ascertained that Tartarin, the pharmacist Bézuquet and Father Bataillet were then the most popular and trustworthy citizens in town. He assumed with them a "mysterious air," looked grave, and talked gravely to them — although in such a low voice that Pascalon, who was listening at the door, could not hear anything he said. But he spoke so convincingly that within a few days the whole Tarascon population became excited about the prospect of founding a "Colonie libre de Port-Tarascon" in the South Pacific.

To be sure, the good people of Tarascon would never have dreamt of giving up their homes had they been motivated only by the love of gain. The fact was that at this time they were much dissatisfied with "the establishment," which they called then "the state of things in France." There were two main reasons for their discontent. First, a government decree prohibiting bullfights. This gave the author an opportunity to recount the old story of the man who lost paradise by rushing out of it to fight the bulls. Secondly, a government order to close the convent of the White-Fathers. When the latter refused to leave, the Tarasconnais, led by Tartarin, moved in to help them resist the troops sent to expel them. No clash took place as it turned out that the so-called besieged were never attacked. They had to surrender at the end of two weeks for lack of food and water, perhaps more especially, as suggested by the author, because Tartarin could not get his cup of good, hot chocolate in the morning.

In turn the monks themselves moved into town and soon every family could boast of having a White-Father in its midst, a real blessing for the home: "From then on men avoided swearing, women almost quit telling fibs, and children sat up straight in their high chairs." But the occupation of the convent by the troops "had left in the Tarasconians' hearts a dark rancor."[4]

When a telegram from Marseilles announced that a first shipload consisting of eight hundred emigrants had left with Bompart as an acting governor of Port-Tarascon, enthusiasm reached a climax. Then came another inspiriting, exultant message, this one from the colony itself, so that within a few months every citizen, from the common herd to the upper cut, including "the nobility," had packed up for the great adventure. The grumblers like Costecalde, the weak, the wobblers, and disbelievers were now the most eager to go. In their eagerness and excitement they almost forgot the Tarasque.

Perhaps it should be recalled here that the Tarasque, from which the name of Tarascon is derived, was, according to legend, a terrible monster, a dragon that in ancient times lived in the marshes along the Rhone river and devoured cattle and children until Saint Martha tamed her. "Captivated by the innocence and pity of the saint," she let herself be brought downtown on a leash consisting of a blue ribbon. Ever since then, the Tarasconians have now and then celebrated the event by taking through the street an effigy made of wood and pasteboard roughly representing the old Tarasque. In Daudet's time it was still venerated as an idol, considered as part of the city, as its very soul. Obviously the Tarasconians could not leave her behind.

Neither could they leave "le Romain," the most famous bull of Camargue who had won so many victories in the arenas of the Midi. Three cows were added to insure the survival of bullfighting, the most venerable tradition of the South. Along with objects such as dog collars and umbrellas to barter with the savages were various kinds of seeds and, naturally, an enormous amount of garlic "whose delicious fragrance marked the wake of the ship, thus mingling the smell of Tarascon with that of India."[5]

Unfortunately, the Tarasconians were not to be luckier than the Bretons. It soon appeared that the "duke" was an impostor. The island supposedly bought by him from a native Papoua king belonged to the English, who eventually repatriated all the emigrants who had been dumped there.

When the main body of emigrants, among them Tartarin now "invested by the duc de Mons with the fine title and the important functions of Governor,"[6] arrived at Port-Tarascon, they expected also to find a town, a port, a fine harbor with docks and shipyards. Two ships of emigrants having preceded them a year before, they expected also to find a crowd to greet them upon their arrival. Instead, all they found was an old pier made of rafters and planks, a half demolished shed, and a "deserted cemetery." Except for the pharmacist Bézuquet who was to tell their plight, all the first comers had been eaten by the cannibals. When asked why he himself had been spared, Bézuquet answered that having spent most of his life among jars, "soaking in pharmaceutic products," his flesh had probably acquired a flavor not quite to their taste; unless of course, precisely because of this peculiar aroma, they had on the contrary, decided to keep him as a tidbit for the end of the festivities, which lasted a whole month.

Everything kept on going from bad to worse. The most courageous had immediately started clearing and planting, but the soil was so bad that nothing would grow normally. Vegetables would either grow overnight as big as trees or not at all: "nothing would come up or would come up too much." It rained most of the time, ten months out of twelve, "more than at Lyons or in Switzerland." This lack of sunshine, so detrimental to those used to the Provençal sun, the combination of dampness with bad diet, homesickness, and boredom made the number of sick people increase every day. Luckily, the director of the health center was a clever man. Instead of prescribing drugs, as Bézuquet would have done, he merely prescribed for every patient, "a nice good garlic soup (three cloves of garlic, three spoonfuls of good olive oil with some toast on top)." Even those agonizing individuals who could no longer speak would exclaim: "Boy that smells good! . . . and the smell alone would revive them." And this explains why everybody was appalled when they realized that this universal panacea, "garlic the healer and savior," which could not grow on the island, would soon be lacking.[7]

Then le Romain had escaped and was roaming the forest, no longer a bull, but a true wild buffalo. Instead of being baited, he was now the one baiting, frightening people and making them run! Nevertheless, one day, the sun having miraculously appeared, Tartarin tried to recover his popularity by organizing a bullfight (the bull race) with the three remaining cows. Unfortunately, the first one did not move after reaching the center of the arena; the second, probably too weak, absolutely refused to come out of the stable; and the third, on which the last hopes were set, rushed out straight into the sea, where she drowned.

The Governor was naturally held responsible for everything bad that happened and he had to defend himself by making speeches and dictating to his secretary Pascalon "general orders" meant to reassure the population. A most effective one consisted of cleverly suggesting that the supply of garlic would be maintained (*l'ail ne manquera pas*). Other important crises took place. Tartarin managed to keep his authority, his popularity, and even his dignity. However, after his confrontation with the English the colony agreed unanimously that time had come to evacuate Port-Tarascon and return to Tarascon, France, which they did. But Tartarin's troubles were not over. Fate seemed to dog him on board ship. As it was to be learned later, the Tarasque had been washed off the ship. When he saw her in the distance, half covered by the waves, he took her for a whale and shot her, to his dismay and the astonishment of his countrymen. The Tarasque had been rolling on the high seas and had outlived the most dreadful typhoons. Being strongly built, "indestructible," she had remained undamaged. But now her first and only wound had been inflicted by Tartarin de Tarascon: "Pascalon, I am telling you, that is a shot that will bring me bad luck."[8] All day long, he worried, full of remorse and sacred terror.

Yet, most of Tartarin's experiences at Port-Tarascon had made him very happy. He had enjoyed his popularity and his power as a governor, he had married the daughter of His Majesty King Negonko, princess Likiriki, who decided to stay at Port-Tarascon, and perhaps more than anything else he had enjoyed comparing himself, his personality and destiny, to Napoleon's. His vanity was enhanced once more on the ship, when the commodore's wife seemed to get seriously interested in him.

Upon reaching Gibraltar, he and Pascalon were arrested by French police officers armed with warrants and writs of extradition, transferred to a French ship, taken to Tarascon in handcuffs, hooted by the populace, jailed in King René's castle, accused of gross fraud, of manslaughter through criminal neglect, and of violating the laws of emigration. His trial is described at length in a most amusing and satirical mood. He was finally acquitted, but he considered himself as "fallen, knocked off his pedestal."

Tartarin confided to Pascalon: "I see through it now. The Tarasconians have opened my eyes. It is as if I had been operated on for cataracts."[9] He thought also that his countrymen themselves had been operated on, that they could see now, "but he found them cruel." Thoroughly disgusted, he left Tarascon and went to live across the river, at Beaucaire, where he died three months later. Thus ends this work which Anatole France called a "creation unique among his creations," a character he conceived in his youth and whose accomplishment he pursued almost to "the end of his life."[10]

Throughout this book the reader feels the underlying sadness, the anquish that beset Daudet. It is truly remarkable that in his condition he could write a story as entertaining as this one. Not a great novel to be sure — Daudet himself did not claim to have written a masterpiece — but one that will be appreciated by anyone having previously enjoyed the first two volumes of the Tartarin trilogy. "Its only defect," said Henry James in the preface of his own translation, "is that it leaves no more to come to Tartarin's dramatic life, that it exhausts all possibilities."[11]

The question having been raised as to a possible reaction of Tarascon against the author of the novel, Mistral wrote the following

in defense of his old friend: "Daudet a bad Provençal? . . . Just
because, given to mockery and teasing, he made fun of the minor absurdities of our country, Tarascon would harbor resentment against
him? No! Mother lioness does not bear any, and never will, against
her cub which, in play, for fun, scratches her!"[12]

II   Léon's Marriage

One day in the summer of 1890 Léon arrived unexpectedly at
Champrosay to inform his parents that he had become engaged to
Jeanne Hugo, the heroine of Victor Hugo's famous poem "L'art
d'être grand-père." While Julia was "in seventh heaven," Alphonse
made some reserves. But he himself was very fond of Jeanne whom
he had known since she was a little girl. He regarded her as an "exquisite, good, affectionate person, with an original mind," and he
did all he could so that his future daughter-in-law would not be
"under the impression of sickness."[13]

Unfortunately the Daudets' relatives, except "l'excellent Ernest,"
objected strenuously because of religious and political con-
siderations. This they did, according to Lucien, "without any
thoughtful or sympathetic regard for Alphonse's frightful state of
health and unremitting courage. They harassed him till the last
minute "with thousand of objurgations, refusals, and baneful predic-
tions" which collided with his sole, single aim: his son's happiness.
The marriage, which took place in January, 1891, had to be a "civil"
one, that is, without a church wedding. For reasons perhaps related
to the political career of Jeanne's stepfather, the official press (la
presse gouvernementale) acclaimed the event as "the beginning of a
new era originated in high circles, as a victory of enlightenment over
obscurantism. . . ." The "mundane" newspapers limited themselves
to comments on the dresses, the flowers, and the music played at the
wedding. But the Catholic, "right-minded" (bien pensants) newspapers were venomous and acted atrociously toward Alphonse
Daudet.

Lucien saw in these attacks mostly a revenge of jealous, envious,
and frustrated authors and critics. Alphonse Daudet "was being
made to pay dearly" for his past success, he said, "for the high
position" he had been occupying during the last sixteen years in the
literary world, "the exceptional diffusion of his works — comparable
only to Zola's — and the amazing offers made to him by publishers
and newspaper editors for the privilege of being the first to publish
his work." Many of these attacks came from the small, unimportant

reviews and some from "Felibres who had never forgiven Alphonse Daudet for Tartarin and Numa Roumestan."[14]

III *Cultural Background*

During 1891 and 1892, referred to as "two terrible years" by Lucien, Alphonse Daudet tried to forget, ignore his pain, seeking refuge "in time and space" by reading "from morning to night history books, memoirs and works of explorers like Stanley, Livingston, and Nansen, following them from "the dark Continent" to the North polar regions. His fondness for books, inherited from his mother, had never subsided since the days when he read *Robinson Crusoe*, the *Aventures de Robert Robert et de son compagnon Toussaint-Lavenette*, or the *Théâtre du Seigneur Croquignole*.

He had never ceased adding to his cultural background. In addition to hunting stories and voyages of discovery, he had read the great works of antiquity and the classics of French and foreign literatures. We learn from his son Léon, who used to have long literary and philosophical discussions with him, that he appreciated particularly "the beauty of Lucretius, Virgil, and Tacitus — the latter "always to be found on his table by the side of Montaigne." Among the philosophers he had been impressed mostly by Spinoza and Descartes, "as much for their lucidity of mind as for their minute and anxious researches into the play of human passions." Léon states further that he had a "very pronounced taste" for Schopenhauer, which is evidently a statement calling for some qualification, since Alphonse Daudet became much concerned about the influence of the German philosopher on youth.

In the field of modern foreign literature, his admirations went first to Cervantes, Shakespeare, and Gœthe. The latter's *Conversations with Eckermann* was his breviary for a long time. To Alphonse Daudet, Gœthe's motto "Poetry and Reality" (*Dichtung und Wahrheit*) seemed "to sum up the wisdom of mankind." Among the French writers, Montaigne, Pascal, and Rousseau were, again according to Léon, "his three chief and violent admirations." He admired their sincerity and proposed them as examples for himself. We must not forget that Alphonse Daudet never separated life from literature.[15] The importance of his rapport with Mistral and the "Felibres" has already been emphasized.

Now, at the age of fifty-one, he enjoyed greatly the novels of George Meredith, which his friend Marcel Schwob used to translate to him at sight. Then he immersed himself in the works of Pascal, who, however, brought him back to his pain rather than helping him to forget it. Sometime earlier he had jotted down .this line in his *carnets*: "I have given to my son, as a thesis subject, Pascal's neurosis." He also jotted down the following: "Two and a half years without notes. I have worked, I have suffered. Lassitude. Despondency."[16]

IV   Rose et Ninette

In the fall of 1891 Daudet mustered enough courage to write a short novel on the problem of divorce, *Rose et Ninette*,which was published in 1892 by the Librairie Flammarion. To what extent he was moved to write it as a warning to Léon whose marriage seemed to lack the desirable stability is perhaps not as clear as it would seem at first sight — even though the book was dedicated to him;

> To my dear son Léon Daudet
> To the Poet and Philosopher
> I dedicate these pages out of contemporary life

The law permitting divorce, passed in 1884, had never ceased being a controversial subject. The fate of the family considered as a social unit had become one of the most discussed among sociologists and was soon to become an important theme with the "traditionalist" writers, perhaps provoking later André Gide's notorious utterance "Family, I hate you." Daudet realized the danger and somehow foresaw the effect it would have on the structure of twentieth-century society. At that time, his own career and reputation had ceased to be his main concern. Being primarily preoccupied with the general question of Man's happiness, that of divorce was naturally in his mind, long before Léon had announced his intention to marry Jeanne Hugo. In fact, its presence is manifest in the powerful scene of *La Lutte pour la vie* where Paul Astier tries to poison his wife, the former duchess of Padovani. There, divorce is finally accepted by the wife as the lesser of two evils.

At the outset of *Rose et Ninette*, we learn that its main character, the well-known dramatist Regis de Fagan, has just been divorced. He has two daughters, Rose and Ninette aged sixteen and twelve, whom he will be allowed to see twice a month. The first time they come to spend the day with him, he realizes that their mother, his former wife, has worked on their feelings and set them against him. His landlady, a woman by the name of Mme Hulin who lives on the ground floor of the house with her young son, has brought flowers for them. But the girls are suspicious about their father's relationship with Mme Hulin and make unkind and undeserved derogatory remarks about it. The following reunions merely stress the progressive estrangement of the girls from their father.

Then, while de Fagan is becoming better acquainted with Mme Hulin and slowly is falling in love with her, his former wife remarries and his spoiled daughters remain under her sway. Through them he learns that Mme Hulin, whom he believed to be a widow, was visited by her husband, from whom she was only separated. This adds some element of mystery to the plot. Then Mr. Hulin commits suicide when his wife refuses to take him back. The last sentence of the book suggests that she and Fagan will "probably . . . remain strangers to each other forever."

The case against divorce in that story is not at all convincing. First, it is Fagan's story rather than that of Rose and Ninette who, anyway, appear quite satisfied with the new situation and do not seem to deserve all the consideration he has for them. Second, his wife is so mean that we may easily imagine him unhappier had he not divorced her. Finally, the story suggests that a marriage between Fagan and Mme Hulin might solve the problem. Evidently, the family has been destroyed and "divorce is not the solution," but keeping the family together in this particular case would not have been one either, with such a partner as Mme de Fagan. The main arguments for and against divorce were to be examined again later, but only briefly, in *La Petite Paroisse*.

V La Menteuse

Alphonse Daudet had agreed to collaborate with Léon Hennique in the dramatization of a short story, "La Menteuse," which Alphonse had published in *Les Femmes d'artistes*. The new play, bound to fail on the stage, offers nonetheless rather pleasant reading. Its conventional plot (two women in love with the same man) was reduced to the bare essentials. Less pretentious than *L'Obstacle*, short, straight to the point, devoid of didactic intentions, even lacking the minimal analysis that would have endowed its characters with life, *La Menteuse* possesses nevertheless some qualities that reveal the hand of an experienced dramatist.

The main character, Marie Deloche, has evidently been inspired by Marie Rieu, whose chief traits can also be found in at least half a dozen other Daudet characters, such as Irma Borel, Sapho,

Madeleine Ogé, and La Fédor. Like her prototype, Mme Deloche has had many lovers and is still involved with one or two of them while deeply in love with a young man four years her junior. She marries the latter but takes poison when she realizes that it has become impossible for her to hide her past life.

Performed at the Gymnase theater on February 4, 1892, *La Menteuse,* was Daudet's last play to be put on the stage. Its failure did not surprise anyone but Léon Hennique and the producer himself. As for Daudet, who in reality had not put his heart into it, he had now more important cares on his mind than that of lingering and moaning over this minor disappointment. Having just been informed that his dear friend Timoléon Ambroy had suffered a heart attack he left immediately for Provence. When he arrived there he had the pleasant surprise of finding Tim partly recovered, but he himself had been dangerously ill during the trip. Upon his return to Paris he hastened to take medical advice from several renowned physicians. Again, none of them could procure him the relief he was seeking.

Now that because of his illness his social life had perforce been reduced, the number of visitors in Paris or Champrosay multiplied. Lucien and Léon have named dozens of writers, artists, scholars, and politicians of the various "generations" who came then to honor the master. Among the writers were the old Leconte de Lisle, the already famous Anatole France, Maupassant, Loti, and Bourget, the young Barrès and still younger Marcel Proust; among the artists could be seen the American painter James Whistler, Degas, Renoir, the sculptor Auguste Rodin, the composers Massenet and Reynaldo Hahn; and among the politicians Georges Clemenceau and Raymond Poincaré. Also, critics among whom were Gustave Laroumet, Jules Lemaître, and the well-known Danish scholar George Brandes. There were many others whose names have now fallen into complete oblivion, and even some who remained unknown in their own time. When, many years later, Julia was asked how it happened that she and her husband would unearth these nonentities, she answered: "They were the ones who 'unearthed' us."[17]

Alphonse Daudet never looked down upon anybody. He viewed scorn as a form of stupidity and always maintained that in every human being lies something worthy of interest and consideration. And this is why he had always made it a point to help the young and lay himself out to please the humblest.

VI   *Batisto Bonnet*

One of these humble individuals who entered his life at that moment was Batisto Bonnet, a proud Provençal poet stranded in Paris. Bonnet became the faithful friend who helped him most, during these terrible years of 1890 - 1897, to recover and keep up his spirits, to forget his physical as well as his mental sufferings.

How this new friendship originated has been told separately by the two individuals concerned. Daudet has recalled how on two or three occasions in 1889, he had been impressed by the "easy and delectable" provençal prose of rustic scenes signed Batisto Bonnet which he had read in *Lou Viro-Soulèu* (The Sunflower), a Provençal review then published in Paris. Having discerned that this author was "neither a dilettante nor a philologist," and having discovered that he was a genuine peasant from Bellegarde (a small town between Nîmes and Arles) now working in Billancourt (a suburb of Paris), Daudet became actually interested in him and repeatedly invited him to call at Rue Bellechasse. However, when his reiterated invitations were left unanswered he reasoned that "talent and mind are not born on the same day," concluded that his Billancourt "felibre" must be "one of those boobies" who had not yet forgiven the creator of Tartarin, and decided not to trouble himself any longer with him.

For his part, the surprised and overwhelmed Bonnet had felt very eager to meet the great man who had so honored him. However, partly because he could not afford decent clothes, and partly because he feared that Daudet would take advantage of him, "utilize him," put him in one of his books and then reject him, he allowed "Sundays to pile up for a whole year," without daring to appear. Then, on a cold December day in 1890, having finally procured a new jacket and a top hat, he gathered the necessary courage to face the master. He went to Rue Bellechasse and, somewhat hesitatingly, rang the bell of the Daudet's apartment. He was immediately put at ease by the warm welcome of the master who greeted him in Provençal. Daudet asked many questions: "Tell me my friend, what are you doing? Do you have a position? Are you happy?" "Nothing of the sort," answered Bonnet, ". . . I came precisely to ask you if you could help me find a job. . . ." Thus began this most wonderful friendship which was to bring so much relief to Alphonse Daudet during the last six or seven years of his life.

Daudet immediately detected in Bonnet the qualities of a man deserving to be helped. Pulling him out of his financial difficulties was easily done, but finding employment for him took a long time. When finally a small position as a clerk in a publishing house was secured, a new life began for Bonnet, who, now freed from dire necessity, could take care of his family (his wife and two daughters), and look serenely into the future. Determined to give him a start in his literary career, Daudet coaxed him to write the story of his childhood in Provençal. From then on, he never stopped encouraging him. "How holy is the enthusiasm of friendship!" exclaimed Bonnet. Going and attending to his work took most of his time, but he would have done anything to please his *baile*, his "foster-father" and Maecenas. To remain worthy of "his noble intention" he kept on writing in spite of all kinds of material difficulties. He wrote "in bed, on the bus, on the boat, at meal time, while standing in front of his bookstall. . . ."

Mistral who also had congratulated Bonnet for his articles in *Lou Viro-Soulèu*, now asked him to contribute regularly to *L'Aiòli*, the Provençal trimonthly paper that he had just founded in Avignon. Bonnet's first contribution, "Lou Baile-Pastre," appeared on the seventeenth of January, 1891. He worked daily on his *Memòri d'un gnarro* ("farmhand"), which began to appear by installments in *L'Aiòli* a year later, in January, 1892. On one of his visits to the Daudets, a real festivity during which "the Provençal language was the queen," Alphonse suddenly asked his protégé whether he would like to have him translate his work into French. "I want to make your fortune," he said, "and I will; I want you to be happy, and you will."[18] He added that he would write a first-rate preface. And so it was done.

Bonnet's story of his childhood, translated by Daudet under the title "*Vie d'Enfant*," was published by Dentu in 1894. The "first-rate preface" in question, entitled "Présentation," has been reprinted in the *Oeuvres complètes* (XIV, i-x), where will be found also the *Valet de Ferme* translated by Daudet with the help of Henri Ner, and prefaced by Léon Daudet. Although at first a little skeptical about Bonnet, Léon had become fond of him, and like his father, was now a sincere admirer of his talent. In fact Bonnet had become the object of a special attention in the Daudet family. Julia herself realized fully how much his presence, even the mere sound of his voice, helped her husband to forget his present condition.

Bonnet was like Daudet a prose writer endowed with an extreme sensitivity. They were born and raised under the same sun, and the same stars, but in a different class and social environment. They did not belong exactly to the same world. On the other hand, they both knew rustic life firsthand for having lived in its midst during their childhood — though in a different way and contrary circumstances. From their early experience both had retained a keen feeling for nature and a deep love for the unsophisticated, simple country people. Also, each had suffered from want at some time during his youth. They were kindred souls, generally animated by similar ideals and sentiments.

During Bonnet's frequent visits, Daudet spoke very seldom about his own work.

If asked, he would only name the book he was working on and, immediately, the French writer would disappear yielding to the Nimese, to the Felibre. . . . And what a Felibre he was! . . . He would start by humming some old Provençal tune, then suddenly his face would light up and . . . in a subdued voice he would sing:

Moun galin-galant	My gay gallant
Me menavo	took me
Me menavo	took me
Moun galin-galant	My gay gallant
Me Manavo per la man	Took me by the hand
Amai quand me tenie,	And while holding me,
Me manavo	He took me
Me menavo,	He took me
Amai quand me tenie,	And while holding me
Me menavo is oulivie	He took me to the olive tree

And Bonnet continues: "In luminous evocations of his Provençal education he would show me his father's factory, tell me how he had been indulged, coddled by his mother, how he would kick his cousin Leonce under the table. . . ." In thought, together they went

through olive orchards, wasteland scented with mint, lavender and thyme, soothed, lulled by the chirping of the cicadas among the flights of white and blue butterflies, and bees which would loll in the foliage, on the bunches of flowers. . . . We went and went on and on —— then, suddenly, like a lightning that spreads, streams, frolics in its gleam, like a dazzling forked lightning, my master's thought would take us to the shores of the Vistre, to the Alpilles, the Crau, the White Mas, into the Camargue, by the ponds, the water trenches, the marshes. . . . We would jump over ditches filled with reeds shivering in the sea-breeze, under the flights of partridges, flamingoes, and sea-gulls who would flee from us, fly away in the sunshine. . . .[19]

And Bonnet would joyfully listen to him reminisce about his past, "in which he saw himself as in a mirror." Daudet would then comment on remembrance: Time, which "withers our cheeks, weighs down our gait, whitens our beards and hair," he said, "respects our remembrance." He considered Youth as a dream during which we long to age while we do not know how to enjoy "the secret perfumes of the flower of life. . . ." At times, his voice would deepen, his fancy play about the idea of some kind of a pilgrimage during which both would visit again the places where their hearts had "uttered their first cries of joy."

"Thus his high spirit, and hopes," Bonnet comments, "adorned life as a Springtide that blossomed in his eyes, on his lips, and radiated and strewed gaiety around him."[20]

VII *Gonzague Privat and Gaston Boissier*

Two other meridional "expatriates," Gonzague Privat and Gaston Boissier, contributed also, though for a shorter time and in a different way, to the well-being and delight of their famous compatriot. Boissier, like Daudet a native of Nîmes, was a well-known scholar, author of important studies on Roman literature and civilization, a professor at the Ecole Normale Supérieure, and the administrator of the Collège de France. He called periodically at rue Bellechasse to chat with his friend.

Gonzague Privat was in every respect an entirely different man. The fantastic individual and peculiar artist to whom Alphonse Daudet had dedicated *Tartarin de Tarascon* in 1869 ("A mon Ami, G.P.") had been the most faithful friend in the group of "bohemians" who surrounded Alphonse and Julia during the first years of their marriage. Privat possessed some of the characteristic traits of Tartarin. While he spoke French without any southern accent whatever, he had a tremendous imagination. His "stupefying exaggerations and unparalleled inventions" amazed his friends. He could have become a great artist, as testified by a full-length portrait that he made of Daudet, a beautiful portrait "down to the waist only," writes Lucien Daudet, "the rest ending in a mermaid tail, because drawing legs bothered him."

Privat arrived unexpectedly at Champrosay toward the end of the summer of 1892. He had not been heard of for twenty years. Now he told all about his life in Algeria during the past two decades: His marriage, the death of his wife, his young son whom he brought with him . . . : "There he was, full of life, in high spirits, laughing and weeping at the same time," asking a thousand questions which he would answer himself. He had not forgotten anything about his youth: "Privat remains Privat, he has not changed! How could he suspect what Alphonse had accomplished during that length of time?" The latter was moved. He now realized that he had never been able to compare so neatly the bygone days to the present ones. As Privat, Julia, and her mother recalled the past, Alphonse would visualize everything that he had been expecting from the future. He wondered whether "this cheerful ghost" had returned to make it possible for him "to say good-bye" to his youth once for all "and even to stop regretting it." For several weeks Privat "filled the house and the gardens with his good humor and wit. He started painting portraits and landscapes full of dreams and fancy. He announced he was going to settle in Paris, in the neighborhood of Rue Bellechasse. Everything would be again like in the past. Now the leaves were falling, his trunks ready. . . . He promised to return two days later. He hugged once more his dear Alphonse. . . . But never, never again did anyone hear of him. . . ."[21]

As we have seen, friends and admirers would come also from foreign countries. At this point should be mentioned at least Robert Harborough Sherard, an English novelist who was living in Paris as a correspondent for the *New York World* and who became the author of the first book written in English on Alphonse Daudet; and Marie Belloc, born of an English mother and a French father, but raised in England. She was received "with kindness" by the Daudets, and Alphonse "encouraged her in her literary ambitions." She became a faithful friend of the family.

Alphonse Daudet did not produce anything new or important from 1891 to 1894. However in 1893 the publisher A. Lemerre published a book consisting of excerpts from Daudet's works entitled *Les Mères* — a title which, as will be recalled, Daudet himself had used in one of his "Lettres à un absent." Here can be seen the importance given by the author to mothers and to the idea of motherhood, from "la mère Jacques" to "la duchesse Padovani."

Another volume of Daudet's previous writings, *Entre les frises et la rampe*, was published by Dentu in 1894. These were extracts of articles dealing with the theater which he had contributed to various Parisian newspapers around 1880. He had now reshaped and improved them for this collection. They dealt mostly with the art of acting and with the problems encountered by the actor. Two of them in particular, "Travail du Comédien" and "L'ivresse à la scène," deserve consideration — as does also "Le Rêve de Mme d'Epinay," which dwells on the same theme. Others dealing with staging and rehearsals and other questions of dramatic art such as the role of the producer or "metteur-en-scène" and that of the author in the production of a play should be enjoyed by anyone interested in the modern theater. They can be found in the 1929 - 30 edition of the *Oeuvres Complètes* (vol. XIII).

During the year of 1894 Daudet's health seemed to have improved somewhat. To be sure, his pains did not subside much, but "the sharp stomach attacks which for the past two years had left him prostrate with grief for hours, were now less frequent and his face had brightened up."[22] Now he regained his courage, made new projects, returned to an active life. Now he would read less and write more. He finished *La Petite Paroisse*, which began to appear in *L'Illustration* at the end of the year.

Having returned to his regular schedule, he did his best to solve family problems. On one misty, icy December day, accompanied by his second son Lucien, who has told the story, Alphonse Daudet went secretly to see Edouard Lockroy (Jeanne Hugo's stepfather) in an attempt to save Léon's marriage. He failed thoroughly. On the way back home, Alphonse ensconced himself in a corner of the cab, once in a while uttering exclamations, outcries, and words that revealed the intensity of his feelings. In view of the importance he gave then to the question of divorce, it is both relevant and pertinent to quote his son's account and interpretation of his thoughts on the matter:

This instinctive horror he always had for divorce, the need he had felt to sound the alarm at a time when he could hardly write [the reference is probably to the writing of *Rose et Ninette*], as if he had foreboded that divorce would cruelly affect him and his dear Julia by half depriving them of their grandson, that divorce would destroy a new home, a young couple who had everything to be happy, who in fact had too much for being happy. . . . Happiness must be deserved. . . . Happiness is not available as a matter of course. One must have known misfortune in order to enjoy happiness. . . . That law, that abomination! Formerly, when between husband and wife there were no more clashes than those due to differences in character, when nothing serious came between them, would they have thought of separating? . . . Different views, quarrels, utterances thrown at each other's face without believing one word of it? What did that amount to? Next day it was all forgotten. . . . But then in order to justify their law [the new law allowing divorce], to multiply its victims, they invented an expression, empty and grandiloquent as they are themselves, an oratory expression: "Incompatibility of temperament." Too bad for the parent's future, too bad for the future of the children, now forever amputated of one half of their heart. Incompatibility of temperament! Oh! such scoundrels, speechifiers, phrasemongers!

And Lucien concludes by saying, "No, he will not die before having uttered a last cry and stigmatized the government that leads to family dissolution, death, putrefaction. . . ."[23]

VIII La Petite Paroisse

As early as July 3, 1888, Edmond de Goncourt had entered the following in his journal: "This evening Daudet talks about his next novel, *La Petite Paroisse*, a work still in embryo, now germinating in his mind. . . . He wants now to write a work in which he will put all that is good in him, compassion, his pity for the poor, the outcasts of fortune, the tramps and hoboes of the highways." But this natural compassion and pity for the poor, which had already found an expression in *Le Petit Chose, Jack* and other earlier writings, was now to be extended to man in general, whatever his station in life and whatever the nature of his unhappiness. "His book," Goncourt continues, "will be the story of a husband who forgives," and he expands on the stupidity of killing for the man who is in love, who destroys forever the object of his love! . . . Yes, he goes on, it will be a work of gentleness."

As suggested by both the subtitle of the first edition, *Moeurs Conjugales* (Conjugal morals or customs), and the epigraph, "Jaloux n'a paix ne soir ne matinée (Vieux Texte)" ("A jealous man has never peace either day or night [old text]"), the *Petite Paroisse* (*The Little Parish Church*) is fundamentally a study of jealousy as considered in its various aspects and manifestations. It is the story of a cheated husband who is neither the traditional, ridiculous cuckold of the Middle Ages, nor the jealous and tragic hero who kills his unfaithful wife with the blessing of the law. Nor is he the sophisticated and refined modern man who now, at the end of the nineteenth century, could resort to divorce to solve his matrimonial problems.

In fact the protagonist of *La Petite Paroisse*, Richard Fénigan, appears as an ordinary human being whose unimpressive character somehow epitomizes the virtues and faults of the upper middle class to which he belongs. His story will be that of a sincere but timid individual at first struggling against circumstances and against

himself, but finally revealing himself as a man endowed with an unusual strength of mind that commands respect and admiration.

Encouraged by his mother, he has married a girl of unknown
parentage, Lydie, a foundling who has been raised in a convent and
has become an accomplished young lady. Lydie appears as a very
sensitive person. Like Emma Bovary and Mme Loisel (in
Maupassant's "The Necklace"), she soon gets tired of the monotony
and dreariness of married life, and dreams of beautiful dresses and
romantic adventures. However, it will take ten years before her
attendance at a social function — in her case an evening at the opera
in Paris — leads her into an unhappy love affair. By the help of circumstances she lets young Charlexis, the debauched nineteen-year-
old prince of Olmütz, who is ten years her junior, enter into her life
and seduce her. They elope and, as would be expected, difficulties
arise, and Lydie is left in the lurch by her irresponsible and cynical
seducer. She attempts suicide, but is finally rescued and brought
home by Mme Fénigan senior. Then Charlexis is killed by his
father's gamekeeper as he leaves the room of a new mistress who
happens to be the gamekeeper's daughter-in-law. This murder leads
to the arrest of Richard Fénigan, who had repeatedly proclaimed
that he was determined to avenge his honor. He is accused of the
slaying, then released from prison when the killer has confessed and
convinced the police that he himself is the author of the crime. Now,
partly owing to the influence of Napoléon Mérivet, the other
betrayed man in the story, who has built the little parish in memory
of his unfaithful wife, Richard Fénigan forgives his — and all's well
that ends well.

Among the minor characters which hold the reader's attention
must be named Mme Fénigan senior, the stern and domineering
mother; the now disabled paramour, the duke of Alcantara; the
somewhat naive and at the same time very austere and devoted Ab-
bot Cerès; the vagabond Père Georges, Lydie's grandfather, whose
identity is discovered at the end of the book, and Mr. Alexander, the
contemptible flunkey, a villain without the charm however of the
other villain, Charlexis, whom he serves.

The part played by the Little Parish itself, called by the common
folk "la Paroisse du bon cocu," has been criticized as a failure to
dramatize the power of religion, and the author himself, was accused
of having lost his sense of humor, a deficiency attributed to the state
of his health. These are sweeping statements and generalizations
which call for many reservations. To be sure, the *Petite Paroisse* is

not a great masterpiece, but it should be appreciated for what it is and what it was meant to be, neither a sermon nor a treatise of psychology. It was conceived merely as a novel. "a short, very simple, straightforward novel," with man's happiness in married life as its main concern. It was certainly meant to be didactic, but in no way a roman à thèse, not a novel written with the purpose of proving a point, the verity of a statement or of a theory, but only with that of showing humanity as the author saw it, with both its virtues and its defects, in order to suggest to man a way of alleviating both his physical and mental troubles.

It should be added that besides the theme of jealousy, in which Alphonse Daudet had been interested for a long time, this novel offered him an opportunity to treat another favorite subject, that of life on the highway, which like the river seems to unroll indefinitely, and toward the unknown. His two main characters, Richard and Lydie, had been fascinated, in their childhood, by the spectacle they could watch from the homes where they happened to be confined. Every day they saw the itinerant merchants, the peddlers and street hawkers (whose halloos Daudet listed in his notebooks); they saw beggars, tramps, and hoboes going their way, just as country boys and girls, shepherds, truck farmers, and many others went theirs.

Richard and Lydie were somewhat embarrassed the first time they met, but their conversation was soon enlivened by an exchange of their impressions of the road. To them the highway had been a kind of clock and calendar. They both remembered Robin the road-mender sitting at lunch time in the shade of a tree, with his two younger sons. On Saturdays, they had watched the wedding processions headed by the fiddler "swinging his hips to mark time"; right behind him came the bride and bridegroom, the former "flushed and perspiring beneath her orange blossoms," the latter with his silk top hat and black frockcoat picking up all the dust on the road; then the guests, two by two, the women very proud of sweeping the road with their big shawls, whereas the men "were ill-at-ease for being seen in their Sunday best (their arms dangling) on a work day." Richard was particualrly interested by a group of orphan girls taking a walk under the supervision of "three winged cornets."[24] Lydie had been one of them.

There are many other pages such as these in which a mere description becomes a series of animated scenes skillfully integrated in the novel, where the reader always finds a picturesque expression of the author's sensitivity and, in Zola's words, "the throb of his soul."

Alphonse Daudet himself was keenly conscious of that intense sensitivity, which has been emphasized by all critics (some considering it a good quality, others a defect), and has referred to it on many occasions.[25]

La Petite Paroisse was published in book form by Alphonse Lemerre at the beginning of 1895 and acclaimed by one critic as a miracle in that it had "revived the old theme of adultery," by others as a new penetrating study; most critics judged it to be a work of pity and tenderness.[26]

IX *Supreme Hope*

Alphonse Daudet was determined not to allow his pain and general physical condition to stop him from writing a book he had had in mind for some time. He wrote the following in his cahiers: "Today, January 28, 1895, I am beginning with a feeble hand the *Support of the Family [Soutien de famille]*, a book of anger and compassion which I may not have the strength to finish. May God help me!"[27] The writing of *Soutien de famille* was to be interrupted several times, but it was finished in September, 1896.

X *Alphonse Daudet and Edmond de Goncourt*

The importance of Goncourt's place in the life of Alphonse Daudet cannot be overemphasized. It is revealed on almost every page of the Goncourt *Journal*, where Daudet's name appears more and more frequently during the period 1880 - 1896. When the "dîner des auteurs sifflés" ceased to exist, after the death of Flaubert and the departure of Turgenev in 1880, Daudet and Zola encouraged Goncourt in a project to keep up its spirit by entertaining a literary group once a week in his home at Auteuil, a former township of the Seine department which was integrated with Paris in 1860. Goncourt was only too glad to acquiesce, as the idea fitted in with his plan for an academy. He had part of the upper floor, or attic, of his house, transformed into a kind of large living room, the now well-known and famous "Grenier." It opened for the first time in 1885. The following invitation had been sent to some twenty-five, well-selected writers or artists: "The Grenier des Goncourt will start its literary Sundays on February 1, 1885. It will be much honored by your presence."[28]

Daudet and Zola, their friends Céard, Huysmans, Alexis, and others of the same generation were among those who attended this first reunion. There were those eager to meet the great masters and also perhaps, as it has been suggested, some young hopefuls primarily interested in a possible invitation to become members of the then much discussed academy. Be that as it may, the Grenier soon became a popular and famous literary center. Later its popularity declined. Goncourt's courteousness had been found at times "a little cold," too formal; his handshake "a little too mild," wanting vigor; his conversation scrappy. On February 6, 1889, Goncourt wrote in his *Journal*: "People come when they know dinner will be served but if it is a dry party . . . all you have . . . is the very intimate friend and two or three nonentities. . . ."[29] That "very intimate friend" was often Alphonse Daudet, very greatly missed whenever absent. Goncourt is quoted as having said: "It's dreadful how one can get bored when Daudet is not present."[30] The following description and comments from an enthusiastic admirer deserve to be quoted in full:

How many times, between 1885 and 1896 have I witnessed this spectacle!
We are, on a Sunday afternoon, at Edmond de Goncourt's house at Auteuil in his famous "grenier." There are writers, artists — some who have "made it" and others only beginners — all in love with literature and the fine arts. They talk about various things, but, the general conversation remains somewhat dull, long, drawn-out. . . . They look at rare engravings, at admirable Japanese drawings and sketches that Goncourt pulls out of his precious folders.
Suddenly, the door opens. Alphonse Daudet appears, leaning on his cane, holding fast to his son Léon's arm, or to some friend's arm, such as Léon Hennique, who often went to get him at Rue de Bellechasse. At first, he does not see anyone in the cloud of cigars, and cigarette smoke of the long three-windowed room. His uncertain myopic eyes look without seeing. He shakes hands at random, recognizing people by the sound of their voices and goes to sit on the large low sofa between the fireplace and the window, beside *his Goncourt*, as he calls him familiarly.
There, once settled, having adjusted his monocle, having found his friends and greeted them with a friendly smile, now warmed up by his affectionate surrounding, at times controlling the twinge or throbbing caused by an acute pain, he talks. Around him, immediately everything livens up, glitters, blazes; conversation becomes general, rises, shines; discussion sparkles.
The apostle of life has come. His speech, the sound of his voice, his moral and physical contact, have been sufficient to fill the "grenier" with intense life. It is as if sunshine, but a southern sunshine, had entered the room which had grown numb in milky, veiled quietness, and had illuminated everything; the smallest things take on a dazzling splendor, the smallest words a surprisingly enhanced meaning: upon coming into contact with this

incomparable brain, brains get inflamed, and thoughts burst forth toward high summits.

It is not only the picturesque, amusing and interesting, varied conversationalist, the stunning storyteller, with an encyclopedic memory who has just appeared among us, it is also, and above all, the Thinker. . . .[31]

In the winter of 1894 - 1895 a few enthusiastic "habitués du Grenier" conceived the project of offering Edmond de Goncourt a dinner to celebrate his seventy-third birthday. They asked Alphonse Daudet to preside over the committee in charge of the fiesta. He accepted with pleasure but requested that the occasion be improved to organize the affair on a much larger scale, so that it would not appear as the work of a coterie or clique. Accordingly, hundreds of people were invited to attend, and Daudet and Zola took the necessary steps to have Raymond Poincaré, then Minister of Education, preside over the reunion and award Goncourt the rosette of the Legion of Honor.

The banquet took place on March 1, 1895, at the Grand Hôtel. Three hundred and ten places were laid in the dining room and most of the important writers and artists in Paris at the time were present. Goncourt had expressed his wish that Princess Mathilda and Mme Daudet should be invited, but the lady writers ("les dames de littérature") having rebelled, it was finally decided to have men only. Letters and telegrams of excuse and congratulations from all over France and from foreign countries were read and followed by many speeches. The speakers were Poincaré, Clemenceau, Zola, Heredia, Henri de Régnier, and, naturally, Alphonse Daudet.

Goncourt, who had expressed a certain annoyance regarding the banquet, stating that having one of his plays interpreted by talented actors would give him much more pleasure, was nevertheless very deeply moved.[32] The audience shared his emotion, and he was told that such complete adherence by those present on similar occasions had never been witnessed.

Nevertheless, when asked to give a toast he said perhaps inadvertently to the three hundred people present: "I drink to the health of all those who are my friends and they do not swarm [*il n'y en pas des foules*]." Léon Daudet called it "a slip of the tongue" and exclaimed! "Dear Goncourt!"[33] In his *Journal* Goncourt quoted passages from several speeches, particularly from Poincaré, the minister who in the name of the government "almost humbly" asked him to "allow himself to be decorated." Some forty years later Lucien Daudet wrote that the audience was moved upon seeing his disabled father, who had gathered enough strength to extol, "in a musical and fascinating voice," his friend Goncourt, "the faithful and affectionate companion of both good and bad hours."[34] However, other accounts of the affair at the time were less enthusiastic. Robert de Montesquiou found the reunion "monotonous, cold, and boring" and Daudet's speech "almost inaudible."[35] Jules Renard wrote in his own *Journal*, where he gave a very picturesque and amusing gallery of portraits of those in the limelight, that Daudet had remained seated while reading his speech, looking much "as a schoolboy bent over his table, over his trembling sheet of paper, reading an assigned essay on friendship under the stern eyes of the master."[36] Nevertheless, it may be said that, under the circumstances, Daudet's performance was quite admirable and indeed beyond all expectation.

XI *Visit to England*

In the month of May 1895, Alphonse Daudet realized a wish he had entertained for some time: a visit to England with his family. They were met at the station by Henry James who, like Robert Sherard and Marie Belloc, was to show them around London. The Daudets were abashed by some of the things they saw in the English capital, as for example the poor wretches in Hyde Park wallowing in the high grass, separated only by a low railing from riders on horseback and wealthy ladies in beautiful carriages. However, the Daudets' sojourn turned out to be a very pleasant one. They went to the zoo as well as to the British Museum, and visited Oxford, Eton College, and Windsor Castle. They met George Meredith, Edmund Gosse, and many other writers and artists, had tea with the Dean of Westminster Abbey, and were guests of honor at various club dinners. But what pleased Alphonse most, what he considered "perhaps the high light of his experience" was, according to G. V. Dobie, "the visits he paid to H. M. Stanley and George Meredith."

Stanley was sensitive to Daudet's admiration and felt much honored by his visit. Using his best French, and occasionally resorting to Spanish, the great explorer managed to answer all the questions asked by his visitors, told anecdotes about his travels, and commented upon his African museum. We learn also from our well-informed biographer that Meredith received Alphonse Daudet with open arms. Their conversation was lively from the outset and their friendship was "sealed over some choice bottles," which Meredith claimed to have set aside for the occasion. They had dinner together some time later, and Meredith joined the party that went to Victoria station to bid them farewell when they left for France. A rather dramatic incident that might have turned to tragedy occurred at the time of their departure: As the train began to move — Daudet being in the car and Meredith on the platform — it was suddenly discovered that "Meredith's gouty fingers were still clasping Daudet's crippled hands and that neither could release his hold of the other." All felt relieved when Sherard "seized Meredith round the waist and held him firmly to the ground as the train gathered speed and steamed out of the station."[37]

CHAPTER 6

The Last Two Years

I   La Fédor

U PON his return from England Alphonse Daudet wrote a short
novelette which appeared in the fall of 1895 under the title of
"L'enterrement d'une Étoile" and then, a few months later, under
that of *La Fédor* (Flammarion, 1896), which was the name of the star
in question. The story of *La Fédor*, which has been acclaimed as a
little masterpiece, perfect of its kind, consists mainly in the reflections, actions, and reactions of François du Bréau upon the death of
his former mistress, Louise La Fédor, a famous actress with whom he
was involved before his marriage.

We learn at the outset that La Fédor had created endless trouble
for Du Bréau, including threats to kill him and his wife, and his child
if one should be born. When told by a friend that La Fédor's funeral
is to take place that very afternoon in a nearby town, Du Bréau
decides to attend it with his friend who has prevailed upon him to do
so. They go the the village, but Du Bréau is not allowed either to
enter the house of the deceased or join the burial procession. He
leaves alone, then enters a café and has a drink served him on a table
near a window from where he can watch the procession without
himself being seen. He is recognized by the orchestra leader
Desvarennes, who is sitting at the next table and in the process of
getting drunk. He happens to have been Du Bréau's successor as a
lover of La Fédor. He introduces himself, talks about La Fédor's
various love affairs, names her former lovers as he spots them in the
procession, which they are both watching through the window. Then
he falls asleep on the table and Du Bréau leaves the place.

On his way home, Du Bréau travels part of the way in a comedian's carriage. Neither the comedian nor his wife knows him but
they are both very talkative individuals. They, too, seem eager to tell

everything they know about the great actress. As they go through a storm, Du Bréau recalls that the most stormy hours of his life with La Fédor were the happiest. He now understands that she had come to live in the vicinity in the hope of seeing him again, and he feels quite sure that she has loved him until the end: "Is that possible? But is it not all over? Is it not true that it was all broken long ago?" Now he wonders whether he did the right thing. However, the more he thinks about it, the more he is convinced that he did. He has no guilty conscience. Suddenly the storm subsides and stops. He arrives home under a clear, blue sky. His wife is waiting for him. His little girl, who had a fever when he left is now well, and Du Bréau delights in the bosom of family life. "How comfortable one feels, how far away is everything else, how restful forgetting the world can be!"[1]

The reader knowing the essential facts about Daudet's two-year love affair with Marie Rieu (when he was 19 or 20), cannot fail to recognize her under this name of La Fédor as he had already recognized her under that of Sapho and of other characters in his works — which testifies to the firm hold Marie Rieu had gained over him. We agree with Lucien Daudet that the story of *La Fédor* can be considered as a kind of conclusion, a post-scriptum to *Sapho*.

II Premier Voyage, Premier Mensonge

It may have been during that same summer of 1895 that Daudet finished *Premier Voyage, Premier Mensonge*, which is another story based on personal experience. He had begun to dictate it to Robert Sherard in London for an English magazine, but it did not appear in French until 1900, published in book form by Ernest Flammarion. The English version, under Daudet's and Sherard's joint names, and entitled *My First Voyage, My First Lie*, was published by Digby, Long and Co., in 1901. The story is, like *La Fedor*, a little jewel, but of a very different character. It differs from it not only in subject matter, but also in style, mood, and tone.

The "first voyage" in question actually took place in 1854 or 1855 when Alphonse Daudet and his cousin Léonce, both of them in Nîmes at the time, were allowed to return to the Lycée de Lyon all alone, unaccompanied either by parents or teachers. They went to Beaucaire by stagecoach and from there to Lyons by boat on the Rhone river. The two boys, aged fourteen or fifteen, were very excited to be free on such an adventure, and Alphonse particularly, at the prospect of setting foot on a boat. They did not have much money, but Alphonse carried proudly two letters of recommendation, one for the innkeeper in Beaucaire where they were to spend one night and the other for the "captain" of the boat.

Nothing spectacular happened between Nîmes and Beaucaire. Daudet reminisced later that they had traveled "through undulating landscape, olive orchards, vineyards and mulberry fields" on a road covered with "two feet of white dust cracking like snow, a whirling dust that obscured, masked the view," and so added to the confusion of "the first stage of their journey."

The "first lie" began the next day when, while waiting at the wharf, boisterous, bumptious Alphonse pretended that he and Léonce had graduated from the Naval College of Varna (Bulgaria). Then one lie leading to another, his fantastic imagination helped by his boyhood readings — in which *Robinson Crusoe* held the largest place — he succeeded in convincing most of his audience, consisting chiefly of soldiers on sick leave from the Crimean War. These veterans unconsciously fed his imagination by naming persons, places, and events which he promptly utilized. They soon became his friends and enthusiastic listeners, the more so because he provided them with food and delicacies from the basket of provisions given to the boys in Beaucaire. But his lies were "neither perverse nor utilitarian." Only his imagination and vanity made him a liar: "I felt the need to animate my dreams, to endow them with life."[2] He ended by imagining that he really was that midshipman he wanted so much to become! Eventually his bluff was called by a man who made the embarrassing remark that the buttons on Léonce's vest bore the words "Lycée de Nîmes," which are not usually found on that of midshipmen.

Four major adventures took place during the voyage between Beaucaire and Lyons — four episodes on whose authenticity Daudet has greatly insisted. Once the *Bonardelle* (name of the boat) had berthed for the night, Alphonse led his habitual audience, chiefly composed of soldiers from northern France, on a kind of pilfering party in the surrounding country side, where they found delicious muscat grapes, jujube fruit, figs with reddish flesh with which they gorged themsleves. Meanwhile the southerners Alphonse and Léonce expressed their preference for the small "figues blanquettes" which, as Alphonse described them, are indeed "true bags of sunshine" whose skin is "wrinkled and fine like Suéde cloth."

"But where shall we find such wonderful figs, officer? Are there not any around here?" Just as he was being asked this question, the "officer" detected in a yard on the other side of a crumbling wall,

big trays in which the small white figs had been drying in the
sunshine for the winter supply. He pointed to them and, followed by
his "friends," jumped over the wall. They were beginning to fill
their mouths, pockets, and hats when suddenly lights pierced the
darkness, while furious voices set two mastiffs against the invaders,
who retreated as fast as they could toward the *Bonardelle*. The next
morning, the "officer" had to empty his pockets in order to pay the
damages.[3]

The second episode also took place at night, when he made passes
at a waitress, who had him slapped by her "uncle." The third one
deals with the two Lyonnaise "ladies" already referred to, whose
own stories are as extravagant as Alphonse's. He nevertheless
swallowed everything they said: "How is it that being such a liar
myself I remained so naïve and credulous?" In the last one, his
braggadocio put him into another critical situation from which
ironically he comes out unscathed thanks to the very man who called
his bluff and whom he hated most on the boat.[4]

Premier Voyage — was told also to Batisto Bonnet who transcribed it in his book *Lou Baile*. It is an excellent story whose value
resides not only in the manner in which it is told, in the language,
the style and that undefinable Daudet charm which is typically his
and not, as has been vaguely suggested, that of his English translator
— but also in the biographical facts regarding his adolescent years as
well as in information about some aspects of life in the 1850s. There
is also a good deal of humor which originates not only from the
behavior of the two teenagers but also from the author's own observations. Here again, truth and poetry, fantasy and reality, imagination and plain observed facts are perfectly blended and hold the
reader's attention. There is no sign of weariness or decrepitude of
either the artist or the man, whose verve is as keen and sunlit as ever.

III   *Again the French Academy*

We have seen that the question of the Academy was raised in
favor of Daudet as early as 1883, when he asked his friends Zola and
Goncourt what they would think of his possible candidacy for the
Academy (this was the year of his duel with Delpit). Now, at the
beginning of 1896, a few friends, foremost Anatole France, assured
him that if he should agree to becoming an academician he would
not have to do anything about it, neither write letters nor visit
anyone. The matter was seriously discussed in the Daudet family.

Julia insisted he should accept, Lucien, "whose opinion was not requested," would have been all for it, but Léon was against it. As to Alphonse himself, he had no hesitation: his answer was again a positive no. And he set forth the reasons for his attitude: first, while admitting that one may change his mind, he thought that it would not be honorable to reverse his judgment to that extent, to stultify himself that thoroughly; second, his feeling toward the Academy had not changed; and third, he could not betray Goncourt who had selected him to preside over his future academy. And he stood by his decision.

Goncourt, who had heard about such a possibility, was considerably upset because he had counted on him to be the executor of his will and to take charge of the contemplated academy foundation. So, on March 21, 1896, in Daudet's apartment he asked Alphonse point blank: "What would you do if you were offered an opportunity to become a member of the French Academy without having to go through the customary formalities?" It was Mme Daudet who answered, rather vehemently: "Well, he would accept!"[5] And Goncourt concluded that Daudet was as eager as Zola to belong to the French Academy.

IV *Trip to Venice*

Meanwhile, the trip to England, where they had spent several weeks, having proved to be a success in every respect, Alphonse felt the urge of making another sojourn abroad. This time it was decided that the family would visit Italy. They apparently left for Venice on March 29: ". . . his hair trimmed, a tobacco-colored felt hat on his head," wrote Goncourt, "Alphonse is quite lively, brimming over with the light joy of a school boy on his way to a vacation." From Venice, they intended to go to Florence, then to Rome. . . . The regular attendants of the Grenier concluded that this was a "diplomatic trip" destined to facilitate or rather insure the election of Daudet to the French Academy.[6]

Alphonse Daudet was literally captivated by Venice. They hired a gondolier and they spent many hours rambling through the canals. As usual, Alphonse jotted down his impressions. Unfortunately he became suddenly ill and had to take to his bed for several days. When the news reached Paris, the Grenier came again to the conclusion that Daudet's illness was "diplomatic," and Edmond convinced himself that he, Goncourt, was the only writer left in France without an "academic ambition." It occurred to him that if he should die while Daudet was in Italy, the fulfillment of the clauses of his will might be hampered.

As soon as he had regained some of his strength, Alphonse declared he was ready to proceed to Florence, but cautious Julia had already reserved seats for the trip back home. Soon after their return to Paris, the Daudet family was very much concerned over Léon who had become seriously ill with typhoid fever. Then they received a telegram announcing the death of Timoléon Ambroy, Alphonse's most intimate friend, with whom he had corresponded for thirty-five years. Lucien Daudet has suggested that his father's love and understanding of Provence was mostly due to Timoléon Ambroy, which of course is an oversimplification. There is no doubt however that to Alphonse's mind Timoléon symbolized friendship and personified a period during which he had enjoyed some of the finest experiences of his early youth, first at Fontvieille and then in the Camargue, where some thirty years before he and Timoléon had gone to hunt in the marshes, fish in the Vaccarès, and dream in the moonlight. Upon hearing the bad news Daudet interrupted all the work he was engaged in at the time and began writing a short novelette, *Le Trésor d'Arlatan*, as a kind of memorial to his old friend.

V   Le Trésor d'Arlatan

The dedication and the poem that follow constitute an appropriate prelude to the work:

Au cher Souvenir de Timoléon Ambroy

En Camargue[7]

Coumo fai bon quand lou mistrau
Pico la porto emé si bano
Estre soulet dins la cabano
Tout soulet coumo un mas de Crau,

E vèire pèr un pichot trau
Alin bèn liuen, dins lis engano
Lusi la palun de Girau;

E rèn ausi que lou mistrau
Picant la porto emé si bano,

Enterin pièi quauqui campano
Di rosso de la Tour-dóu-Brau.

In Camargue

How good it is, when the mistral
Knocks at the door with its horns
To be alone in the cabin
All alone as a ranch in the Crau desert

And see through a little hole
Far away in the glass-worts
The Giraud marsh glisten;

And hear nothing but the mistral
Knocking at the door with its horns
And then at times the tinkling bells
Of the wild mares of the Wild-Bull-Tower.

While the impressive and mysterious silence of the marshy plains of the Rhone delta is neither the subject nor the main element in this story, it seems evident that the use of the poem as an epigraph was meant to emphasize the importance of the background. It also illustrates the author's ability to express himself in Provençal. However, as if to reassure the reader, he immediately stresses the human interest through a letter supposedly addressed to Henri Danjou, the character telling the story. This realistic approach will be maintained throughout the book, which closes with another letter.

Through the introductory letter we learn that the "northerner" Danjou, who wants to break with his mistress, has been offered a refuge in the wilderness of the Camargue, far from the charms and seductions of Parisian life. Hoping he will thus be able to forget and be forgotten, he accepts the invitation. A cabin located a few hundred feet from that of Charloun and his wife Naïs, the people committed to watch over his material comfort, has been put at his disposal. Naïs will cook for him, and her sister Zia will bring his meals to the cabin. At first, Danjou feels secure, "sheltered and protected" by the blue sky and distant horizons he can contemplate from his retreat. However, his passion for Madeleine Ogé, the woman he wants to forget, will be revived by contact with other human beings. Similarly, his presence in this neighborhood will affect the lives and conduct of Zia and Arlatan, the other two main characters in the story.

Arlatan is a former hero of the arena, now a mere horse herder in the process of regaining fame, this time as a healer, a quack specializing in the cure of swamp fever and rheumatism. All kinds of drugs, some of his own invention, will be found later in his treasure box, which is a large trunk containing also such heteroclite items as dried flowers and plants, butterflies and cicadas preserved in camphor or alcohol, faded ribbons and tarnished gilt, druggist's notices and pamphlets, cockades snatched from famous bulls and, particularly, portraits of actresses, dancers, and "pretentious nudities with naughty implications," among which is the portrait of Madeleine Ogé. This gives a fair idea of what could be seen in this sort of "Mohican hiding place," this "hole (or nest) of a thieving magpie" which Arlatan called his "treasure" and which will be mostly responsible for the development of the action.

Zia is a fifteen-year-old girl who lives in Arles but comes once in a while to stay with her married sister Naïs. Zia is unhappy because her *bon jour,* that is, the day of her first communion, has been repeatedly postponed by the priest. The reason for the priest's refusal will be disclosed only toward the end of the novel, when it can be surmised that Zia has seen Arlatan's treasure and apparently has been fascinated by the "forbidden things" that the old cowboy has shown her.

Danjou also has seen the treasure, which he describes, and has been upset by it, but for a different reason, at first by the suspicion, then the certitude, that his mistress had a love affair with Arlatan when, some ten years before, the latter was at the height of his fame. Danjou's jealousy is aroused; he is tortured mentally, troubled with nightmares:

In the morning, . . . while not quite asleep . . . he glided from insomnia into a half dreaming state, under hallucinations due to fatigue. . . . It was the Camargue, but the Camargue in the summer . . . when the ponds are dry and the white mud of the irrigation ditches cracks in the intense heat. The ponds here and there smoked like huge vats, retaining in their depths a remnant of life, a swarming mass of salamanders, spiders, and water insects seeking moist corners. And over it all a pestilential air, a mist heavy with miasma, made dense by eddying millions of mosquitos; and the only personage on that vast and dismal stage was a woman, Madeleine Ogé, with Naïs' head-dress and her yellow wrinkled cheeks, Madeleine panting and shivering on the seashore, beneath the inexorable sun which burns the fever-stricken without warming them. . . .

The shrill cries of a flock of early birds flying over set him free from his nightmare. . . .

Danjou tries to comfort Zia and perhaps does not fully realize, says the author, that by so doing he "comforts himself and is encouraging his own distress."

Meanwhile Zia considers herself as being cursed because she cannot forget "these things" in the treasure nor resist the urge to return to Arlatan's cabin and see them again, thus damning herself. They seem to pursue her, "burn her" everytime she closes her eyes and, she says, "even when she keeps them open." A last trip to Arles has convinced her that she is unworthy, not in the proper state of mind and soul to receive communion. She concludes that "it is the end of everything, that people will point at her, run after her because of her "bon jour." Desperate, she drowns then in the Vaccarès lagoon in order "to escape that cruel obsession."[8]

"You must have heard of Arlatan's treasure," writes Danjou to his friend. "Little Zia died because she longed to look at it; while I, on the contrary, hope that I have found in it a cure and renewed life. I shall know in a few weeks. I was warned however by these words of the herder: 'I have in my treasure the herb that cures and the herb that kills.' Does not this 'treasure of Arlatan' resemble our composite and diversified imagination, which is so dangerous to explore to its lowest depths? Of such an exploration one may die or live."[9] Danjou chose to live.

Here again it can be easily established that Madeleine Ogé is the fictitious name for Marie Rieu and Danjou for the author himself. T. de Logeret, the author of the first letter and adressee of the last one, was Timoléon Ambroy. What has impressed both the reading public and the critic is the classical perfection of the work.

VI *Strained Relations with Goncourt*

The tighter the twenty-or twenty-five-year-old Daudet-Goncourt friendship became, the more fragile and perilous it seemed to be. While they had many things in common, shared the same enthusiasm and passion for art and literature, they both kept their individuality, each moving in his own world. When we compare their lives we cannot help noticing one striking difference between them; whereas Daudet kept social commitments reduced to a minimum, spending all the time he could on his works, Goncourt spent most of his at dinner parties and social gatherings. They were both very sensitive men, Goncourt at times morbidly so. He often misinterpreted what he saw and heard, or gave it undue importance. His ideally realistic objectivity had degenerated into a subjective, unhealthy state of mind which occasionally made of his remarks and observations a mere superficial and gossipy reportage.

A tremendous pressure was put on Daudet, as we have seen, by other friends and by his family, to become a candidate for the French Academy. On the other hand, Goncourt insisted on having him as the executor of his will (Edmond was Alphonse's eighteen year senior) in connection with his own academy, and this was the main source of the frictions that now occurred between them almost daily; next, and mostly, were of course Goncourt's indiscretions in his *Journal* regarding the Daudet family, and finally Alphonse's and Edmond's poor health at the moment.

We have seen also that on April 12, 1896 Goncourt had become distressed and distrustful of his best friends. However, when he heard that they were back from Italy he rushed to Rue de Bellechasse. He found Alphonse "his face melted, drawn and yellow" on account of a terrible stomach attack. Except for his god-daughter Edmée Daudet, they had all returned from there with a damaged stomach, and Goncourt wondered to what extent this "poisoning" was due to the oysters they ate or to "their endless, lingering sojourns on the most stinking canals."[10] He felt very sympathetic and once more everything seemed forgiven and forgotten. But then Goncourt received a letter from Julia reproaching him for a number of statements in the press for which he did not feel responsible. This letter made Goncourt very unhappy. For a whole week he was awakened every morning at four o'clock by gnawing pains due to his worries regarding its contents: ". . . the gloomy thoughts that haunt the brains of this married couple and the blind injustice of the woman make of our friendship a friendship that resembles a love no longer completely trustful. . . ." When, on April 25, he went to the Daudets' apartment; he was "very nervous and ready to break on the first unpleasant remarks from either the wife or the husband." However, he found both wife and husband so upset because of Léon's grave typhoid fever that his "wicked disposition" disappeared immediately: "I was disarmed and I shared their distress. . . ."

A month later, Alphonse Daudet himself was reported as saying to Barrès that he considered his friendship with Goncourt as finished, that he could not stand it any more, that it was all over. And so Goncourt now found the Daudets a little cold.[11] When he went to Rue de Bellechasse Madame Daudet would not come to shake hands with him. On one occasion they almost showed him the door. But on June 4 he was invited to a dinner in celebration of Léon's recovery. Léon and Alphonse welcomed him very warmly and they expressed the hope that he would return to Champrosay in July, an invitation that was reiterated three days later. But then came an article by Ernest Daudet in *Le Figaro* condemning in no uncertain terms "this foolish obstinacy of a writer of the rank and value of Mr. Edmond de Goncourt to persist on a road where scandal borders so closely on indiscretion and slander borders on truth," almost spoiled everything. Now the Daudets were deeply concerned, wondering whether after this hostile criticism from "la mère Jacques,"[12] Goncourt would still want to come to visit them at Champrosay, and Goncourt seemed indeed wanting to reassure them by inviting them to the Grenier on June 16. He himself dined again at Rue de Bellechasse on the eighteenth, which is also the date of the last entry in the *Journal* concerning Alphonse Daudet. At this point the reader feels that difficulties will arise again, and also that they will be overcome, that wounds will be dressed and breaches healed.

VII   *Death of Edmond de Goncourt*

Alphonse Daudet has given a day by day account of Goncourt's last days of life in a twenty-five-page memorial article which appeared first in *La Revue de Paris* (August 15, 1896). The following information is taken from this most interesting text which is written in the form of a diary.

On July 11, 1896, Daudet went in his landau to the railroad station of Ris Orangis to meet Goncourt, who, accompanied by Lucien, was coming to Champrosay. When he first saw his old friend in the distance, svelt, erect, brisk, walking nimbly toward him, Daudet's impression was that Goncourt indeed looked twenty years younger than his age. When close however, he appeared to be nervous, tired, and preoccupied. At the house, Goncourt was warmly welcomed by Mme Daudet, as usual in the past, by her mother and ten-year-old Edmée, Goncourt's goddaughter. Léon was then convalescing in Guernsey with Georges Hugo. That afternoon Edmond and Alphonse took a walk round the garden. They were soon joined by Mme Daudet who showed Goncourt her roses. He spoke about his own and about his espaliers. At the dinner table he told of the numberless worries originated by the publication of his *Journal*. They discussed various subjects.

Among these was that of the transformations of man during his life time. Daudet had remarked once that man's first impressions are about the only ones that stay with us: "At the age of fifteen or twenty at most," he said "we are printed off (achevés d'imprimer)." Both Goncourt and Mme Daudet disagreed throughly. As they had just been talking about a friend whose disposition, morals and talent had undergone a curious modification," Goncourt exclaimed: "What becomes of your theory?" Mme Daudet proclaimed: "That theory of his is distressing, abominable," and Goncourt expressed once more his belief that "man changes constantly to the last day of his life, that we change our skins an infinite number of times, as snakes do." And Daudet answered: "You are probably right, Goncourt, and this shows to what extent any formula is a dangerous thing to handle. . . . Opportunism and Naturalism, for example, are not bad in themselves, but the tag has no value. Do you remember our saying so to Zola, one evening?"[13]

Then they discussed the value and beauty of prose as compared to poetry, which Goncourt detested. To punish him, Mme Daudet compelled him to listen to two or three pieces. They reminisced about Jules Vallès, Turgenev and others. That evening they went to bed late. Goncourt's room was above the Daudets'. Alphonse heard him walk: "the only thing about him that betrays his age is his footstep, a heavy, tired step as would be that of a laborer at the end of a full day of hard work."[14]

The next morning Goncourt complained about the heat and the fact that he could not quench his thirst. He harked back to the trials he was subjected to by the publication of his *Journal* and declared to Alphonse that he was through with it, that he was stopping it. Mme Daudet who had just heard his last words as she was coming to join them, hurled at him:"I'm glad of it for you. I do not like it anymore, your journal. It has made you too many enemies." Alphonse remarked that it would not be becoming for him to criticize the *Journal des Goncourt* because his own novels, all written from life, had also aroused people's anger. But Daudet added that for some years he had felt less free to talk with his friend: "I did not know any more how to confide, to expand, as I used to in the past. The mere idea that everything I said would appear in the *Journal* bothered me, made me awkward, as if I spoke facing the public. He may have thought that I was failing. That was the reason. . . ." Goncourt laid softly his hand on his: "My dear, be yourself again. The *Journal des Goncourt* is closed." And "the two old famous men"[15] remained a long time motionless on their bench "in the vast silence of a Sunday in the country."[16]

Later in the day they went for a ride, as far as Corbeil, along the cliff road between the river (la Seine) and the Forest of Sénart, the road that runs through some of Daudet's books. They talked about the reasons for writing — Goncourt for posterity, Daudet for the simple pleasure of writing.

On Monday, July 13, they again took a walk, and the subject of both the French Academy and the Goncourt Academy came up again. Then Goncourt talked about his brother Jules, deceased in 1870; about his own life, that of a lonely bachelor having only his art collections for company: "That is rather cold, you know; that does not speak to you every day."[17] At noon he could not eat and he retired to his room. On Tuesday he spent most of the day in bed. On Wednesday he took a bath, then felt very tired. They thought at first he had one of his sharp liver attacks. However, they called the doctor and his diagnosis was pneumonia. Goncourt died on Thursday, July 16, his hand in those of his friend Alphonse Daudet, who finished "Ultima"[18] on August 5, the day of the funeral.[19]

VIII   *The Goncourt Academy*

Two other dear friends, Timoléon Ambroy and Paul Arène, had passed away during that eventful, mournful and memorable year of 1896. His turn was to come exactly seventeen months later.

When back in Paris, Alphonse Daudet was still busy with *Le Trésor d'Arlatan*, which he finished one evening while Batisto Bonnet, then working at his table, marveled at the steady flow of his inspiration. Now he would be concerned with the second half of *Soutien de Famille*. However, as the executor of Goncourt's will, he had to engage in a kind of work which to him had always been an irksome task. To complicate matters, it happened that Goncourt had been dissatisfied with the language used by his *notaire* — the man who, in France, executes authentic deeds among which are those dealing with successions and sales or real estate — and had rewritten his will in his own personal style, no doubt in better and more literary French. Unfortunately, the wording was now quite litigious, disputable at law. Goncourt's relatives, including distant cousins whom he had never met, claimed they had a share in the inheritance. According to Lucien Daudet, the notaire himself did not take Goncourt's will seriously and advised Alphonse not to bother with it any longer because, he said, Goncourt's fortune was mediocre and could not provide the necessary capital for the foundation of his literary society. "But you forget what the sale of the collections will bring," said Daudet. "Pooh!" retorted the notary scornfully, "a man of letters's collections! We know what that means in value!" However, the sales were to produce three million francs, in gold, which at the time meant naturally a great deal more than it would today. Finally, realizing the near impossibility for him to carry on his task successfully, Daudet put the business affair in the hands of Raymond Poincaré, whom he trusted entirely. The legal proceedings took a long time, but the Academy des Goncourt was finally constituted in 1903.[20]

More than ever, Emile Zola and Anatole France bestowed their affection on Daudet when they realized to what extent their friend was downcast, saddened by his recent hardships, more specially by the death of Goncourt. Having decided that a new monthly literary dinner would somewhat take his mind off his sorrow, they proceeded to organize one under his presidency. This "Balzac dinner," as they named it, took place only two or three times attended by Emile Zola, Anatole France, Paul Bourget, Maurice Barrès, Léon and Alphonse Daudet. Unfortunately, it was marred by the Dreyfus affair which was beginning to stir the nation and could not be ignored. It soon prevailed in discussions supposed to remain strictly literary. Zola and France had already sided with the Dreyfus party. Paul Bourget, Barrès, and no doubt Léon — though his brother does not refer to him in this connection — were in the other camp. As to Alphonse, he had not yet formed any opinion, feeling that politics, which he had always hated, played a part in the quarrel. Indeed the judiciary affair was fast becoming a strictly political one.

IX   La Caravane *and other Projects*

This was also about the time when Alphonse Daudet spoke of another book that he had in mind and which he named *La Caravane*. Here the fictitious element would be reduced to a minimum, its only thread consisting in a journey made by several persons in a trailer through the French provinces. These ramblers would be naturally all sensitive and intelligent individuals but of different ages, sex, character and background. The author intended to pour all his knowledge and life experience into their conversations. From the "fragments" of the *Caravane* published in *Notes sur la Vie* can be deduced that the book might have been indeed the most interesting in his career.

The droll idea of the two trailers, one to live in and the other for the kitchen, the servants, and food supply, was perhaps derived from the novel of the Provençal poet Valère Bernard, *Lei Bóumian* (the Gypsies) in which the two main characters are two well-meant artists who begin their adventure by getting in trouble with the real gypsies. Daudet had imagined a caravan started by two old friends and their wives, the latter two hardly knowing each other. Hence all kinds of discussions, amusing and perhaps serious conflicts could be foreseen.

Daudet had previously promised the *Revue de Paris* a work entitled *Quinze ans de mariage* in which he would have summed up his experiences as a husband and father. Obviously *La Caravane* had a more ambitions purpose. He had also pondered the idea of founding a *Revue de Champrosay* in which the question of the antagonism between Paris and the province would have been discussed by competent contributors to the review. But Alphonse Daudet was also keenly aware that the necessary time to write these works or carry out such projects might be denied to him. And this is precisely what happened, thus leaving the question open for later critics to speculate on what the work could have been and indulge in making gratuitous assumptions or suppositions. Some of the notes meant for *La Caravane* were utilized in other less ambitious works like *La Petite Paroisse*. Others were published later in *Notes sur la Vie*.[21]

During the summer 1897 Mme Daudet accompanied by Lucien, Edmée, and her nieces, went to Switzerland for a few weeks. Eager to finish his book, and also a little apprehensive because of his physical condition, Alphonse had decided to stay at Champrosay with Léon. Two or three times a week Batisto Bonnet who was now attaché to the library of the Department of the Interior, came to Champrosay to join them for the evening. In his book, *Lou Baile Anfos Daudet*, he has written that he had never seen "Anfos" as cheerful, exhilarated, and exhilarating, as he was during those weeks. Alphonse would sing drinking songs, dictate to the cook recipes for Provençal dishes, then talk about the near and distant future. He fancied that the next year, while Mme Daudet and the children would enjoy the seashore, he, Léon and Bonnet, would go to the land of sunshine. They would live in a cabin or hut in the Alps or in the Camargue with the gardians or cowboys, listen to their stories and to the lowing and mooing of the cows, the bellowing of the wild bulls, and the neighing of the horses, while Léon would hunt rabbits and other game which they would cook with all the Provençal seasoning. Then, after watching the beautiful sunset and dreaming in the moonlight, everyone would write his impressions of the day. "Oh! what a beautiful and kingly life the three of us would have led, lost in the ponds and the jointed glassworts of the Camargue!"[22]

The Rue de Bellechasse apartment having become inadequate when Léon returned home after his divorce, the Daudet family decided to look for one better suited to their needs. They found one at 41 Rue de l'université after several months of intensive search. But now Mme Daudet had serious trouble with her eyes (they feared for a while that she would lose her sight), and moving had to be delayed until October, after her condition had sufficiently improved. Alphonse was very much pleased with the new place: "How beautiful is my home," he exclaimed. "If only mother (Julia) would soon recover, we could still be happy."[23] His wish was granted. One day in December, Mme Daudet came home with good news: The doctor had declared that for her to be completely cured was now only a matter of time.

During that year of 1897, Alphonse had corrected proofs of *Premier Voyage, Premier Mensonge* and finished *Soutien de Famille*. We have seen that he had begun this work in 1895 and interrupted it several times, first to write *La Fédor*, which deals with the woman he could never forget, and another time to write *Le Trésor d'Arlatan*, to honor the memory of his best friend, Timoléon Ambroy. In that same period he had also worked on plays, written a short story for children, "La Fille de l'Ogre," for a German magazine, and started his work on *La Caravane*.

X   Soutien de Famille

Soutien de Famille, his last work, is the story of a young man on whom falls the responsibility of heading the family after the death of his father. It is also an indirect, but unmistakable and powerful denunciation, of the political and social regime of the time. The work is headed by a sixty page "Prelude" which opens with a conference between Victor Eudeline, an honest but insolvent manufacturer, and the principal of a Parisian lycée. Eudeline approaches the latter to solicit a favor for his two sons, Raymond and Antonin, who are unable to attend the lycée because of their father's financial difficulties. To his surprise and dismay the principal's answer to his request is an absolute no. He then applies to political "friends" for help, but again all in vain. Desperate and realizing that it will be impossible for him to avoid bankruptcy, he commits suicide in order to "save the honor of his name and family." As a result, it will later behoove his elder son Raymond to support his mother, sister, and younger brother Antonin.

But Raymond soon reveals himself as a weakling afflicted by "an infirmity of the will." He "confuses acts and words," talks endlessly on the great things he intends to accomplish and "believes the task is over while the most important and difficult part of it, still remains to be done." The support, the real "breadwinner" of the family, will turn out to be his younger brother Antonin. Toward the end of the book Raymond finally admits his insufficiencies and ends by enlisting in the marines, supposedly to substitute for his brother who has drawn a lot calling for a five year period of military service. However he explains in a letter that instead of accomplishing a noble act by so doing he was indeed merely running away, shirking his duties, not only those he had assumed as the "support of the family," but also those he had toward Geneviève, the fine girl he has ruined.

The characters are taken from various environments, chiefly from the world of business, industry, and politics. Antonin becomes the true hero of the novel, but perhaps its most likable and truest character is that of old Izoard, the old revolutionary of 1848, who, in spite of his great disappointment with the politicians of the Third Republic has remained a firm believer in the princples and ideals that inflamed his youth. Izoard is the man who answers Raymond's question on how to cleanse and improve the political regime of the time: "Before anything else," he said, "close the Chamber of Deputies for two years. During that time the French would learn how to seek their livelihood anywhere but in the pantry of the State, of the nation."[24] Fascinating also is Dr. Sophia Castagnozoff, the daughter of a Russian grain dealer at Odessa who had come to study medicine in Paris against the will of her parents. To make a living and pay her tuition fees she had given private lessons "in all dead and living languages," and in all the knowledge that "her Slavic memory and vast intelligence" had stored in her mind. Paradoxical "Casta," as her Parisian friends called her, became a great humanitarian, a foundress of charitable dispensaries and hospitals for children while remaining to the end a staunch friend of the anarchist Lupniak, a murderer whom she protected and hid from the police.[25]

Soutien de Famille, finished in September, 1897, was currently appearing in *L'Illustration* at the time of Daudet's death. It was published in book form in 1898, but it did not receive much attention. Biographers have suggested that it might have received more had it not been published at the height of the Dreyfus Affair. Later critics have dealt with it rather summarily, and some quite unfairly. It is perhaps not a great masterpiece, but it contains many beautiful and powerful pages, and unquestionably possesses a great documentary value.

XI   *Days of Respite*

Both the members of his family and Batisto Bonnet have shown Alphonse Daudet during the fall of 1897 as a very active man who, in the midst of his suffering and struggles with various problems, managed to keep his chin up, help others, and continue to write and supervise theatrical productions. Léon Hennique, his former collaborator of *La Menteuse,* now came regularly to Rue de L'Université to discuss the stage version of *La Petite Paroisse* on which they were working. Other collaborators and friends would often drop in for a short visit. Léon has described a charming scene which took place in the month of October, and must have given Alphonse some respite from the terrible physical and mental distress he was then experiencing and more or less successfully hiding. It concerns a visit made by composer Jules Massenet, the author of the operas *Manon* and *Werther,* who had come to report on his completion of *Sapho,* Henri Cain, the author of the libretto, and Mme Calvé the famous prima donna who created the part of Sapho. "Alphonse is the one," said Cain, "who has put us all in the right mood." Mme Calvé sang. Alphonse was deeply moved and so were the others, including Léon.

Some time later in November, the day after the dress rehearsal, which Julia and Alphonse had attended, Mme Calvé came to ask for his criticism. "You were admirable . . . , absolutely admirable," said Alphonse. Pressed further for a sincere criticism, he finally quoted Baudelaire's famous line, *"Je hais le mouvement qui déplace les lignes,"* and suggested that she had indeed "displaced the lines" a little too much, a remark which Mme Calvé accepted gratefully. She also accepted graciously Mme Daudet's answer regarding her velvet gown, which Julia had found too much like a piece of furniture, "trop meuble," that is, too correct, prosaic. It made Sapho look like, said Julia, "a mother at her daughter's wedding."[26] Bonnet who was present, is the one who wrote about that delightful conversation, which ended with an affectionate embrace between the author and his interpreter. *Sapho* was performed at the Opéra Comique on November 12, with huge success.

Alphonse Daudet attended the "Balzac dinner" on December 9, accompanied by Léon. Present, also were Emile Zola, Anatole France, Paul Bourget, and Maurice Barrès. Zola wrote later that he found the reunion "un vrai délice" and added that Daudet had never appeared younger and "more charming," that his fortitude and clearness of mind had defeated his pains. "We were delighted as if the whole past had flourished again."[27] To Léon it was "a cordial and charming meeting at which many subjects were discussed including that of death. As he and his father were returning home in a carriage, "happy and deeply moved," Alphonse expressed the opinion that such gatherings of "love-feast" are indispensable, that they stimulate the spirit, enrich and embellish it.

XII   *Death of Alphonse Daudet*

On December 16, Daudet and Hennique worked as usual on *La Petite Paroisse*. They were both in high spirits as they had just finished the play and apparently had spent most of the day telling jokes while working. When Batisto Bonnet called for a short visit on his way home, Alphonse asked him whether he had corrected the last chapters of his *Valet de ferme*. Upon Bonnet's affirmative reply he announced joyfully that he himself had the preface all prepared in his head and that he would begin writing it the next day.

After Bonnet and Hennique had left, the Daudet family — including Mme Allard — sat at table for dinner. The conversation was running upon Edmond Rostand's new play, *Cyrano de Bergerac*, and Alphonse, who was fond of the young author, spoke enthusiastically about him and recalled the real Cyrano (Savinien Cyrano de Bergerac, 1619 - 1655). As he was commenting on the latter's *Voyage dans les Empires de la lune et du soleil*, he suddenly slumped in his chair. An awful rattle was heard, and he collapsed. They rushed to him. Léon auscultated his father. He was dead!

Till the last moment his mind had remained clear and his conversation fascinating. The news spread through Paris in no time, and friends and relatives rushed Rue de l'Université. That evening an elated Batisto Bonnet was eagerly rereading and correcting his manuscript so that his "baile" would not find too many mistakes in it. The next morning he went to his office exulting with joy. As he arrived, the office boy exclaimed: "How come? You here? Don't you know? . . ."

A few years later Léon wrote the preface to *Le Valet de ferme*, but the trio's jaunt to Provence that his father had dreamed of was never to take place.

Alphonse Daudet was not given a national funeral apparently because he had derided the Republic and the politicians in *Soutien de famille*, which was now appearing by installments in *L'Illustration*. But, according to Léon, people by the thousands lined the streets to watch or join the burial procession to the Père Lachaise cemetery where his father was to be inhumed. Drumont and Zola were among the pallbearers, who, on that occasion were all united in a common feeling in spite of their violently conflicting opinions on the accursed Dreyfus Affair which had already begun to tear them apart. Zola gave the funeral oration in which he extolled both the man and the writer:

. . . Daudet represented what is rarest, most charming, most immortal in a literature: an exquisite and vigorous originality, the very gift of life, that of feeling and expressing himself with such a personal intensity that the slightest, least important page written by him will keep the throb of his soul as long as our language will last. . . . His eternal merit will consist of this compassionate love for the humble, of this victorious laughter pursuing the fool and the wicked, and of all the extreme kindness and fair satire which impregnate each of his books with shuddering humanity.[28]

Georges Clemenceau expressed a similar opinion the next day: "His work will survive as long as our language because of the clear filtering of thought, the exquisite charm of a limpid intelligence, in love with beauty, perfumed with a subtle love of all that exists and wishes to exist."[29]

CHAPTER 7

Main Aspects of His Works

I *Posthumous Publications*

SOME of Alphonse Daudet's writings were published posthumously. *Soutien de Famille* appeared in book form in 1898, and *Notes sur la vie* the same year. The latter consisted of notes collected by Madame Daudet from the *cahiers* he had filled between 1868 — the second year of their married life — and 1897. In a short preface she explained that her husband had never published any of his thoughts separately, that he would simply jot them down in a notebook for further reference and then cross them out as he utilized them in his works. She had made a choice from the "unused" notes, those left uncrossed, and published them under the appropriate title of *Notes on Life*, first in the *Revue de Paris* (March 1 and 15) and then in book form a few months later. They will be found in volume sixteen of the 1929 - 30 Ne Varietur edition of Daudet's *Oeuvres complètes*. The importance of *Notes sur la vie*, which have been quoted here several times, cannot be overemphasized. Like *La Doulou*, published in 1929, it is of paramount importance for a good understanding of Alphonse Daudet, the man and his works. *Premier voyage, premier mensonge* was published by Flammarion in 1900.

The Ne Varietur edition contains also, under the title "*Pages iné-dites de critique dramatique,*" a certain number of articles that Daudet had contributed to the *Journal officiel* during the period 1874 - 1880 (vol. 18); others will be found in *Femmes d'artistes* (vol. 4) and *Etudes et Paysages* (vol. 5), both published in 1874; in *Trente ans de Paris* and in *Souvenirs d'un homme de lettres* (vol. 12), both published in 1888; and *Entre les frises et la rampe* (vol. 13) in 1894. This volume contains also a collection of articles dealing with the stage.

II *The Critics' Attitude*

Most of the critics and book reviewers quoted so far in this work had nothing but high praise to bestow on Alphonse Daudet during his lifetime. They all recognized his mastery of the language, his verve, his knowledge of life and respect for it, the human quality of his realism, his charm. Some reserves were made regarding his technique as a novelist, especially with regard to the structure of his books, which usually consists of a succession of pictures, perfect ones to be sure, but only loosely connected.

This method of juxtaposing scenes or episodes hardly linked together, leaving it up to the reader to make the connections, has naturally been used by many other novelists. It was regarded by some of Daudet's critics as neglecting the analysis and development of emotions, weakening their dramatic interest, and being detrimental to the ensemble: "Is this what a true novel should be?" asked the otherwise favorable critic Armand de Pontmartin.[1]

Similar remarks were made by others who, however, agreed that those scenes or "pieces" were all "perfect jewels" in which the characters appearing in them were so active and so much alive, that they suggested the ensemble appearing to have been thoroughly neglected by the author: "Those characters live only during the few minutes we see them, but then," exclaimed Jules Lemaître, "how they live!"[2] Yet, a case regarding this "weakness" was made by both the French and foreign critics in the countries where Daudet's novels had been translated. Henry James's statement that *The Nabob* was not a sustained narrative, "but a series of diabolically clever sketches"[3] paralleled those of French critics. Some of the latter who had wondered about Daudet's ability to develop a single theme, later conceded that he had successfully done so in *L'Evangéliste* and in *Sapho*.

Other minor reserves were made. As for the violent reactions that took place in southern France upon the appearance of *Tartarin de Tarascon* and *Numa Roumestan*, or in Paris upon that of *Le Nabab*, *Les Rois en exil*, and *L'Immortel*, they could likewise be expected, in those days. What is significant is the fact that Daudet's reputation as a writer was never seriously challenged by the unbiased and competent critics of his time. After his death, however, adverse criticism of the man and his works has reached such a systematic disparaging character that it has become impossible to trust either the sincerity or judgment of some scholars of our generation.

Two recent works of literary history by French scholars will illustrate the point. The first one, meant primarily for college and university libraries, is the kind of book that only specialists in the subject — or students badly in want of a thesis subject — would read; the other is destined to have popular appeal as a guide for the history of the French novel. They are both impressive and monumental studies in which are piled up, spelled out, or suggested, all the shortcomings, defects, and weaknesses, real or imaginary, that have been imputed to Alphonse Daudet during the past hundred years: accusations of plagiarism, guilefulness, ungratefulness, and unreliability. They accuse him of having lied every time he said something in his favor, but praise him for saying the truth whenever he charged himself with some kind of mischief or misdeed. Unrelenting censors, they find his jokes insipid and pointless, his codumentation imperfect and incomplete, his descriptions and depictions unrealistic and lacking in subtleness. Withal, they regard him as a poor imitator of Dickens and other writers, always inferior to his models, inferior to most of the novelists and dramatists of his generation.

The most violent diatribes have appeared in periodicals. Some of them are couched in journalistic prose and have reached the point of ridicule. They hardly deserve our attention. Such an attitude on the part of a few of Daudet's contemporaries is of course quite understandable, but we are at a loss to explain that of his twentieth-century critics. What may have been their true motive for starting a campaign against the man and his works twenty-five years after his death remains a matter of conjecture. The possibility of a posthumous reprisal or revenge for the political activities of his son Léon — who was then very much in the limelight as "député" and codirector of the now defunct Action Française — has been suggested and should not be left entirely out of consideration. But the recurrence of the same savage attacks in our days is a question that will probably never be elucidated. Their authors' main purpose seems to be the gathering of enough evidence to prove that for one hundred years the world has been sadly mistaken about Alphonse Daudet, fooled by him, his family, and a few friends. We may wonder to what extent these critics themselves inwardly recognize the greatness of the man to whom they have devoted so much attention.

Contrary opinions on Alphonse Daudet will naturally be found under the pen of his famous contemporaries. Among those on the favorable side can be named Jules Lemaître, Emile Zola, Anatole France, Barbey d'Aurevilly, Gustave Lanson, Paul Bourget, and the then young Marcel Proust; on the other side, Jules Vallès, Léon Bloy, occasionally Sarcey, and Brunetière, Octave Mirbeau (who after some vicious attacks changed his mind), and Remy de Gourmont. To the latter group could be added the names of those who, in the words of Antoine Albalat, "poured barrels of dung" on Daudet's public and private life. The books and articles listed in our Selected Bibliography contain a great variety of opinions.

Albert Thibaudet recalled that Alphonse Daudet did not start any literary school, which is true, and added that he has not exerted any influence, which is perhaps an oversimplification. We may wonder for example how many, and to what extent, Provençal and provincial writers (from Paul Arène and Jean Aicard to Jean Giono, Henri Bosco, and Marcel Pagnol — and from Le Goffic, Eugène Le Roy, and Barrès to André Chamson and Mauriac), who have contributed to regional literature in France, have been inspired at some time in their career by the works of Alphonse Daudet. Some interesting comparisons could also be made between a few ideas and impressions noted by Daudet and later developed by Marcel Proust.[4]

III Daudet as a Dramatist

The hostile criticism expressed by the stereotyped, assertive statement "that's not playwriting [ce n'est pas du théâtre]," has been applied to most of the plays written by Alphonse Daudet from 1862, when La Dernière Idole enjoyed a certain success at the Odéon, to 1892, when La Menteuse, his last play put on the stage, failed miserably at the Théâtre du Gymnase.

La Dernière Idole, which de Morny and the brilliant audience surrounding him applauded enthusiastically (Mme Morny "so violently that she broke her fan") was censured as being "undramatic." L'Oeillet blanc, called a "polished trifle," and Le Frère aîné were generally described as overly sentimental plays, Lise Tavernier as melodramatic, L'Arlésienne in 1872 as ridiculous and impossible to understand, L'Obstacle and La Menteuse as too artificial and didactic, the latter being regarded, even by Lucien Daudet, as the story of "an uninteresting adventuress."

While much of this adverse criticism is understandable, although not always justifiable, it remains that L'Arlésienne has been reviewed favorably by several generations of authoritative critics, that it was for years a staple in the repertory of the Odén theater and that it has been played in various other theaters in France and abroad over three-fourths of a century; also that La Lutte pour la vie enjoyed about one hundred performances in 1889, and *Sapho* about eighty in 1892 — a real dramatic triumph with Jane Hading, and later with Cécile Sorel and Réjane, each in the part of Sapho — which after all constitutes a rather remarkable achievement on the stage.

To be sure, Francisque Sarcey's remark that the success of *L'Arlésienne* in 1885 was mostly due to the music of Bizet was quickly picked up. Others suggested that *Sapho* and *Numa Roumestan* owed theirs to that of the novels from which they were drawn.

Anticipating a repetition of this kind of criticism, which annoyed him considerably, Barbey d'Aurevilly wrote the following in his appraisal of *Le Frère aîné:* " 'No, this is not a play!' pedants will say, Let them talk! That lacks action, lacks plot, motion . . . that lacks everything! But what if "that" needs nothing! If that thing is done with nothing! What is a spark made of? What made the fragrant molecule of the rose?"[5]

It could be added that even *Lise Tavernier* is not such a bad drama if considered as one of its kind.

After rereading some of the plays in question, one comes to the conclusion that Alphonse Daudet as a dramatist has not quite been the failure that the critics have so often pictured him to be. Also, that his biographers have taken his expression of despair too literally, given far too much importance to his 1872 "threat" to give up both playwriting and literature altogether.

IV   *Universality in Daudet's Characters*

The preceding pages have made it sufficiently clear that in the case of Alphonse Daudet the man and his works cannot be separated. They explain each other. It has been shown also that they must be considered from the point of view of time and environment, in this instance the South of France, Paris, and the Parisian region during the second half of the nineteenth century. In fact, it soon becomes obvious to the reader that the presence of the "southern spirit" prevails in Daudet's writings from the *Lettres de mon Moulin* to the *Trésor d'Arlatan*; that a firsthand account of the activities of the Parisian society gravitating in the orbit round the duc de Morny pervades the pages of the *Nabab*; and that various aspects of political life under the Third Republic are described, explained, and dramatized in *Soutien de Famille*. It could be claimed also that the industrial and business world is depicted in *Fromont jeune et Risler aîné*, the intelligentsia in *L'Immortel*, the working classes and bohemian life in *Jack* and *Sapho* and in other novels and plays. In short the importance of Daudet's works as social documents of the aforementioned places and periods of history cannot be overlooked.

It does not follow however that these temporal and geographical limitations have prevented Alphonse Daudet from reaching universality. Under his pen, some otherwise simple thoughts or remarks have indeed acquired a universal value that makes them applicable elsewhere, regardless of time and place. And there is no doubt, for example, that his comments on bohemia in the Paris of the 1860s would apply as well to the various bohemias and bohemians of our time, wherever they are and whatever we call them; that those he made in 1870 and 1871 about the incompetence and indifference prevailing in the French armed forces in time of national emergency, or about the corruption in government and the entanglement of business and politics, would certainly apply to the years 1914 - 1919 and 1939 - 1945. There are naturally other more recent cases both in France and elsewhere, which would have aroused similar reactions and comments on his part.

Anatole France and Paul Bourget among others considered works like *Le Nabab*, *Numa Roumestan*, and *Les Rois en exil* as historical novels. And indeed they can be regarded as such. It remains however that, while he was quite aware of the social and political problems of his time, and while he occasionally found it necessary to deal with them, Alphonse Daudet's main interest lay first of all in those purely human values that are unrelated to history, completely independent of the particular status of society at a given time. Daudet concerned himself with people of all kinds of social environment and background, from the farmhand and plain workman to the tycoon of finance and the powerful politician — one could even say from the beggar or vagabond to royalty — but in each case, from the humblest to the proudest and most vainglorious, he treated them primarily as individuals, as human beings rather than as members of a class or of a particular social group.

The preponderance of the universal element, which makes it possible for subsequent generations to consider him as a contemporary, is naturally more evident with respect to his chief characters, which were his main concern. The novelist's "real joy," he declared, will always be "to create beings, to put on foot, by dint of resemblance, types of humanity who, from then on, move about in the world with the name, the gesture and grimace with which he has endowed them, and which make people talk about them." His greatest pride resided in the fact of having created such characters. He had for them the feeling of a father for his children:

"As for me, my emotions are always the same when, with regard to a life transient, to one among the thousand marionettes of the political, artistic human comedy, I hear people say: "That's a Tartarin . . . , a Monpavon [in *Le Nabab*] . . . , a Delobelle . . ." I am thrilled, the thrill of a proud father hidden in the crowd while people are cheering his son, and who feels all the time like yelling: "That's my boy! . . ."[6]

Daudet's keen interest in man whatever his station in life, appears in the least developed or sophisticated of his characters. At first he only sketched lightly the country folk among whom he had been raised, but there cannot be any question about their human quality: Rose Mamaï *(l'Arlésienne)* in her motherly love, Maître Cornille *(Le secret de . . .*) in his determination to save the mill from "dishonor," M. Seguin in his failure to understand his carefree goats, the old man and his Mamette *(les Vieux)* — both with "every wrinkle in their faces smiling" and each asking "the friend of Maurice" to speak a little louder for the other's sake — in their concern for their grandson, are only slightly sketched, but a single trait as reported by Alphonse Daudet has been sufficient to make of them all unforgettable characters.

Later he drew more elaborate portraits of the so-called social bohemians whose lives on the fringe of society he had shared and partly enjoyed for a long time. In bohemia he had met talented young men who, like him, were then struggling to make a living while pursuing their literary or artistic goals. In those days, and afterward through life, he also rubbed elbows with the well-known type of would-be artists and self-styled writers, those who delude themselves into believing that they are unappreciated geniuses victimized by family and society. It was in this last category that he found most of those whom he called the *ratés*, that is, the dissatisfied individuals who hasten to blame others and "the establishment" for their shortcomings. We may wonder how many young men today consider themselves beaten before beginning, as they did in Daudet's time, just because they lack confidence in life and lack the necessary courage to face it.

Alphonse Daudet has illustrated and dramatized in his so-called realistic novels some of the reasons that may prevent a man from realizing his ambition. His most famous raté is the boastful and pretentious poetaster d'Argenton, who always assumed the attitude of a talented writer without himself ever being able to write one worthy page. Also in *Jack* should be recalled the educator Morenval, who is responsible for the death of little king Madou-Ghézo, and Dr. Hirsh, a raté of the medical profession. In *Fromont jeune et Risler aîné* we have met two spineless misfits: the businessman Ferdinand Chèbe, who squanders his wife's dowry in foolish enterprises, and the ham actor Delobelle, who, claiming that he has no right "to renounce the theater," lets his own wife and his daughter support him. They both have such a high opinion of themselves that they consider it beneath their dignity to accept the positions offered them in order to relieve their wives' anxieties. The case of Raymond Eudeline, the supposed support of the family (*Soutien de Famille*), is a little different. It will be recalled that he was at first a well-meaning, ambitious young man who, like the others, had no will of his own and soon turned out to be a vain, spineless, and selfish weakling.

When Alphonse Daudet became deeply concerned about the cynicism tending to prevail among the younger generation in the 1880s he dramatized the type of the cynical "go-getter" or thruster, the "struggle-for-lifeur" Paul Astier, in *L'Immortel* and in *La Lutte pour la vie*. Paul Astier and the young blasé, reckless débauché Charlexis, in *La Petite Paroisse*, are two impressive characters who have survived even though not supported by outstanding master-pieces.

V   *The Gap between Generations*

It was chiefly through them that Daudet made his readers conscious of the seriousness of the old and universal problem of the gap between generations — a problem that haunted him during the last twenty or twenty-five years of his life. An expression of that concern found its way in this terse and pessimistic *note sur la vie:* "Communications broken off between this generation and ours; incomprehension that goes as far as hate."

He was horrified by the bitterness and "ferocity" of envious young men in all classes of society, but especially in the literary and artistic world. He often heard the latter tear to pieces their elders whom they hated and whose works they wished they could blast, destroy, annihilate: " . . . and what offended me above all," says one of his characters in *Soutien de Famille*, "was that these gentlemen pretended to speak in the name of French youth, which is an awful lie — for youth does not consist of a few hundred would-be authors intoxicated with ink and vanity, but of all the others . . ."[7] Jules Huret's famous "enquête sur *l'évolution littéraire"* published in 1891, is quite enlightening and conclusive in this respect. Alphonse Daudet himself was among those whose workd were derided by the interviewed young hopefuls. From this viewpoint he could be called again a contemporary, or better still a seer, a prophet who predicted the future development, intensification, and multiplication of the social ills he was then witnessing.

But Daudet understood, and was in sympathy with, the younger generation as can be seen in this most interesting page of *L'Immortel* where he puts the following reflections in the mouth of the painter Védrine, his spokesman in that novel. Védrine is addressing his wife as they are getting ready to row across the Loire River in a small boat, just before an oncoming storm. Members of a rowing party have already left in a hurry, following each other in a single file because of the narrowness of the channels:

Look at this Mom . . . you know, when speaking of one of my chums I say that we belong to the same boat . . . well, there is my image, quite visible and alive . . . all these boats filing away in the wind, dark night drawing nigh, are our generations of art, of artists. . . . Being in each other's way does not make any difference if we are in, or belong to, the same boat; we know each other, we touch elbows, support each other; we are friends without our wanting or knowing it. But those, who are ahead of us, how they linger, block our way! Their boat and ours have nothing in common. We are too far from each other, we do not understand each other any more. We pay attention to them just enough to shout at them: "Hey you over there, keep on going, get on! Clear out of the way!" While, to the boat following us, whose youthful impetus pushes us, follows on our heels and would like to ride us down, we hurl angrily "Hey now, slowly! — What's the hurry?" Well! As for me, I belong to my boat, to be sure, and I like it; but I am interested in those ahead and those behind as much as in mine. . . . I hail them, beckon to them, I try to communicate with them all . . . for all of us, followers and predecessors, we are threatened by the same dangers, and for each of our boats the streams are swift, hard to negotiate, the skies are treacherous — and the night comes so fast! — Now let us move off darling, here is the shower — .[8]

There are other sorry specimens in Daudet's minor novels and plays, as there are attractive, outstanding, and unforgettable figures: the heroes facing the villains. Some of his best-known characters are among those whose names or nicknames are to be found in the titles of his works: Tartarin, Jack, Numa Roumestan, Fanny-Legrand-

Sapho and Jansoulet-le-Nabab. This category could include Robert Helmont and Risler Aîné. Helmont arouses and retains the interest of the reader who sees in him a real, living character, a "regular fellow" caught in an unusual situation, living character, a "regular fellow" caught in an unusual situation, at grips with life in difficult circumstances, and who manages to remain equal to the occasion. Obviously the author's interest was in this case far more centered on what he had observed than on Robert Helmont, who happened to be himself. Neither is Risler Aîné a great character of a national or universal type, but he holds his own in the novel.

No more space can be devoted here to Jack's tragic life or to Sapho's strange personality and magic powers that have fascinated generations of young men. Neither do Tartarin's inner conflict and numberless adventures in Africa, the Swiss Alps, and the South Pacific islands require further comments. And it may be agreed that enough attention has also been given to the Nabob's fantastic rise and downfall. On the other hand, the novel *Numa Roumestan* calls for some additional remarks with regard to the North-South question.

VI   *The Midi in the Works of Daudet*

A thorough discussion of the subject would require naturally an analysis of the many southern characters in Daudet's works, such as for example Jean Gaussin, "l'oncle Césaire" and "La tante Divonne" in *Sapho*, Elysée Méraut in *Les Rois en exil*, and especially Jansoulet in *Le Nabab*. But neither of these works was written primarily to convey a message, to present and defend a thesis, as is the case with *Numa Roumestan* which, from this particular point of view, must be reexamined through its main characters.

An interesting fact about this novel is that it is not so much the portrait of its hero that is exaggerated, turned into an amusing caricature, but rather those of its minor characters, such as, for example, picturesque Aunt Portal and Bompard, whom we have already met in the Tartarin trilogy. Bompard is presented here as one of Numa's fellow countrymen who has become a regular member of his household in Paris:

Right at the beginning of her married life, Numa's young bride found comfortably installed in her house, at the place of honor, like a piece of family furniture, this lean, skinny person with the head of a palikar, with a big eagle beak of a nose, eyes like agate marbles popping out of his saffron skin which resembled embossed Cordovan leather, slashed with those wrinkles that are peculiar to clowns, common to all faces that are strained by continuous contortions. Yet Bompard had never been a comedian. . . . Bompard had seen everything, tried every trade, gone everywhere. You could not mention a famous man or refer to a great event without his asserting: "He is a friend of mine" or "I was there, I have just come from there . . ." and immediately a story to prove it. . . . This delirious southerner was Roumestan's joy. He always took him along, wherever he went . . ."[9]

More developed, and perhaps truer to life even though more extravagant, is the portrait of Aunt Portal. Here the satire is still gentle and the emphasis on the likable side of the character; also, the references to the supposed characteristics of "the race" appear more frequently:

The race is proud in the land of Aps [an imaginary town in Provence] and good-natured; but with an extreme sensitiveness and unrestrained use of language of which Aunt Portal — a true type of the local bourgeoisie — can give and summarize the idea. Enormous in size, apoplectic, with all her blood flowing into her purplish red cheeks that contrasted with her skin, the skin of a blond, that which could be seen of her very white neck, of her forehead on which beautiful bows of ribbon, carefully done, like mat silver, sprang from a bonnet with mauve ribbons, her blouse fastened askew, but just the same striking one with respect, a majestic look and pleasant smile, such was your first impression of Mme Portal . . . You could say she was like a family portrait, an old marchioness . . . But if in a conversation with the aunt you unfortunately suggested that the Protestants were as good as the Catholics, or that Henri V was not likely to ascend the throne very soon, the old portrait would dash violently from its frame and, with the veins of her neck swollen, her irritated hands mussing by the handful the fine arrangement of her ribbons and frills, she would fly into a passion, a terrible fit of anger mingled with abuse, threats, and curses, one of these tantrums so famous in the town.

Once, at one of her evening parties, the servant knocked over a tray loaded with drinking glasses; Aunt Portal yelled, little by little got excited, through reproaches and lamentations arrived at a state of violent delirium in which indignation could not be expressed through words. Then, choked by what she wanted to say, unable to hit the clumsy servant who had prudently got out of her way, she pulled her silk skirt over her head, hid under it, choking down her rage, grunting and grimaces, not caring at all whether, or not she let her guests see the starched white underwear of a portly lady. . . . In the long run an excellent person, . . . passionate and generous, with that desire of pleasing, of devoting herself, and doing her best to please others, which is one of the traits of the race.[10]

No one will question that Alphonse Daudet's intention in writing *Numa Roumestan* was to give a complete picture of the Midi as he saw it, with its scorching sun, with the manners of its people and their peculiarities, including their language and pronunciation of French with a Provençal accent. Some reserve can be made regarding Thibaudet's statement that with *Tartarin de Tarascon* and *Numa Roumestan* it is a question of a Midi "fabricated" for exportation, as a contribution to caricature. But it would be still harder to accept the idea that Daudet is not to be considered as an "evocator" of the Midi. It must be granted also that Daudet was keenly conscious of the North and South conflict and that he dramatized it in his novel, insisting on the idea that the people of southern France belonged to a different "race," the "southern race" exalted by his friends the Felibres, and symbolized by the hero of his novel. But attention should be called to the fact that Numa's portrait is not a mere caricatural sketch like those of Bompard and Aunt Portal. It was elaborated little by little almost imperceptibly throughout the book. Numa does not appear as a type but rather as a rich, complex, living individual.

College and university professors may appreciate the following sketch of Numa as a student:

Numa was twenty-two when he went to Paris to finish the law studies he had begun at Aix. He was at that time a good-natured fellow, full of high spirits, noisy, florid of complexion, with fine golden-brown eyes, and a lock of black hair that fell over half his forehead like an otter-skin cap without a peak. Not the shadow of an idea, of an ambition, beneath that sumptuous covering. A regular student of Aix, very good at billards and pool, without an equal at drinking a bottle of champagne at a party, at hunting cats with torches till three in the morning in the broad streets of the aristocratic and parliamentary town, but interested in nothing, never opening a paper or a book, steeped in the provincial foolishness which shrugs its shoulders at everything and clothes its ignorance with a reputation of plain good sense.

The Quartier Latin enlivened him a little. . . . In this limited milieu Numa was easily an eagle. He was more noisy that the others, and he enjoyed a superiority, at any rate a reputation, for originality because of his lively liking for music. He went to the pit of the Opera two or three times a week, and returned full of recitatives and tunes, which he sang in a fairly good voice. . . .

As for the lectures, he was similarly easy going. Though only half prepared, for he was lazy, feared work and solitude, he wrote rather brilliant examinations, thanks to his boldness and his southern subtlety, which always enabled him to discover the weak point in a professor's vanity. Moreover his face, with its frank, amiable expression, helped him, and, as a lucky star, lighted the way before him.[11]

Numa Roumestan managed to become a lawyer, later secured a position in a law office and finally made his career in politics, in which he succeeded splendidly. As we study him, we realize that he does not appear as the symbol of the ridiculous and hateful southerner that so many have seen in him. The author has been careful to minimize the seriousness of Numa's faults. When he lies, for instance, we are told that it is not with the intention of hurting anyone. On the contrary, Numa knows that those listening to him will admire his fluency of speech and imagination for which, at any rate, only the southern sun is to be blamed. He may be "all speech" and "all gesture," but attention will be called to the fact that his words are "musical." Indeed he may speak in court for two hours with "an insolent verve" and yet manage to have the judges listen to him. And if, as a politician, he makes promises that he does not intend to keep, it is because he knows, or has so convinced himself, that no one will be too upset by his failure to honor them. Nevertheless, Numa's shortcomings are real. Daudet has shown him as being invincibly indolent, "dreading steady, constant office life and work, and "radically wanting in concentration." In short he is one of those weaklings we have already met in Daudet's works — a type who seem to be found as often in the North as they are in the South.

Numa is an opportunist. He does not hesitate to shift to Bonapartism as soon as he realizes that the cause of monarchy is a lost one. When his wife criticizes him severely, he gives way to her arguments, but soon manages to acquire a new prestige as leader of the Royalist party, which he had at first intended to disown. It certainly may be contended that acting thus characterizes him more as a politician than as a Méridional. Let us further recall that Daudet's novels and dramas abound with such a large number of unreliable individuals — weaklings, windbags, braggards and liars, choleric and unfaithful husbands, "struggle-for-lifeurs," and plain scoundrels — that it would be as impossible as otiose and tedious to name them. The above passages do not represent Daudet at his best, but they deserved to be recalled in view of the importance that both the author himself and his critics have given to the book.

Daudet satirized the South through Numa Roumestan as he had satirized it through Tartarin, one of the differences being however that Numa is hardly the type that makes one laugh. Being less ludicrous than Tartarin, he has been taken more seriously and his defects, emphasized by the author himself, have often overshadowed his good qualities. Moreover the pressed, hurried critic or book reviewer of the 1880s whose dormant prejudices had perhaps been awakened or reinforced by the epigraph of the book, usually followed the author to the end of his demonstration, imputing Numa's more or less unpleasant or condemnable traits entirely to his "race" rather than to his original personality. It is rather disturbing to find that critics who take Alphonse Daudet to the letter when, for example, he satirizes or rails his compatriots' abuse of imagination, forget so easily and so conveniently that he himself was a southern poet, thus doubly liable to indulge in both imagination and exaggeration. It was certainly an overstatement to write that Numa represented exactly "the southern type," and an oversimplification to present him and his wife as symbols of the North's and South's supposed inability to come to an agreement — an assertion which, for different reasons, has equally offended or irritated readers of both the North and the South. Incidentally, Alphonse Daudet's own marriage weathered many storms whose origins had nothing to do with either.

Numa is unquestionably a genuine Méridional, but he is an exceptional one, a fascinating and living character, created partly in the author's image. He is one of these types of humanity who still "move about in the world with the name, gesture and grimace with which the author has endowed them."[12]

VII Alphonse Daudet's Regional French

So far, then, the characterization — whether complimentary or derogatory — of Alphonse Daudet's works as social documents has led us to some remarks on the universal element found in his short stories and novels, particularly in *Numa Roumestan;* the book he preferred, the work into which "he poured the wealth of his experiences, as a son of the South."[13]

The importance and significance of these southern experiences have been questioned. Professor Louis Michel, author of a good study on Daudet's use of the Provençal language in his works, remarks correctly that Alphonse Daudet, who grew up in a bourgeois family disdainful of the Provençal language and culture, never was himself a bilinguist; that the amount of time he spent in the Midi during the forty-seven years of his "Parisian life" did not amount to more than six or seven months in all; and that his knowledge of the South, which he left at the age of nine, "the age when one knows only the boys in the neighborhood and a few local expressions," was quite limited and artificial.[14]

One must take into consideration the fact that, as a child, Alphonse Daudet had had the opportunity of spending many weekends and vacations with his foster parents (his *nourriciers*) in the villages of Bezouce or Rodessan, where he played passionately with the boys on the farm, spoke their language, and listened attentively to the stories told in Provençal by his foster father. It may be assumed that he acquired then much more knowledge of southern life than the above-mentioned "few local expressions." Another experience, which no doubt compensated appreciably for the lack of a long and direct contact with his native region, was that of visiting it, at the age of twenty, after a few years of absence. Finally, we may imagine how much his knowledge of the South must have been enriched through his contact with the Félibres.

Alphonse Daudet resorted to every means to make his Parisian readers understand the Provençal turn of mind and arouse their interest in his native land. Besides characterizing its landscape, its people and their manners, referring to its folklore and its institutions, he repeatedly called attention to the linguistic peculiarities of its regional French, which he himself had probably spoken very little in his childhood. But Daudet was a keen observer. Not only did he, like every northerner or "exiled" southerner, note the accent, which he associated with gestures, but he also made pertinent comments regarding the alteration of French words, the use and abuse of diminutives, the misuse of articles, prepositions, reflexive and pronominal verbs and idiomatic regional expressions, proverbs and popular sayings usually translated into French from the vernacular. That he should have made some mistakes and failed to satisfy every critic could be expected — especially in view of the fact that he claimed the right of the poet to use freely his imagination and poetical instinct.

Daudet's errors, inaccuracies, insufficiencies and oversights listed by Professor Michel are unquestionably real and quite interesting. They constitute a welcome statement of facts as well as a necessary warning to the reader inclined to take the author of *Tartarin* and *Numa Roumestan* too literally. In order to create local color, Daudet studded repeatedly some of his texts with a certain number of picturesque expressions and words, particularly those belonging to the effective and exclamatory vocabulary, whether in the original Provençal or in the regional French, such as *pecaïre, Vé, Té, Zou, Pardi, Autrement* (pronounced *autremain*), *Pas moins, Tron de l'ér,* etc. While being currently used by some people in Provence — as for example *n'est-ce pas* (or *spas)* is used in Paris, or "you know" is used here — these provençalisms are far less common than the reader is led to suppose.

Daudet's process of repetition tends to become fastidious to the average reader and, at times, quite irritating to the well-informed southerner. The latter is prompt to notice the author's errors, and he resents his satire and misleading generalizations — such as, for instance, the suggestion, repeated to satiety, that the average Provençal pronounces the French word *accent* as *assent, exemple* as *ezemple, exagérer, ézagérer, pauvre, povre* or *pavre, non, nan, certainement* as *certainemain,* etc., etc.

Other writers and actors have since then amused their readers or listeners by calling their attention to the southerner's pronunciation of French, which of course is quite natural in the South but sounds ridiculous in the North. It can be said that the degree of success enjoyed by actors like Raimu or Fernandel varied according to latitude. Alphonse Daudet's language was partly, but only partly to be sure, responsible for the popularity of his works with the public for whom he was writing, that is, mainly the Parisian public. Its artificiality stands out when compared to that used by other French writers of Provence, particularly Jean Giono.

Even though they were written in French, Giono's first novels were actually "thought" in Provençal, or in the regional French of Provence, which in most cases is a literal translation of Provençal. Contrarily, Daudet wrote and generally thought in pure, correct French, while consciously trying to give his text a Provençal color and flavor. Thus Giono's language was, in these first novels, a more or less unconscious but authentic *regional* French, whereas Daudet's turned out to be a more or less artificial one. Yet Daudet's genius was such that he usually managed, through his so-called *style méridional,* to give an impression of authenticity to the language he put in the mouth of his characters.

VIII *Alphonse Daudet's* Style Méridional

This "southern style," whose main characteristics are spontaneity and mobility, is lively and dynamic. It presupposes a state of mind that pervades the Provençal language itself. It is characterized by the cheerful attitude of the individual whose imagination and emotional behavior sometime lead him to exuberance and exaggeration. Paul Bourget, who found it "unfortunate" that *Numa Roumestan* "illustrated rather than told" the North-South conflict, wrote that "never had style better gesticulated in the manner of the characters it creates."[15]

As in Provençal, the rhythm of southern regional French varies considerably according to the mood of the speaker or writer particularly eager to communicate his emotions to his readers or listeners. Much closer to the style of the spoken language than to that of grammatical literary French, it entails the abuse of question and exclamation marks, elipses, inversions and interruptions, as it can be seen in some of the above-quoted passages. Alphonse Daudet defined it perhaps inadvertently when, appraising his own *Tartarin de Tarascon,* he called it "stand up literature" *(la littérature debout)*: "The grain of my writing is neither very fine nor of very close texture," he said. "It is what I call "standing literature," spoken and gesticulated with my heroes's bursting enthusiasm. But I must confess," he added, "that great as is my love of style, of beautiful, melodious and colored prose, in my opinion, there is something else for the novelist to consider."[16]

The "something else" concerned evidently the picture of the world and the creation of living characters. Written in a different language and style, *Numa Roumestan* or any of the Tartarin trilogy might have gained appreciably in harmony, elegance, dignity, and perhaps even in a sort of realism, but it is very likely that the characters in these books would have lost much of what gives them life. We may wonder what would have become of that particular Daudet humor which can hardly be conceived apart from his style and language. The question may be asked, for instance, what the tragic story of the Bretons told in *Port-Tarascon* would have been without the Tarasconians and their tarasconades. No doubt either that transferring the action of "Les Vieux" from Chartres to Provence saved this delightful short story from being a mere sentimental, listless, lackadaisical anecdote. As for the "Curé de Cucugnan," originally written in French by a "northerner," it is possible, by comparing the now available versions, to appreciate the improvement realized by Daudet's translation from a Provençal text.

IX *Varied Aspects of his Style*

This is not to say however that Daudet's style lacks originality or that it does not bear the mark of other influences. That it changed considerably under the sway of the various literary movements of his time, from the beginning of his career when he espoused the ideals of the *Revue Fantaisiste* to the heyday of Realism, Impressionalism, and Naturalism is a matter on which all critics have dwelt, as they have on the help he received from his wife Julia. The technique of using long and somewhat involved sentences, or contrarily a sort of telegraphic style, omitting conjunctions and verbs, replacing articles with demonstrative adjectives or the past definite tense with the imperfect, resorting to slang terms, or having one's characters think aloud, addressing the reader as if interested in his feelings or judgment, are among the many aspects of Daudet's technique that could be found in the works of many of his contemporaries. Albert Thibaudet's remarks, particularly with reference to Goncourt's and Roumanille's influence, are worth quoting: "The artistry of the Goncourt brothers has seriously endangered the lasting quality of their prose. But when Daudet grafted this *écriture artiste* on his French filled with Provençal sap and juice, the result was a perfect success. Daudet's style makes one see, live, gives pleasure...."[17]

A great deal has been written about Daudet's Realism and many critics still insist on classifying him among the Naturalists in spite of his numerous protests and of the very nature of his works, which should preclude any such conclusions. In a preface to Lepelletier's *Les Morts heureuses,* he wrote the following, in 1886 after the publication of *Sapho,* which some critics had regarded as the best expression of French Naturalism:

Your book thus sheds light, without your intention to do so, on a very delicate point of literary controversy and once more shows that the theories I have so often discussed and maintained are right, even against these two masters of the modern novel Edmond de Goncourt and Emile Zola.

Is it indeed necessary to tell everything one has seen, with his own eyes, and nothing else; or does the artist have the right to extend, enlarge his horizon, look in front and behind, very far, not with his myopic eyes, those of a passer-by, but with this predatory vision that Michelet had over the Middle Ages, Flaubert over Carthage, Leconte de Lisle over primitive civilizations?

Would not Goncourt himself, if he should decide "to put on foot" some of these creatures of the eighteenth century which he has rediscovered — give us a work as true, as much seen and "lived," as his most admirable studies of modernity? . . . And since I have named Zola, who will believe that we owe the beautiful evocations of *Germinal* to a few moments spent in a mine and to a compilation of statistics? . . . It is not a question of having seen, but one of making people see. There are no bones too fossilized, no dead too old, no past too much frittered away for the wizardry of a poet, who is the only true seer, the clairvoyant. That one belongs "to all time and to the whole earth"; he rediscovers ancient souls, upsets the notions of centuries and distances, dominates and holds humanity. . . . Oh! Yes indeed, no systems, no "schools," especially, no inflexible criterion! . . . Let us think of the sailors who make everything float on their ship . . . even their compass in the middle of the deck, under the stars. Thus must go (float) our opinions on people, on art, on life. Any kind of stability is impossible, as is any absurd and dangerous inflexibility on board our big ship, which rolls and pitches eternally, on the way toward the unknown.[18]

X   *The Originality of his Style*

It would be hard to say where exactly Daudet's originality begins or ends. Daudet's originality consisted precisely in his ability to adopt the literary devices in vogue during the various periods of his career, and adapt them to his needs. There is quite a difference in style between the above quoted passages of *Numa Roumestan* and those of *Tartarin* or *Sapho*. Anatole France has described *L'Evangéliste* as "light, flexible, skilled to perfection. . . ."[19] However, it seems that the southern element, whether it proceeds from the Felibres or directly from his southern origins and personal experiences, is the predominant one in his works dealing with the South or with southern characters.

It should be kept in mind that, while he loved Paris and was a genuine French patriot, Daudet never disowned, forsook, or forgot his native province. He returned to the land of sunshine as often as he could, and the chances are that he enjoyed the crowd in the arena as much as Numa Roumestan did in the novel. His family and all his friends in Paris or in Provence have insisted on the authenticity of his enthusiasm. His visits, excursions, and parties with Mistral and the Felibres were recorded in their publications and he himself often referred to his sojourns with his friends at Fontvieille and Orgon. Léon insisted on the vivifying effect of the Provençal air on his father. Perhaps the most persuasive written account was that given by Batisto Bonnet whose mere presence sufficed to launch him into lyric effusions and endless reminiscences about his youth and the Midi.

The question involved is not entirely one of form, language, and literary technique. It is also one of tone and contents, one concerning the author's general attitude toward life and his ideas about such subjects as religion and politics.

CHAPTER 8

Conclusion: Daudet's Attitude toward Life

I Attitude toward Politics

SETTLING the political regime and determining what the power of the Church should be are probably the two problems that most occupied the French mind during the nineteenth century. The solution of these problems had become the main subject of discussion since the French Revolution of 1789. They concerned all classes of society, affected the lives of the old and the young — women and children included. Yet, generally speaking, neither politics nor religion as such have received much attention in the works of Alphonse Daudet. There are a few exceptions, *L'Evangéliste, Soutien de Famille,* and *Numa Roumestan* among them. But, even here, the emphasis is on the characters, on the politicians rather than on politics, on the clergy (both secular and regular) rather than on religion.

This is not suggest however that Alphonse Daudet might have remained unconscious of, or indifferent to, the existence and importance of these problems. We have seen that he was born and raised in a Catholic and Royalist family. As he grew up he heard endless political discussions at home and elsewhere. In Paris, first in the taverns he haunted, where he heard "men with long beards" discussing endlessly the "social regeneration" of a "new France" — muddling their thoughts "a little more with every beer mug" — and then in the circle of the duc de Morny, he must have listened to many different points of view. His position was a marvelous observation post which enabled him to watch the behavior of high officials in government. He recalled having been "at first quite amazed, then quite disgusted with their incapacity and silly blind self-conceit. . . ."

When later, during and after the war and the Commune (1870 -

71), he found himself again in the midst of political activities, again in a favorable position to observe the working of government, he "solemnly and sincerely" declared that what he was then witnessing grieved him and scared him . . . : "All the fools I knew," he said, "the thieves, the stragglers, tricksters and unemployables, those whom the Empire did not want," were now finding their way, succeeding. When he saw "the same slackness, the same lies, the same traffic of decorations" and as much squandering of energy as he had noticed under the Empire, he became really suspicious of the Republic which, at first, he had acclaimed; and when Paris surrendered while the Parisians wanted to continue the fight, he almost cried "Long live the Commune!" But he never could make up his mind as to the kind of political regime that would be best for France. This he acknowledged and explained in his *Confession d'un homme de trente ans.*[1] Like every Méridional, he knew the intensity of political feelings, among the southern "Whites" and the "Reds," who hated each other. The whites were the Royalists, the Bonapartists and the churchgoing Catholics. The "Reds" were the others — those who believed in the principles of the French Revolution and were fighting for social reforms. He knew also the damage that could be caused by unleashed political passions. The following passage sums up his feelings on the subject.

Oh politics, I hate you, because you are coarse, unfair, high-pitched, screechy and garrulous . . . , because you separate good hearts that should remain united; you contrarily bring together beings who are quite different from each other; you are the powerful dissolvent of consciences; you train people to lie, to use subterfuge, and, owing to you, we see honest people befriending knaves and rogues, provided they belong to their political party. I hate you above all because you have succeeded in killing in our hearts the love, the very notion of country.[2]

To the end of his life, Alphonse Daudet held to this conviction and kept aloof from politics, even at the time of the Dreyfus Affair.

As can be seen through his works, his disdain for, and rejection of, politics does not mean disinterestedness on his part. He did not dissociate himself from the fate of the poor or unprivileged individual who is ill provided for life. To him — after 1885, when he had reached the peak of his fame — the main job of the writer consisted precisely in denouncing social injustice, showing the harshness of the rich and privileged, and pleading for the wretch who occasionally rebels against the social order when he cannot stand his plight any more. This may well be the part of Daudet's "charm" which appeals to those not believing anymore in the promises of politicians — demagogues and dreamers who promise wonders, the moon, and stars to ailing humanity.

II *Religion*

Just as he avoided dealing with the political question Alphonse Daudet kept to himself whatever he thought or felt about the religious one. Nonetheless, he was interested in both and tried to understand their champions and supporters. His contact with religion started naturally at home, at the time of his birth. There are records that he attended the Ecole des Frères de la Doctrine chrétienne in the city of Nîmes, where the boys of the Catholic and Protestant schools used to fight, throwing stones at each other. Alphonse Daudet showed his English friend Sherard a scar on his forehead where a stone from the opposite camp had hit him. Such fights were still frequent in various small towns of Provence and Languedoc toward the end of the century, but they now occurred between boys of the lay, public schools *(l'école laïque)*, and those of the parochial schools. Many of them grew up hating those of the opposite camp. After the establishment of the *Ecole laïque* the questions of religion and politics had become more and more intermixed, and conflicts occasionally arose in the family regarding the kind of school, public or parochial, that the children should attend. We may assume that in similar circumstances no such conflicts would have arisen in the Vincent Daudet family, where perfect harmony seems to have reigned in this respect.

Alphonse's faith was not to last very long however. He has explained in his "story of my books" devoted to *Le Petit Chose*, how, around the age of ten or twelve, he was "cruelly shaken" by several "religious crises"; how he violently reacted against the "mysteries and absurdities in which one had to believe." His revolts were followed by remorse and despair that caused him to prostrate himself in churches. He was about thirteen when he suddenly felt an imperative, wild need (un besoin éperdu) to "live," to spend himself, "to tear away from the hardened sorrows, the tears which choked life at home," as his parents were gloomier every day because of their financial ruin. He later attributed his violent reactions to "an effervescence of the southern temperament" and to an excess of "compressed" imagination. Thus "the delicate and timorous child" changed into a bold one, ready for any foolishness: playing truant to go boating, endangering his life every day, coming home late, exhausted, but at the same time feeling a savage "ferocious joy," "an expansion" of his whole being, he explained, a widening of the "dark horizon."[3]

He noted in his *cahiers* a few visits that he had paid to priests in Lyons and Paris. Several of them tried at that time, and also later, to "convert him," rescue him, to bring him back to the fold, but to no avail. He had noted early that his brothers were much more religious than he was. He had often "debated with himself" and had been irritated by his own coldness. More important was the fact that he had been calling for God in vain ("appelant Dieu et Dieu ne venant pas").[4] Léon reminisced that he had heard his father talk of Christ "with an energy and an unction which any preacher might have envied . . . ," and of faith, "with an eloquence that sprang from the intimate sources of religious feeling. . . ." But Léon summed up, adding that his father nevertheless "venerated Montaigne more than Pascal," and wondered whether he [A. D.] was "entirely unbelieving and skeptical."[5] And Lucien wondered what his father meant when, in a period of terrible suffering and despondency, he had written the sentence "Tout ce qui nous manque est le divin."[6]

After his death, Julia wrote to a cousin who was then bishop of Saint Denis expressing her regret that Alphonse had never returned to his faith. The bishop answered on this point declaring that he could not help thinking of "all the sincerity, good faith, respectful and almost melancholy reserve that were in him." His conclusion was that God, "whose kindness is infinite," would take into consideration "such feelings of this noble heart." Benoît-Guyod quotes also the following undated verses written by Alphonse Daudet after the manner of the sixteenth-century French writers:

> A Julia
> Ains ne faut-il, quand orrey l'heur' suprême,
> Vous despiter, ni plurer, ni crier,
> Mais ramenant vos pensers en un même,
> Ne faire qu'un de tout ce qui vous aime,
> Regarder ce, joindre mains et prier.[7]

It is evident from the above that Alphonse Daudet's religious education had marked him profoundly, but it is equally clear that he lost faith when still a young boy and that he never recovered it. Whenever the question of religion comes up in his works it is generally dealt with in a light, detached, or satirical vein, as in

"L'Elixir du Révérend Père Gaucher," "La Mule du Pape," "Les trois messes basses," *Port-Tarascon*, and certain pages of *Numa Roumestan*. Yvonne Martinet expressed it very well when she said that Daudet's religion was "une esthétique" rather than "une métaphysique."[8] *L'Evangéliste* is naturally the most outstanding exception in this respect. But it remains that his spiritual life, as an adult, was not guided by any religious tenets whatever. On the other hand he always respected others' religious beliefs. Léon assures us that no word of impiety had ever come out of his mouth. He despised base anticlericalism while he shunned discussing the subject of religion for the same reason that he shunned political activities.[9] In fact, Alphonse Daudet persistently refrained from using literature as a tribune or pulpit, either for political, religious, or philosophical purposes.

III   *Daudet's Attitude toward Life*

Daudet's philosophy of life is an expression of that particular state of mind that is said to be prevalent in the South and has been labeled *l'esprit provençal* ("the Provençal spirit"). Critics point it out in the works of some great French writers like Rabelais, Montaigne, and Molière who partook of it, each in his own way. It is a philosophy of life akin also to that of Beaumarchais' Barber of Seville who hastens "to laugh at everything for fear of having to cry about it." It suggests a rather deep, and in some cases inescapable, pessimism for the man who cannot find help in religion. As we have just seen, this was precisely the case of Alphonse Daudet. Such pessimism can be overcome, or at least considerably lessened, through a strong belief in certain principles and the determination to live up to them. By the time he reached the age of thirty, Alphonse Daudet had acquired or developed some of these principles which, through fortitude and iron will, he was able to apply effectively during the better part of his life. Whether or not his "passion for indulgence *(ferveur d'indulgence)* and "love of pardon" or sacrifice were due to his "Catholic blood," as claimed by his son Léon, could not affect the fundamental traits of his personality or reduce the importance of his deeds and achievements.

In his life as in his works Alphonse Daudet assumed that realistic attitude which means acceptance of the unavoidable and resignation to suffering. While being at times obsessed by the idea of death he did not spout about the human condition and was less concerned with "the absurdities of life" than with the means to improve and embellish it. And this was precisely one of the qualities that he had in common with Mistral and other Méridionaux who, however deep-seated their pessimism might be, still believed in possible happiness on this earth and regarded as their first task that of creating joy and dispensing it to their readers. To the inquiring Swedish student who found life not worth living and wanted to know why Tartarin and his Provençal friends were the only beings he had found happy, Tartarin made this reply: "Our race is the reason for that, young man!"[10]

Beside the pessimism derived from his personal experiences and from his literary friends' thinking and attitude, Alphonse Daudet had to fight also, and especially, that of the then popular foreign philosophers, particularly Schopenhauer, whom he otherwise admired greatly:

"Worth remembering," he jotted down in his *Notes sur la Vie*, "the sadness and dismay of my big boy [Léon who was then at the lycée] who has read the books of Schopenhauer, Hartmann, Stuart Mill, Spencer. Terror and disgust for life; mournful doctrine, despairing professors. Distressing conversations in progress. Uselessness of everything appears evident to these kids and devours them. I spent last evening trying to put new life into mine, giving him a rub down; and unwittingly comforted myself. . . ." Not having been able to find any kind of formula on any question of philosophy, he concluded: "I know one thing only, cry to my children: "Hurrah for life [*Vive la vie*]! Torn by pain as I am, it is hard."[11]

Not only his family, but also friends and members of his household have testified to the genuineness of his enthusiasm. André Ebner, his faithful secretary, wrote the following in the preface to *La Doulou:*

The love of life: . . . No man has experienced it more than he did. And this beautiful flame that shines through his writings, endows his characters with life and bestows so much glitter on the scenes he describes, would appear in its full radiance to those of us who were fortunate enough to know him. His enthusiasms were splendid. A radiance emanated from them; his great compassion, infinitely delicate, crept in the unfortunate's heart, which it warmed up with an almost divine warmth.[12]

Similar remarks had been made many times by these fortunate ones, among them Gustave Toudouze whose text is quoted on pages 115 - 16 of the present work.

The following is from an article written by Marcel Proust in 1897, four months before Alphonse Daudet's death, in which the future

author of *A la Recherche du Temps perdu* wanted "only to show . . .
how life offers man "beautiful subjects for meditation and . . .
elevation":

Everything has been said on Daudet as an artist. It seems to me that I have
something to say on Mr. Daudet as a work of art. . . . He also celebrated life,
besides making better use of it than many of us, kept on thinking, dictating,
and when he deemed his work could reach and impress his readers he would
write, as eager in the pursuit of truth as a young man, passionately fond of
courage, of beauty, constantly talking to us, and still braver by listening to
us.

We were talking about courage, and as he was reproaching those who
nowadays speak ill of courage and love, for impoverishing, draining the
momentum of life, he left the room for a while. . . . When a moment later he
returned, he resumed the conversation where he had left it, stirring it up
with the same fire — a fire which jets flames and which sings; for his sweet
and crackling voice is like a musical instrument, like a holiday-making music
in a sunshiny country. And yet, as I learned it later, it was because of the intensity of his pain that he had left us. That pain had become so sharp that he
almost fainted just as he stepped out of the drawing-room. . . . And now I
remember that upon his return his forehead was shining with beads of
perspiration. He looked as if coming from a fight, but he was breathing the
calmness of victory. . . .[13]

Lucien Daudet made the following comments on his father's idea of
life:

. . . As to his own life — and yet what is life unless we give this word the
ridiculous meaning of emancipation it had thirty years ago, "to live one's
own life," or that meaning just as much worn out and fallen in the most
sadly public domain, "to live dangerously"? No, he did not aim at either
"living his own life" nor living "dangerously." In short he did not give
much importance to himself nor to those who think too much about
themselves. . . . But he worshipped life, what he called life, that is, a
beautiful hour of sunshine, one of those days when, with tears in our eyes,
we say to ourselves "How good it is!" To him, this plenitude, this fullness is
life. . . .

And Lucien recalls that his father's first concern was his family's
good health and well-being, that he entertained no vanity, that he
was not one of those men of letters who think they must play a role
other than that of writing. In fact his impressions, intense feelings
and sensations, and especially his dreams animated by the most fertile imagination, made up the most important part of his life — of his

personal experiences which he put in his works. "I have not lived," he would say, "I dreamt" my life.[14]

Once, in a conversation with his elder son Léon, he made the following comments on life: "We live two parallel existences which complete each other, one an existence of emotion, the other of observation. To give prominence to one or the other of these existences is to give oneself up to unhappiness. Happiness lies in their equilibrium."[15]

Evidently, the reader's reaction to the above comments and remarks is bound to vary a good deal, not only according to the individual's temperament, education, and experience, but also according to the generation to which he belongs or in which he lives. In any case, the chances are that Alphonse Daudet would not have accepted the translation of his utterance "Vive la vie!" by "Live your life!" that is found in a popular American edition of his works. And this brings us back to the question of happiness.

IV *Marchand de Bonheur*

Daudet's natural, partly innate and partly acquired, passion for life was progressively intensified from the time he suffered from an acute tracheitis in 1861, and then from a violent hemoptysis in 1878, to the last fifteen years of his career, when his physical condition kept on worsening. He believed that everyone should appreciate the joy of living and, in view of his general experiences, soon became convinced that even the most destitute and prostrated human being could find some happiness in this world. Hence the more and more didactic aspect of his works and his cherished idea of becoming a purveyor, vendor of happiness. Lucien Daudet wrote, "My father was often wont to repeat: 'When my task is finished I should like to establish myself as a merchant of happiness [*un marchand de bonheur*]: my profit would be my success.' "[16] This "queer profession" would consist in putting his "experience of life and of suffering at the service of the host of unfortunates who do not know how to discern what there is still good and pleasurable to be found in the least favored existence."[17] Alphonse Daudet knew of course that happiness had to be achieved by the individual himself.

Alphonse Daudet had already expressed his compassion for the poor and the humble, the victims of either social or individual injustice or persecution, the underdog, in *Jack* and in other works. *Jack* may have caused investigations in industrial centers and ultimately led to social reforms regarding child labor. Professor Sachs considers the second part of *Jack* as "one of the earliest and one of the most effective outcries in fiction against child labor and the dehumanizing consequences of industrialisation."[18] *L'Evangéliste* was written to call attention to the plight of an unfortunate mother and to the danger of "excessive proselytism" by denouncing some evils "in a well-documented and convincing novel"; *La Petite Paroisse* dealt with man's happiness in married life, a rather important subject, regardless of a more or less cynical tradition in literature; and *Soutien de famille*, another "book of anger and compassion" concerned with family life struggling against injurious, harmful inclinations (*les volontés mauvaises*), was a book in which the questions of responsibility and reliability were involved and given the proper emphasis. It dealt also with government and politics, thus departing from the rule Daudet had until then imposed upon himself never to deal with either. However, even in this case, the emphasis remained definitely on the characters themselves.

Beside succoring in various ways people in distress, Alphonse Daudet extended his concern to man in general, whatever his station in life and whatever the nature of his unhappiness. He has undoubtedly helped thousands of readers, not only by depicting life as he saw it with its joys and sorrows and successes and failures, its ups and downs, but also by showing convincingly the possibility for man to find some joy in it whatever the circumstances of his life. It was with reference to Alphonse Daudet that, some seventy or seventy-five years ago, Edmund Gosse wrote the following: ". . . in an age when the cynical and the sinister take so wide a possession of literature, our thanks are eternally due to a man who built for us a world of hope and light and benignity."[19]

V   *Daudet's Humor and Charm*

While not agreeing entirely with either the form or contents of Daudet's novels, readers evidently kept on reading them, expressing their enthusiasm for the famous, but somehow undefinable, charm that bewitched them: "Daudet is a great enchanter who charms you even though you do not approve of him; you smile and applaud while grumbling,"[20] wrote Francisque Sarcey in his review of *L'Evangéliste*.

No doubt a good deal of this charm proceeds, as it has already been pointed out, from the classical qualities of his style, especially those of clearness, precision, and concision — his ability "to spare and measure his nerve," said Anatole France — that we find in his best pages; also from his ability to touch the reader in connection with common incidents of everyday life and occasionally by creating or suggesting an intense drama in the course of a very short story; or his ability to reveal a personality, recall an event, or sum up a situation by stressing certain details that may seem insignificant at first sight: for example, the sudden apparition of a forest-ranger's cap *(une casquette forestière)* shouting orders, the different positions of Tartarin's fez during the crossing to Algiers, or again the drawers of the chest in which it landed, crammed down to the ears on the head of its proprietor.

Most readers are naturally and completely won over if in addition they find wit and fine humor in a novel. Daudet's humor, which like Molière's varies considerably in both nature and quality, has undoubtedly procured him many admirers. He felt, however, that a particular aspect of it ought to be explained in order to avoid some misunderstandings — which we know as being of common occurrence.

There is in Mistral language, he wrote, a word which sums up and defines perfectly and thoroughly an instinct of the Provençal race: *galeja,* which means to rail, to joke. In Provence, *galeja* appears at every turn of the conversation, either as a verb or a substantive: *Veses pas? . . . Es uno galejado* ("Don't you see? . . . It's a joke"). *Taiso-te, galejaire!* ("Hold your tongue, you joker!") But being a *galejaire* does not exclude either kindness or fondness and affection. They simply want to laugh; and in Provence laughter goes with every feeling, the most impassioned as well as the most affectionate. . . . And I, too, am a *galejaire.*[21]

And so, the galéjades and tarasconnades of Tartarin and Numa Roumestan are the kind of good-humored banter that, as a matter of course, imply that free use of imagination which leads to exaggeration and at times to plain nonsense. It is not always handled with all the necessary tact and good taste one would expect but it is, notwithstanding appearances, generally devoid of meanness or wickedness — at worst a mild form of teasing. The author of *Tartarin de Tarascon* considered his hero's adventures as "a burst of laughter, a mere *galejado.*"

Daudet's humor can be, and usually is, very subtle and delicate. In his *Partial Portraits,* Henry James described it as "of the finest, . . . never violent nor vulgar . . . part of the high spirits . . . that accompany the temperament of his race."[22] Anatole France, the author of *Crainquebille* and *Pinguins Island,* found "something musical and light" about his laughter: ". . . And how innocent his enormous gaiety can be! . . . this is the beautiful 'galejade,' a whistling of mockingbird under the dark pines in the blue sky, a winged thing, a divine thing."[23]

But besides the charm of his talent, there is that of the man himself. Beside his knowledge of, and feeling for, language, there is his delicate sensibility, his friendly approach, his constant desire to please, his concern for the reader, whom he always respects. Alphonse Daudet is never coarse in his books, not even when dealing with a risqué, scabrous subject. He was, shockingly so, to be sure, in his conversations with his friends at the dinners of the "auteurs sifflés," but Alphonse Daudet would discriminate between the spoken and written language, as he did between his listeners. He was not writing only for himself and a few kindred souls. He wanted to be understood by all, and he succeeded in attracting and satisfying everyone — the common people without appealing to their lower instincts, and the worldly-wise without indulging in their lofty bearing or pretentiousness. And when he appealed to a man's feeling of compassion for the outcast of fortune (les déshérités), or victims of particular circumstances, he won him over by that genuine human warmth, that special charm that has been defined in so many different ways.

But the critics' overemphasis of this charm has undoubtedly irritated the few who are invulnerable to it, and particularly those who, in his time, for some reason disliked him and envied his rising reputation. We have seen how the precocious child, the unmanageable "Petit Chose," and still later the handsome young man spoiled by his various successes, conscious of his own value and concerned only, or mostly, with himself, asserted his independence by indulging in all kinds of eccentricities. He may well have deserved, in those days, all the reproaches he incurred later. The important fact however is that early in life Alphonse Daudet had been keenly aware of his ability to see clearly within himself, as if there were two beings in him, he said, one who felt and acted, and the other who followed him everywhere, observed, and analyzed his actions.[24]

This second self overpowered the other and made the slothful, weakling Petit Chose mend his way and succeed where so many others failed. Thus the once irresponsible, rebellious, and pessimistic individual developed a tremendous willpower, a moral force which enabled him not only to achieve most of his goal as a writer, as an artist, but also as a man who felt that he had an obligation to fulfill.

The attentive reader of his work cannot fail to marvel at the amount of energy, courage, and fortitude which Alphonse Daudet had to summon up in order to avoid interference with the realization of his aim, that of achieving the highest degree of perfection in his art so that, without preaching or moralizing, he could effectively counteract the inherent pessimism of the younger generation.

Perhaps his greatest merit has been indeed his ability to reveal himself not only as an author but also as a man whose personality comes up to the ideal one of the seventeenth-century *honnête homme,* the humble gentleman "who does not plume or pride himself on anything." And this may well be, after all, the most important aspect of his charm.

Notes and References

Chapter One

1. *Le Petit Chose*, in *Oeuvres complètes illustrées*, Editions Ne Varietur (Paris: Librairie de France, 1929 - 1930), II, 3 (hereafter referred to as *O.C.*).
2. "Lyon. Souvenirs d'enfance," in *Etudes et Paysages*, in *O.C.*, V, 125 - 26.
3. *Le Petit Chose*, in *O.C.*, II, 13.
4. Ibid., p. 17.
5. The original story, "Le Pape est mort," will be found in *Contes du Lundi*, *O.C.*, IV, 141 - 44. For a translation into English, see "The Pope is dead," in *The Novels, Romances and Writings of Alphonse Daudet*, III, 270 - 76. (this edition will be hereafter referred to as *D's Writings*).
6. *My Brother and I*, in *D's Writings*, XX, 377.
7. A degree for which a French student registering in an American university is usually given a junior standing.
8. *Le Petit Chose*, in *O.C.*, II, 30.
9. Ernest Daudet, *Mon Frère et Moi*, p. 186 (or *My Brother and I*, in *D's Writings*, XX, 402).
10. *Le Petit Chose*, in *O.C.*, II, 47 - 48.
11. *Trente ans de Paris*, in *O.C.*, XII, 1 - 5.
12. Léon Gambetta (1838 - 1882). One of the most prominent statesmen during the Second Empire and the first years of the Third Republic. He left besieged Paris (Oct. 7, 1870) in a balloon to organize the French army on the Loire river.
13. *Trente ans de Paris, O.C.*, XII, 7.
14. *My Brother and I, D.'s Writings*, XX, 412.
15. "La Jeunesse d'Alphonse Daudet," *O.C.*, I, 104.
16. *Les Amoureuses, O.C.*, I, 31 - 33.
17. Ibid., pp. 1 - 3, 15 - 16.
18. Cf. Paul Ginesty in Henri Murger, *Scènes de la Vie de Bohème*, p. xix.
19. *Scènes de la Vie de Bohème*, Préface, cv, cix - cxvi. Murger comments on those who, having somehow succeeded in "overcoming" bohemia, and chosen to stay with it, "become its authoritative representatives." "They

belong," he explains, "to that class of semifailures" who can be seen everywhere, who are so well known that "they cannot take ten steps on the boulevards without meeting a friend, and thirty steps "without meeting a creditor." But they exploit it to the best of their ability (Ibid., p. cxv).
  20. Pierre Labracherie, *La Vie quotidienne de la Bohème littéraire*, pp. 129 - 30. See also J. H. Bornecque, *Les Années d'apprentissage d'Alphonse Daudet*, pp. 118ff.
  21. For a detailed, complete and fascinating account, see "La fin d'un pitre," where Daudet refers to Georges Destouches, whom he calls Desroches, and further names Courbet, Gustave Mathieu, Monselet, and Alexandre Leclerc.
  22. It has been pointed out that "Marie R. . . ." could be interpreted as referring to Marie (Mariette) Reynaud, his cousin (Cf. Bornecque, *Les Années, p. 157*).

Chapter Two

  1. *Trente ans de Paris, O.C.,* XII, 45.
  2. *The Armana prouvençau* was published for the first time in 1855. Alphonse Daudet could not therefore have seen it when he was twelve or thirteen, as suggested in his preface to Batisto Bonnet's, *Vie d'enfant,* Cf. *O.C.,* XIV, vi - vii.
  3. *The Century Illustrated Montly Magazine,* May 1885, XXX, 416 - 22. Apparently a poor translation of Daudet's original French, which we have not been able to see.
  4. G. V. Dobie, *Alphonse Daudet,* p. 83.
  5. Published in Paris, in 1866, pp. 301 - 303.
  6. Lucien Daudet, *Vie d'Alphonse Daudet,* p. 60.
  7. *Le Petit Chose, O.C.,* II, i - ii.
  8. *Lettres de mon moulin, O.C.,* III, vii.
  9. *Lettres à un absent, O.C.,* III, 13.
  10. *O.C.,* III, 145 - 55; and *Robert Helmont, O.C.,* V, ii - 50.
  11. See paragraph on *L'Arlésienne,* in *Fromont jeune, O.C.,* V, ii.
  12. The Arlesian woman has been identified by name for the first time by Mme Marie-Thérèse Jouveau in a most interesting brochure, *Il y a cinquante ans mourrait l'Arlésienne* (published at Aix-en-Provence by René Jouveau, 28 Rue du Maréchal Joffre, 1972.
  13. Lucien D., *Vie,* p. 101.
  14. *Tartarin de Tarascon, O.C.,* IV, ii.
  15. Ibid., pp. 21 - 23.

Chapter Three

  1. *Fromont jeune, O.C.,* V, ii.
  2. Ibid., pp. vii - viii.
  3. Emile Zola, *Les Oeuvres complètes,* 50 vol, Texte de l'édition E. Fasquelle 1910. Typographie François Bernouard, XLII, 226.

4. Lucien D., *Vie d'Alphonse Daudet*, pp. 121 - 22.

5. Léon D., *Quand vivait mon père*, pp. 16 - 17. Cf. Lucien D., *Vie*, p. 102; G. Benoît-Guyod, *Alphonse Daudet*, pp. 174 - 75.

6. Quoted by Emery Neff, *Edwin Arlington Robinson*, p. 58.

7. G. V. Dobie, *Alphonse Daudet*, pp. 179 - 80.

8. *Jack*, O.C., VI, xii; Albert Thibaudet, *Histoire de la littérature française de 1789 à nos jours*, p. 369.

9. O.C., VI, 481 - 96.

10. Marian McIntyre in her introduction to *Jack, in D's Writings*, XVIII, xxv.

11. Quoted by Lucien D. *Vie*. p. 124.

12. Théodore de Banville in Le National, Feb. 4, 1878, quoted in O.C., VII, 412; also, ibid., 404 - 405ff, 426.

13. Lucien D., *Vie*, pp. 128 - 29.

14. *Journal des Goncourt*, November 23, 1877.

15. Benoît-Guyod, *Alphonse Daudet*, pp. 183 - 84.

16. *Le Nabab*, "Declaration de l'auteur figurant en tête de la 37e éd., datée de 1878". O.C., VII, ii.

17. Edmond et Jules de Goncourt, *Journal Mémoires de la vie littéraire*, January 31, 1876. Henceforth referred to as E. & J. de Goncourt, *Journal*.

18. "Autour du *Nabab*," O.C., VII, 387 - 88.

19. *Le Nabab*, O.C., VII, iii.

20. *Les Rois en exil*, O.C., VIII, i.

21. E. & J. de Goncourt, *Journal*, Feb. 1, 1880.

22. *Numa Roumestan*, O.C., IX, v.

23. Ibid., pp. 25. Indeed the name Rosalie was part of Mme Daudet's maiden name, exactly: Julie Rosalie Céleste Allard.

24. Lucien D., *Vie*, pp. 151ff.

Chapter Four

1. *Sapho*, O.C., X, 114 - 15.

2. Ibid., pp. 159 - 60.

3. Gustave Lanson, *Histoire de la Littérature française*, 22nd ed., p. 1084.

4. Henry James translated and quoted by G. V. Dobie. See James' very interesting letter to A. D., written in perfect French (*The Letters of Henry James*, ed. Percy Lubbock, vol. 1, pp. 108 - 9).

5. *La Revue indépendante*, June, 1884; "Autour de *Sapho*," O.C., X, 196.

6. Léon Daudet, *Quand vivait mon père*, pp. 162 - 67.

7. Lucien D., *Vie*, p. 183.

8. "Autour de *Tartarin sur les Alpes*," O.C., X, 148.

9. Ibid., p. 151.

10. *Tartarin sur les Alpes*, p. 141.

11. *La Doulou*, in O.C., XVII, 5.

12. *Pages inédites de critique dramatique*, O.C., XVIII, 300.
13. Paul Belon in *Le Parti National*, July 14, 1888, in "Autour de *l'Immortel*," O.C., XI, 210.
14. *L'Immortel*, O.C., XI, 211.
15. Ibid., p. 176.
16. *La Lutte pour la vie*, Preface, O.C., XX, 323, 379 - 80.
17. *L'Immortel*, O.C., p. 68.
18. Ibid., p. 29.
19. Lucien D., *Vie*, p. 216; Cf. *La Doulou*, O.C., xvii, 15.
20. *La Doulou*, O.C., xvii, 23.

Chapter Five

1. *Port Tarascon*, O.C., XIII, 3.
2. Ibid., p. 5.
3. Ibid., p. 17.
4. Ibid., pp. 15 - 16.
5. Ibid., p. 34.
6. Ibid., p. 24.
7. Ibid., p. 84.
8. Ibid., p. 112.
9. Ibid., pp. 150, 181 - 82.
10. In *Le Temps*, Nov. 9, 1890, O.C., XIII, 181 - 83.
11. *Port-Tarascon. The Last Adventures of the Illustrious Tartarin*, translated by Henry James, pp. 7 - 8.
12. *Armana prouvençau per 1891*; and O.C., XIII, 185.
13. Lucien D., *Vie* p. 231.
14. Ibid., p. 234.
15. Léon D., *A. D.*, in *D's Writings*, XX, 16 - 19. 35 - 39, 46 - 47.
16. *La Doulou*, O.C., XVII, 27, 29.
17. Lucien D., *Vie*, p. 247.
18. Batisto Bonnet, *Le "Baïle" Alphonse Daudet*, pp. 4 - 10, 62 - 70.
19. Bonnet, *Le Baïle*, pp. 432 - 35.
20. Ibid., pp. 436 - 39.
21. Lucien D., *Vie*, pp. 73, 94, 243 - 44.
22. Ibid., p. 252.
23. Ibid., p. 253 - 55.
24. *La Petite Paroisse*, O.C., XV, 11 - 14.
25. "What a marvelous feeling machine *(machine à sentir)*" I have been, especially during my childhood . . . How porous and penetrating I have been: impressions, sensations, enough to fill piles of books and all of them as intense as dreams." *(Notes sur la vie*, O.C., XVI, 54 - 55.
26. "Autour de *La Petite Paroisse*," O.C., XV, 232 - 49.
27. "Autour de *Soutien de famille*," O.C., XVI, 289.
28. André Billy, *Vie des Frères Goncourt*, III, 32, 36.
29. Goncourt, *Journal*, Feb. 60 1889.

30. André Billy, *Vie des frères Goncourt*, III, 36.

31. Gustave Toudouze, Pages choisies d'Alphonse Daudet, pp. 20 - 21

32. See *Journal*, Feb. 20, 1895.

33. Léon D., *Quand vivait mon père*, p. 290.

34. Lucien D., *Vie, p. 259.*

35. Andrè Billy, *Vie des Frères Goncourt*, III, 107, Cf. pp. 103 - ff., which contain a detailed account of this great social event.

36. *Journal*, p. 267.

37. G. V. Dobie, *Alphonse Daudet*, pp. 270 - 71. More details will be found in "Henry James, Daudet and Oxford," by John C. Major, *Notes and Queries*, Feb. 1966, vol. 211, pp. 69 - 70.

Chapter Six

1. "La Fédor," *O,C,*, XV, 24, 28

2. *Premier Voyage, Premier mensonge, O.C.,* XV, 6, 23.

3. Ibid., pp. 25 - 31.

4. Ibid., pp. 31 - 36.

5. Goncourt *Journal*, March 22, 1896, March 29 & April 12 (XXI, 217), See André Billy for futher details, pp. 116ff.

6. Goncourt, *Journal* March 29, 1896.

7. *Le Trésor d'Arlatan, O.C.,* vol. XVII ("En Camargue": In Provençal, this title would be "En Camargo").

8. Ibid., XVII, 42ff.

9. Ibid.

10. *Journal* . . . , April 18, 1896.

11. Ibid., April 21, 24, 25, and May 30, 1896.

12. On February, 1894, Edmond de Goncourt had written the following in his *Journal*: "A l'heure présente, il n'y a que lui que j'aime parmi mes contemporains, et il n'y a parmi les maisons où je vais où je me trouve du plaisir d'aller." The *Journal* ended on July 3, 1896. For a more detailed analysis of this great literary friendship, see André Billy, *Vie des Frères Goncourt*, 3 volumes, particularly the chapter entitled "Les Amis de Daudet,"and "Les Cinq" (the Five Friends), II, 181 - 95, 107 - 207.

13. "Ultima," *O.C.*, XVI, 102; also, *Notes sur la vie, O.C.*, XVI, 33, 36.

14. "Ultima," *O.C.*, XVI, 104.

15. ". . . they are still quoting Lucien's angry words against his father, after being scolded by him: 'That old famous man!' And suddenly the expression has become fashionable in D's home, where we are referred to as 'the two old famous men'." Goncourt *Journal*, Aug. 4, 1895.

16. *O.C.*, XVI, 105 - 6.

17. Ibid., p. 114.

18. In a letter to Edmund Gosse, dated August 28, 1896, Henry James describes "Ultima" as "a little miracle of art, adroitness, demoniac tact and skill, and taste so abysmal, judged by our fishlike sense, that there is no getting alongside of it at all." (*The Letters of Henry James*. Selected and edited

by Percy Lubbock, vol. I, pp. 247 - 48. New York: Charles Scribner's Sons, 1920.

19. Edmond de Goncourt had written — on Oct. 3, 1875 — the following in his *Journal*: "What I ask above all from God is to die in my home, in my own bedroom. The thought of death at someone else's home is repugnant to me."

20. Lucien D., *Vie*, pp. 269 - 70; André Billy, *Vie des Frères G.*, III, 184.

21. *O.C.* XVI, 89 - 95, 139 - 45.

22. Batisto Bonnet, *Le "Baïle" Alphonse Daudet*, p. 382 ff.

23. Quoted by Lucien, *Vie*, p. 272.

24. *Soutien de famille*, *O.C.*, XVI, 210.

25. Ibid.

26. Batisto Bonnet, *Le "Baïle"*, pp. 442 - 43.

27. Benoît-Guyod, *Alphonse Daudet. Son temps, son œuvre*, p. 247.

28. *Le Journal*, December 18, 1897, in Zola's Oeuvres complètes, XII, 722 - 23.

29. "Alphonse Daudet,"in *L'Aurore*, Dec. 18, 1897, *O.C.* , XII, i - ii.

Chapter Seven

1. Armand de Pontmartin, in *La Gazette de France*, July 15, 1888, and Francisque Sarcey in *Le Parti national*, July 13, 1888, and in "Autour de l'Immortel," *O.C.*, XI, 209 - 11.

2. In *Journal des Débats*, July 16 and August 20, 1888; and *O.C.*, XI, 214.

3. Henry James, *Partial Portraits*, p. 234.

4. As we have seen, Marcel Proust was a great admirer of Alphonse Daudet.

5. Barbey d'Aurevilly, "Le Théâtre contemporain," in *Le Nain jaune*, Dec. 29, 1867. Quoted by Martinet, *A.D. (1840 - 1897)*, p. 257.

6. "Histoire de mes livres," *Tartarin de Tarascon*, *O.C.*, IV, vii.

7. *Soutien de famille*, *O.C.*, XVI, 228.

8. *L'Immortel*, *O.C.*, XI, 143 - 45.

9. *Numa Roumestan*, IX, *O.C.*, vol. 27.

10. Ibid., pp. 37 - 39.

11. Ibid., pp. 13 - 15.

12. Cf. pp. 144 - 45 of this work.

13. "Autour de *Numa Roumestan*," *O.C.*, IX, 237.

14. Louis Michel, *Le Langage méridional dans l'œuvre d'Alphonse Daudet*, p. 228.

15. Paul Bourget, in *Le Parlement*, Oct. 19, 1881, and *O.C.*, IX, 257.

16. "Histoire de mes livres," *Tartarin de Tarascon*, *O.C.*, IV, vii.

17. Albert Thibaudet, *Réflexions sur la littérature*, II, 199 - 204, 182 - 86.

18. Preface to *Les Morts heureuses* by Lepelletier, in "Préface," *O.C.*, XII, 11 - 13.

19. "Autour de *l'Evangéliste*," *O.C.*, IX, 216.

Chapter Eight

1. In *Souvenirs d'un homme de lettres* ("Pages retrouvées"), *O.C.*, XII, 139 - 40.
2. Cf. "Le Rouge et le blanc," in *Etudes et Paysages*, *O.C.*, V, 163; "Epilogue," pp. 167 - 68, 215 - 16. Cf. also "Une champignonnière de grands hommes" in "Lettres à un absent," *O.C.*, III, 94; also, Paul Arène, "Pessègue et Tigassou," in *Au Pays du soleil; Twenty-three Stories from Provence*, ed. Roche & Roche (Boston: D. C. Heath & Co., 1950).
3. "Histoire de mes livres," *O.C.*, III, vi.
4. In "Autour du *Petit Chose*," *O.C.*, II, 258.
5. In *D's Writings*, XX, 174.
6. Lucien D., *Vie*, p. 243; *La Doulou*, *O.C.*, XVII, 29, 39.
7. Benoît-Guyod, *Alphonse Daudet*, Cf. *Notes sur la vie*, *O.C.*, XVI, 73.
8. Yvonne Martinet, *Alphonse Daudet (1840 - 1897). Sa vie et son œuvre*, p. 731.
9. *D's Writings*, XX, 173.
10. *Tartarin sur les Alpes*, *O.C.*, X, 121.
11. *Notes sur la vie*, *O.C.*, XVI, 34.
12. André Ebner, Préface, *O.C.*, XVII, ii.
13. *La Presse*, August 11, 1897, *O.C.*, XVI, 62 - 65.
14. Lucien D., *Vie*, pp. 180 - 81.
15. *D.'s Writings*, XX, 148 - 149.
16. Ibid., p. 189.
17. *Soutien de famille*, *O.C.*, XVI, 62. Lucien reports that, according to his father's contemporaries, it was less his witticisms or his good stories than the propriety of his remarks and the wealth of his knowledge and experience, that made his conversation unique. Lucien supposes that when he referred to the idea of becoming "a merchant of happiness," his father had in mind the possibility of imparting this knowledge, thus enabling his interlocutors to profit by his experience. (*Vie*, p. 248).
18. Murray Sachs, *The Career of Alphonse Daudet: A Critical Study*, p. 102.
19. Edmund Gosse, *French Profiles*, p. 128.
20. Francisque Sarcey, in *Le XIXᴱ Siècle*, April, 1883, *O.C.*, IX, 227.
21. *O.C.*, IV, iv - vi.
22. Henry James, *Partial Portraits*, pp. 217 - 18.
23. In *La Revue de Paris*, January 1, 1898; *O.C.*, 175 - 76. Cf. again Henry James: "there are tears in his laughter and there is a strain of laughter in his tears; and in both there is a note of music." (*Atlantic Monthly* 49 (June, 1882), XLIX, 851).
24. He warned that this "redoubtable, ferocious" overseer, this second self, was not to be confused with what is commonly called conscience, "for conscience," he explains further, "preaches, scolds, gets involved in our acts, modifies or stops them. Moreover, one can easily put it to sleep, this good

conscience." The witness in question did not interfere, it only supervised. It was an inside eye, impassive and fixed, an inert and cold look which during the Petit Chose's most lively, fiery sprees observed everything, and took notes, and the next day would say: "Now, we two will have it out [*A nous deux maintenant*]! . . . Oh! that second self, always sitting while the other is standing, acts, suffers, struggles! . . . He could never make it cry, nor put it to sleep" (*O.C.*, XVI, i).

Selected Bibliography

PRIMARY SOURCES

1. Collected Works

Alphonse Daudet, *Oeuvres complètes illustrées*, Edition Ne Varietur. 20 vols. Paris: Librairie de France, 1929 - 31. Three other collective editions of Daudet's works have been published in Paris: the first one by Dentu & Charpentier in 1881 - 87, 8 vols., the second by Fayard in 1897 - 99, 24 vols., and the third by Alexandre Houssiaux in 1899 - 1901, 18 vols. The 1929 - 31 Ne Varietur edition is the best. It is not quite complete, but it contains many texts that are unavailable elsewhere: prefaces written by Alphonse Daudet, extracts from his notebooks and from reviews of his works, as well as useful information concerning their publication. However, it is not always easy to use. Time should be taken to copy the titles of books contained in each volume, which the editors have failed to do. For example, volume V contains *Fromont jeune et Risler aîné*, pp. 1 - 271, "Autour de Fromont jeune et Risler aîné*, pp. 275 - 308, "Table des matières," pp. 309 - 10. In this same volume, on next page, is *Etudes et Paysages*, with a new pagination (pp. 1 - 221). *(Robert Helmont* is part of it, pp. i - v, 1 - 50), and "Table des matières," p. 223. Volume XII contains *Trente ans de Paris*, pp. 1 - 143 (Pages retrouvées, pp. 95 - 143), "Table des matières" on p. 143; Next, in same volume, *Souvenirs d'un homme de lettres*, pp. 1 - 143 (Pages retrouvées, pp. 71 - 143), "Table des matières" on p 144; and, next again in same volume, *Préfaces*, pp. 1 - 27. "Table des matières" on p. 29, which represents in all 320 pages.
The Novels, Romances and Writings of Alphonse Daudet. 20 vols. New York (The Athenaeum Society) Boston: Little, Brown and Co., 1898 - 1903. With an introduction by Brander Matthews (pp. vii - xlii).

2. Original Editions (Place of Publication is Paris unless otherwise noted)

Les Amoureuses. Poems. Tardieu, 1858.
La Double Conversion. A versified short story. Poulet-Malassis et de Broise, 1861.

La Dernière Idole. A one-act drama in prose. Coll. Ernest Lépine. Michel Lévy, frères, 1862.

Le Roman du Chaperon rouge. Scènes et fantaisies. Michel Lévy, 1862.

Les Absents. Proverbe. Dupré de la Mahérie, 1863.

L'Oeillet blanc, A one-act comedy, in prose. Michel Lévy, frères, 1865.

Le Frère aîné. A one-act drama. Coll. Ernest Manuel. Michel Lévy, frères 1868.

Le Petit Chose. Histoire d'un enfant. J. Hetzel, 1868.

Le Sacrifice. A three-act comedy. Lacroix, Verboeckhoven et Cie., 1869.

Lettres de mon moulin. Impressions et souvenirs, J. Hetzel, 1869.

Lettres à un absent, Alphonse Lemerre, 1870 - 71.

L'Arlésienne. A three-act play and five scenes with musical interlude and chorus by Georges Bizet; first performance at the Vaudeville theater, Oct. 1, 1872. Alphonse Lemerre, 1872.

Lise Tavernier. A five-act drama and seven scenes. E. Dentu, 1872.

Aventures prodigieuses de Tartarin de Tarascon. E. Dentu, 1872.

Contes du lundi. Lemerre, 1873.

Les Femmes d'artistes. Novelettes. Lemerre, 1874.

Fromont jeune et Risler aîné. Moeurs parisiennes. Charpentier et Cie., 1874.

Robert Helmont, Journal d'un solitaire. E. Dentu, 1874.

Jack. Moeurs contemporaines. Dentu, 1876, 2 vols.

Le Char. One-act Comic Opera in Free Verse. Coll. Paul Arène. Charpentier, 1878.

Les Rois en exil. A Parisian novel. E. Dentu, 1879.

Numa Roumestan. Moeurs parisiennes. Charpentier, 1881.

L'Evangéliste. Roman parisien. E. Dentu, 1883.

Sapho. Moeurs parisiennes. Charpentier, 1884.

Tartarin sur les Alpes. Nouveaux exploits du héros tarasconnais. Illustrated with water colors. Calmann Lévy, 1885.

La Belle Nivernaise. Histoire d'un vieux bateau et de son équipage. C. Marpon et Flammarion, 1886.

L'Immortel. Moeurs parisiennes. Lemerre, 1888.

Souvenirs d'un Homme de lettres. Pages retrouvées. Illustrations by Bieler, Montégut, Myrbach and Rossi. Marpon et Flammarion, 1888.

Trente ans de Paris. A travers ma vie et mes livres. Marpon et Flammarion, 1888.

La Lutte pour la vie. A five-act play, six scenes. Calmann Lévy, 1890.

Port-Tarascon. Dernières aventures de l'illustre Tartarin. Dentu, 1890.

L'Obstacle. A four-act play. Marpon et Flammarion, 1891.

Rose et Ninette. Moeurs du jour. With a Frontispice by Marold, Flammarion, 1893.

La Menteuse. A Play. Coll. Léon Hennique, Flammarion, 1893.

Entre les Frises et la rampe. Petites études de la vie théâtrale, Dentu, 1894.

La Petite Paroisse. Moeurs conjugales. Lemerre, 1895.

L'Enterrement d'une Etoile (La Fédor), Flammarion, 1896.
Le Trésor d'Arlatan. A novel. Illustrations by H. Laurent Desrousseaux. Librairie Charpentier et Fasquelle, 1897.
Soutien de famille. Moeurs contemporaines Eugène Fasquelle, 1898.
Notes sur la vie. Bibliothèque Charpentier, Fasquelle, 1899.
Premier Voyage, Premier Mensonge. Souvenirs de mon enfance. Illustrations by Bigot-Valentin. Flammarion, 1900.
Pages inédites de critique dramatique, 1874 - 1880. Ernest Flammarion, 1923.
La Doulou: Extraits des carnets inédits." This volume of the *Oeuvres complètes* edition . . . constitutes the original edition of *La Doulou.*"

3. Writings in Provençal

"En Camargue." A short poem used as an epigraph to *Le Trésor d'Arlatan* (see p. 124).
"La Manécantarié." In *L'Aiòli, que vai cremant tres fes pèr mes* which appears three times a month (on the 7, 17 and 27). No. 11, p. 1, April 17, 1891.
"La Cabro de Moussu Seguin." Ibid., no. 17, p. 2. June 17, 1891.
"La Miolo dóu papo." Ibid., no. 47, p. 1, April 17, 1892.

SECONDARY SOURCES

1. Books

ALBALAT, ANTOINE. *L'Amour chez Alphonse Daudet:* Essai, Ollendorff, 1884. Worth reading as an introduction to the subject.
BEAUME, GEORGES. *Les Lettres de mon moulin d'Alphonse Daudet*, Les grands événements littéraires. E. Malfère, 1929. Interesting historical and biographical details. Also, some penetrating remarks regarding the originality of the *Lettres*.
BENOÎT-GUYOD, GEORGES, *Alphonse Daudet, son temps, son œuvre*. Editions Jules Taillandier, 1947. A reliable biography. Quotes some interesting letters.
BONNET, BATISTO. *Le "Batle" Alphonse Daudet*, Flammarion, 1912. Daudet as seen by a most grateful protégé and enthusiastic admirer.
BORNECQUE, JACQUES-HENRY. *Les années d'apprentissage d'Alphonse Daudet*. Librairie Nizet, 1951. Thèse. A very detailed analysis of D.'s life and works, up to 1886. Much information not to be found elsewhere.
BRUYÈRE, MARCEL. *La jeunesse d'Alphonse Daudet*. Nouvelle édition latine, 1955. Result of research on the Daudet family.
BURNS, MARY. *La langue d'Alphonse Daudet*. Thèse. Jouve et Cie., 1916. A good, thorough study of Daudet's vocabulary.

ULOGENSON, Y. E. *Alphonse Daudet peintre de la vie de son temps*. Janin, 1946. Limited to the subject indicated by the title, but well thought-out and well written.

DAUDET, ERNEST. *Mon frère et moi*. Librairie Plon, 1882. Engl. tr. *My Brother and I* (in *The Novels, Romances and Writings of A.D.*, vol. XX). The first expression of admiration by a member of the family. Limited to Alphonse's childhood and adolescence.

DAUDET, LÉON. *Alphonse Daudet*. Fasquelle, 1898 (in the *Novels, Romances, and Writings of A.D.*, vol. XX). A filial tribute and discussion of A.'s ideas in various fields.

————. *Quand vivait mon père*. Grasset, 1940. Interesting comments on events and people well known by author.

DAUDET, LUCIEN. *Vie d'Alphonse Daudet*. Gallimard, 1941. An honest account, as objective as could be expected from an admiring son.

DOBIE, G.V. *Alphonse Daudet*. London: Thomas Nelson, 1949. A reliable biography; contains interesting facts regarding England and some English friends and writers.

DEGOUMOIS, Léon. *L'Algérie d'Alphonse Daudet; d'après "Tartarin de Tarascon" et divers fragments des autres œuvres. Essai sur les sources et les procédés d'imitation d'Alphonse Daudet*. Genève: Editions Sonor, 1922. The title and subtitles are descriptive of the contents.

KRUGLIKOFF, ALEXANDER. *Alphonse Daudet et la Provence*. Thèse. Jouve et Cie., 1936.

MARTINET, YVONNE. *Alphonse Daudet (1840 - 1897). Sa vie et son œuvre. Mémoires et Récits*. Gap. Imprimerie Louis-Jean, 1940. A very monumental (over 800 pages) and useful work which should be revised by author. Must be used cautiously.

MICHEL, LOUIS. *Le langage dans l'œuvre d'Alphonse Daudet*. Editions d'Artre, 1961. An excellent study.

RATTI, GINO A. *Les idées morales et littéraires d'Alphonse Daudet d'après son œuvre*. Thèse. Grenoble: Léon Aubert, 1911.

SACHS, MURRAY. *The Career of Alphonse Daudet*. A critical study. Camb., Mass.: Harvard University Press, 1965. A solid, well-written and thought-provoking study.

SAYLOR, G. R. *Alphonse Daudet as a dramatist*. Philadelphia: University of Pennsylvania Press, 1940.

SHERARD, R. H. *Alphonse Daudet, A Biographical and Critical Study*. London: Edward Arnold, 1894. More biographical than critical.

TRIVAS, DR. MARY, *Le douloureux calvaire d'Alphonse Daudet. Auto-observation d'un tabétique de qualité*. Les éditions Vegas, 1932.

2. General Articles in Books and Magazines

ALBALAT, ANTOINE. *Gustave Flaubert et ses amis*, avec des lettres inédites. Librairie Plon, 1927.

Selected Bibliography 183

AUCHINCLOSS, LOUIS. *Reflexions of a Jacobite*. Boston: Houghton Mifflin Co., 1961. The first nine pages are devoted to Alphonse Daudet. Reaction of the author upon a second reading of *Fromont jeune* twenty years later.

AURIANT. *Quatre héros d'Alphonse Daudet: Sapho, Flamant, Alice Doré, Tartarin, suivi de quatorze essais* . . . , Mercure de France, 1948. Title is somewhat misleading. Only forty pages devoted to the "four heroes." The remaining 261 pages deal with other subjects.

BADESCO, LUC. *La Génération poétique de 1860. La jeunesse des deux rives*. Nizet, 1971.

––––. "Controverse autour d'Alphonse Daudet." *Revue d'Histoire littéraire de la France*. July - September, 1964, pp. 473 - 78. Controversy with J. H. Bornecque.

BARBEY d'AUREVILLY. *Le Roman contemporain*. A. Lemerre, 1902. Articles previously published in *Le Constitutionnel*. Reviews the *Lettres de mon moulin, Jack, Le Nabab, Les Rois en Exil*. Author admires Daudet as a stylist, but criticizes the naturalistic element in his works, especially in *Les Rois en exil*.

BÉRAUD, HENRI. "Retour sentimental vers A.D." In *Oeuvres complètes d'A.D.*, 1929 - 30 Ne Varietur edition, *O.C.*, I, i-xxviii.

BEUCHAT, CHARLES. *Histoire du Naturalisme français*. 2 vols. Edition Corrêa, 1949.

BILLY, ANDRÉ. *Vie des Frères Goncourt*, précédant le Journal d'Edmond et de Jules de Goncourt. 3 vols. Les éditions de l'Imprimerie nationale de Monaco. Fasquelle et Flammarion, 1956.

BLOY, LÉON. *Belluaires et Porchers*. P.V. Stock 1905. "Le voleur de gloire," concerns A.D. One of those essays that cannot be taken seriously. Written in 1888.

BORNECQUE, J.-H. "Alphonse Daudet et l'amour fatal." *Le Monde*, February 6, 1951. Concerns *L'Arlésienne*.

BRUNETIÈRE, FERDINAND. *Le Roman naturaliste*. Calman Lévy 1882, pp. 9 - 12, 75 - 102.

CARTER, BOYD. "Alphonse Daudet and Darwinism." *Modern Language Quarterly*, March, 1945, pp. 93 - 98. An excellent summary of the question.

––––. "Alphonse Daudet in memoriam, 1840 - 1940." *French Review*, (Oct., 1940), 14, 21 - 25. A praiseworthy homage to A.D.

CÉARD, HENRY. "Préface de l'édition collective, 1899." In *O.C.*, pp. 131 - 68.

DAUDET, ERNEST. "La jeunesse d'Alphonse Daudet." In "Autour des Amoureuses," *O.C.*, I, 99 - 115.

––––. *Souvenirs de mon temps*. Débuts d'un homme de lettres, 1857 - 61. Plon, 1921.

DAUDET, MME ALPHONSE. *Souvenirs autour d'un groupe littéraire*. Charpentier, 1910.

DEFFOUX, LÉON. *Le Naturalisme* avec un florilège des principaux écrivains naturalistes. See especially pp. 70 - 77 and passim. A well-chosen abstract is on pp. 208 - 11.

DOUMIC, RENÉ. *Portraits d'écrivains.* Paul Delaplane, 1892. A short analysis of Daudet's works up to 1892.

DUMESNIL, RENÉ. *L'Epoque réaliste et naturaliste.* Editions Jules Taillandier, 1945. A most interesting "histoire de la vie littéraire" of the period. "Alphonse Daudet à Paris et à Champrosay," pp. 137 - 53.

————. *Le Réalisme* in *Histoire de la littérature française* publiée sous la direction de J. Calvet, J. de Gigord, Editeur, 1936. Pp. 469 - 85 passim are devoted to A.D. See Index.

FAGUET, EMILE. *Propos littéraires,* fourth series. Société d'imprimerie et de librairie. Ancienne librairie Lecène, Oudin & Cie. 1907 pp. 247 - 57. Most interesting remarks on "Les carnets d'A.D." regarding *Notes sur la vie.*

FAVREAU, ALPHONSE R. "British Criticism of Daudet, 1872 - 1897." *PMLA,* June, 1937, pp. 528 - 39. A thoroughly well-organized study.

GONCOURT, EDMOND et JULES DE, *Journal: Mémoires de la vie littéraire.* Avant-Propos de l'Académie Goncourt. Texte intégral établi et annoté par Robert Ricate. 22 vols. Monaco. Les éditions de l'Imprimerie nationale de Monaco. Fasquelle et Flammarion, 1956. Many references to A.D. and his family. At times fascinating but not always reliable. See Index.

GROVER, PHILIP. *Henry James and the French Novel:* A Study in inspiration. New York, Barnes and Noble, 1973. Many references to A. Daudet. Has an index.

GOSSE, EDMUND. *French Profiles.* London: William Heinemann, 1905. A keen and sympathetic criticism of A.D.'s personalilty and works.

GOURMONT, REMY DE. "Alphonse Daudet." *Mercure de France,* January, 1898, pp. 216 - 19 (Same in *Epilogues,* 1895 - 1898, Editions du Mercure de France, 1913, pp. 197 - 202. Maliciously antagonistic.

GUTH, PAUL, "Pour un centenaire d'A.D.," ou "La sensibilité française." *Revue hebdomadaire,* Aug., 1939, pp. 35 - 48.

JAMES, HENRY. *Partial Portraits,* London: Macmillan and Co., 1968, pp. 195 - 242.

————. "A.D." in *Literary Reviews and Essays by Henry James on American, English and French Literature,* edited by Albert Mordell. New York: Vista House Publishers, 1957, pp. 180 - 89.

————. "A.D." *Century Magazine* 4 (1888), 498.

————. *The Letters of Henry James,* selected and edited by Percy Lubbock. New York: Charles Scribner's Sons, 1920.

JOUVEAU, MARIE-THÉRÈSE. "Il y a cinquante ans mourrait . . . l'Arlésienne." Jouveau 28, Rue Maréchal Joffre, 13 Aix-en-Provence, France, 1972.

LABRACHERIE, PIERRE. *La vie quotidienne de la Bohème littéraire au XIXe siècle.* Hachette, 1967.

LANSON, GUSTAVE. *Histoire de la littérature francaise.* 22nd ed. Librairie Hachette, 1894, pp. 1082 - 84.

LEMAÎTRE, JULES. *Les Contemporains:* Etudes et Portraits. 1st series, 1886, 7th séries, 1899, vol. 3, vol. 8.

MAJOR, JOHN C. "Henry James, Daudet and Oxford." *Notes and Queries* 211 (February, 1966), 69 - 70. Contains letters written by H. James.

MIRBEAU, OCTAVE. *Les Grimaces,* no. 21, December 8, 1883. Accuses A.D. of taking credit for letters written by Paul Arène.

MISTRAL, FRÉDÉRIC. *Moun Espelido. Memori e Raconte* ("La Riboto de Trenco-Taio," and "La Proso prouvençalo," pp. 323ff and 292ff. Also, *L'Aiòli,* Dec. 7, 1894, on Bonnet and Daudet.

————. "Anfos Daudet." *L'Aiòli que vai cremant tres fes pèr mes,* no. 252, Dec. 1897. Daudet considered as a friend, a gay companion, and a successful French writer who has remained loyal to his native land.

MATTHEWS, BRANDER. Introduction to *The Novels, Romances and Writings of Alphonse Daudet.* Boston: Little, Brown & Co., 1898 - 1903. An original, but favorable review of A.D.'s works.

NEFF, EMERY. *Edwin Arlington Robinson.* New York: William Sloane Associates, 1948. Refers to Robinson's opinion on Alphonse Daudet., p. 58.

PONTMARTIN, ARMAND DE. *Souvenir d'un vieux critique.* 1883 - 1889.

————. *Nouveaux Samedis.* Calman-Lévy, 1878, 1881.

RAIMOND, MICHEL. *Le Roman depuis la Révolution.* Librairie Armand Colin, 1967, pp. 119 - 20 passim.

RENARD., JULES. *Journal,* Gallimard., 1935.

ROCHE, ALPHONSE. *Provençal Regionalism.* A Study of the Movement in the *Revue félibrénne, Le Feu,* and other reviews of southern France. Evanston, Illinois: Northwestern University Press, 1954. Now published by AMS PRESS, Inc., New York, N.Y. 10003. Title and subtitle are descriptive.

————. "La part du Provençal dans 'Le Curé de Cucugnan,'" *French Review,* March, 1941.

————. "La Camargue et ses poètes." *French Review,* vol. 32, no. 1 (1958).

SACHS, MURRAY. "The Role of Collaborators in the Career of A.D." *PMLA* 73, (March - June, 1958), 1. A thorough and convincing study which, to my mind, settles the question once for all.

————. "Daudet and Paul Arène: "Some unpublished letters". *The Romanic Review.* Confirms the above remark.

————. "Manuscript Evidence Concerning *Les Lettres de mon moulin.*" *PMLA* (December, 1959), p. 638.

SYMONS, ARTHUR. "A.D." *Athenaeum* (London), no. 3661 (1897), p. 887. A rather severe appraisal of A.D. as a novelist and humorist.

THIBAUDET, ALBERT. *Réflexion sur la littérature.* 2 vol. Gallimard, 1938 - 40, II, 182, 199 - 201.

————. *Histoire de la Littérature Française de 1789 à nos jours.*

Toudouze, Gustave. *Pages choisies des grands écrivains. Alphonse Daudet.* Paris, 1900.

Veran, Jùli. "Daudet e Lou Felibrige." *L'Aiòli que vai cremant tres fes pèr mes,* April 7, 1898, no. 262. This is a very interesting discussion of the Provençal influence on Daudet.

Vier, Jacques. "Sur la jeunesse d'Alphonse Daudet." *Revue d'Histoire littéraire de la France,* April - June, 1956, pp. 243 - 51. This is a review of J. H. Bornecque's thesis, *Les Années d'apprentissage d'Alphonse Daudet,* but mostly a pretext for the author to express his own views on Daudet, whom he calls "one of the cleverest parasites in our literature" (p. 244). Vier suggests the best part of the *Lettres de mon moulin,* were written by Paul Arène, which remains to be proven.

Zola, Emile. *Les Romanciers naturalistes.* Bibliothèque Charpentier, Eugène Fasquelle, éditeur, 1910. First published in 1881. Covers A.D.'s life and works from *Les Amoureuses* to *Le Nabab.* An extremely favorable article in which Zola persists in considering A.D. as a naturalist.

Index

187